SATHER CLASSICAL LECTURES

VOLUME EIGHTEEN

1945

OVID: A POET
BETWEEN TWO WORLDS

OVID

A Poet between Two Worlds

BY

HERMANN FRÄNKEL

UNIVERSITY OF CALIFORNIA PRESS

BERKELEY AND LOS ANGELES

1945

UNIVERSITY OF CALIFORNIA PRESS
BERKELEY AND LOS ANGELES
CALIFORNIA

◇

CAMBRIDGE UNIVERSITY PRESS
LONDON, ENGLAND

PRINTED IN THE UNITED STATES OF AMERICA
BY THE UNIVERSITY OF CALIFORNIA PRESS

TO

MY WIFE

PREFACE

THIS IS *a short book on a large and complex, yet well-defined, subject. Dealing as it does with a single writer, it is meant to make a comprehensive, fairly balanced volume. Thus I have chosen to sin on the side of omission rather than on that of profusion, and have offered only part of the material I believe to have at hand to support my somewhat heterodox position. At the same time, I hope that the work is soundly based, and I have striven to be correct in what I say or imply. But I know there are errors, for I have caught some myself, and I shall be grateful for any corrections and criticisms, in print or otherwise.*

Brevity seemed essential, but still no poet can be properly appreciated unless he is given a direct, unhurried hearing. Hence significant passages from Ovid's works have been treated in some detail, especially in the beginning; and throughout the book much of what I wanted to bring out has been said, not in my own words, but by selective quotation and paraphrase. The numerous bits of translation are intended to render the bare meaning of Ovid's lines, with no attempt to reproduce his art. Even so, I must ask the reader's indulgence for them.

Least of all could I pretend to completeness in the matter of bibliographical reference, and I have been chary of direct polemics. We cannot hope to give a nice accounting of our overwhelming debt to all those who have either clarified the issues and taught us to see what they saw, or sharpened our discrimination by proposing opinions we have felt unable to accept, as well as those who have put the facts within our easy grasp and given us the tools with which to work. But I ought to mention here one unpretentious and yet very useful tool, the "Concordance of Ovid" compiled by Roy J. Deferrari, M. Inviolata Barry, and Martin R. P. McGuire (Washington, D.C., 1939).

For the sake of convenience, I use the verse numbers of the Teubner edition.

When the University of California honored me with the invitation to serve as one of the Sather Professors of Classical Literature, I was generously permitted to select a subject on which I had never pub-

lished a line previously, although I had been engrossed in it, and had developed the views set forth here, in the course of a good many years. I enjoyed writing this study more than anything before. Likewise, the delivery of the lectures and the sojourn among my Berkeley friends will remain one of my most cherished memories.

While preparing the lectures and book, I was benefited by the advice of my colleague Lionel I. C. Pearson (until he joined the British army) and of Dr. Maurice Cunningham of Berkeley. Between them, they have read every page of my manuscript to help polish my diction, and moreover they have mellowed many a passage by criticisms and suggestions. I am also indebted to my colleague Frederick Anderson and other friends whom I consulted about matters of style. On myself, however, falls the responsibility for the many rough spots that undoubtedly still remain. Mr. Harold A. Small, Editor of the University of California Press, and his collaborators have nursed the book to publication with competent and loving care.

H. F.

CONTENTS

1. APPROACH AND PERSPECTIVE

As STUDENTS of classical literature, we cannot expect to have new material wafted onto our desks year in and year out in bountiful quantity; most of the time, we find ourselves handling objects that have been known and used for many centuries. The priceless documents from olden times entrusted to our temporary care remain the same, but each of us will make a fresh effort to comprehend and assess them according to his own lights. There are any number of aspects, all of them equally legitimate, under which a great work of literature may be correctly understood; it is the ephemeral product that allows of one explanation only. On the other hand, any person or generation that is keenly responsive to certain values will inevitably be blind and deaf to certain others, and in the march of literary criticism not every step moves forward. Thus it is only natural that we should frequently be obliged to revise opinions handed down to us.

About the merits and failings of the Roman poet Ovid there is, and has been for some considerable time, a remarkable unanimity among scholars.[1] The dissenting voices are few.[2] This settled state of affairs itself invites question. However valid a critical judgment may have been in the first place, it will lose some of its cogency with each reiteration, and by the time it has become a truism it has little truth left in it. The reasons for this strange fact seem to be these. Unchallenged perseverance in a belief leads to complacent oversimplification; the complex setting on which the assertion was originally projected gradually fades out, and with its background its justification will be gone; a criticism, in order to be revealing, must stir the mind rather than put it to rest; and we know least about those things we take for granted.

In Ovid's case, the reputation of the poet has been under a cloud for more than a hundred years. Again and again we hear it said and see it written that, charming as his poetry is, Ovid was never himself serious and must not be taken seriously by us. Is he not the man responsible for the dubious accomplishment of introducing rhetoric into Roman poetry—whatever the term rhetoric may

---

[1] For notes to chapter 1, see pages 167–170.

mean?[3] Against this verdict of a mere century or so, we may set
the estimation which Ovid enjoyed for a considerable part of the
preceding 1,800 years.[4] In the 12th century, Ovid's popularity rivaled
that of Vergil and Horace. Before the century came to a close, "his
fame was established, and the authority of his writings had been
widely accepted not only among poets who wrote in Latin, but also
in centers of culture dominated by the aristocratic circles, among the
Troubadours and Minnesänger, and the poets of northern France."[5]
In the 13th century, the works of Ovid were read more widely than
those of any other Latin poet.[6] It cannot be an accident that the age
which saw the culmination of medieval poetry gave Ovid the first
place among the poets of the past. Although Ovid's prestige was
never again to be supreme as it had been in the 13th century, his
influence, both direct and indirect, remained a major factor in subsequent times. Dante (in the *Inferno* 4, 90) ranged Ovid with
Homer, Horace, and Lucan. The literature of the Spanish *Siglo de
Oro* gives ample evidence of an intensive study of Ovid's works and
of "the vitality and force of the Ovidian tradition."[7] It was the same
story, in the 16th and 17th centuries, throughout the rest of Europe.
In all countries "Ovid's popularity ... was securely established ...
and ever enlarged its bounds. . . . Painters and sculptors no less than
poets turned to the *Metamorphoses* for stories and themes." His
work became "an authoritative Bible of Art."[8] In the 17th and 18th
centuries, Ovid's *Metamorphoses,* in conjunction with two other
books, the *Amadis of Gaul* and Ariosto's *Orlando Furioso,* held
a monopoly for providing subjects for the writers of opera libretti.[9]
It was only in the 19th century—a century which we are not accustomed to regard as an *arbiter elegantiarum*—that Ovid's prestige
fell as low as it stands today.

⟡ ⟡ ⟡

It is, then, for us to recover some of the ground the critics of the
last century have lost, and to try to advance in some direction or
other. It may be interesting, for instance, more closely to determine
Ovid's position amid the shifting lines, rising and falling and cross-
ing one another, of historical evolution. His literary personality is
more complex and more dynamic than his portrait as drawn by

the consensus of scholars would make us believe. For one thing, his poetry had a special and lasting appeal to the Christian era. No doubt in some ways Ovid's writings mark the beginning decline of Antiquity; should they not also contain elements indicating the emergence of a new world?

If the question is to be answered in the affirmative, Ovid's poetry will, after all, prove to have some deeper significance.[10] As we shall see, he expressed in his writings, along with well-established views, certain others strikingly novel. Not that he wanted to make innovations; but he was born a true child of an age of transition, and thus he could not help feeling as he did and betraying the forces that were at work. We, on our part, shall try to make explicit some of the factors involved. Ovid himself knew only a fraction of the implications; he was not a philosopher, but a mere poet. "Not by virtue of philosophy do poets create what they create," says Plato in the *Apology* (22B–C), "but by virtue of their specific gift and inspiration, like diviners and soothsayers, who also say many fine things but do not understand their meaning."[11] "There is hardly a person here who would not talk more sensibly about the meaning of their writings than did the poets themselves."

◇ ◇ ◇

Trying, as we shall do, to stress the positive qualities of Ovid's work, we shall not make a vain attempt to build the poet up to the stature of, let us say, a Vergil. His shortcomings are far too obvious, and as we shall soon see, he was more interested in character than in faultlessness. Often we have to regret his lack of restraint, discipline, and poise. He overdoes things, and again he does them by halves; he cannot make up his mind between two alternatives and tries to combine them both. His taste and tact are not infrequently impaired, sometimes by inadvertency, sometimes by an almost incredible naïveté, and sometimes by a childish spite. He is more frank than we should wish in matters of sex.[12] On the other hand, it does him credit that, in contrast to the other poets and the whole body of society of his time, he demurred at homosexual love, and offered a characteristic reason for his heterodoxy.[13] But even if we admit all his defects, he deserves praise for something more than just his superb craftsmanship in handling the word and the verse, in picturing a scene, telling a story, adapting material of any sort and origin to his own purposes, organizing an ambitious and novel epic, and fascinating his readers. His Pygmalion story alone, properly understood and appreciated, should suffice to prove that Ovid is not only a very successful entertainer, but has substantial ideas of his own to offer.[14] Apart from his artistry, there is enough in his writings which we shall have to admire, and enough in his personality which some people will love. In addition, the whole course of his life lies open for our inspection in the series of his many and many-sided works. Thanks to the fact that they are candid and very personal, and that they can be dated with reasonable accuracy, we have the material for a full biography such as can be envisaged for very few writers of Antiquity.

◇ ◇ ◇

These, then, are the matters which will be on our program of discussion. Their scope is far too broad for an adequate treatment in this narrow compass, to say nothing of my personal limitations. We can only try to analyze a few selected poems and passages from Ovid's writings, all through his career; to ponder the significance of what we may find in them; to apprehend some salient features of each work; and to connect our various observations in such a way as to draw an outline of his biography, both literary and personal. Nevertheless I trust that, once a beginning has been made, Ovid will step in and start speaking for himself. Fortunately, he speaks exceedingly well.

2. OVID GROWS UP

OVID WAS a Roman knight by right of birth and inheritance, and more than once he insists that, although he was not prominent by nobility or wealth, on the other hand he did not belong to the then numerous class of upstarts and *nouveaux riches*.[1] He was born, then, as the son of well-established middle-class parents at a small town in the mountains of central Italy, and was educated in Rome.[2] The date of his birth was March 20, 43 B.C.; that is to say, one year after

---

[1] For notes to chapter 2, see pages 170–175.

Caesar was murdered, and nine months before Cicero was assassinated. The last convulsions of the dying republic were about to end when he saw the light; and the flaming greatness of Cicero's oratory, of Lucretius' missionary enthusiasm, of Catullus' lyrics had burned out before he learned to speak. He was twelve years old when the battle of Actium established a paternalistic autocracy and the *Pax Augusta* began to blanket the wide world. Not until his own life was drawing to a close would Ovid's destiny cease to be in the hands of Augustus; and when the change did come, it dashed the poet's last hope for his release from unbearable misery. Ovid died before Jesus in distant Palestine had begun to preach his new gospel which in centuries to come was to conquer the civilized world. But without knowing of his own mission, Ovid was one of those to help prepare the passage from Antiquity to Christianity.

From boyhood, Ovid was interested only in poetry; "stealthily," so he said later, "the Muse forced me to do her work" (*Tr.* IV, 10, 20). His father, however, reminding him that not even Homer had gathered earthly riches, insisted on an education which would prepare him for public office or for the career of a pleader in court, and sent him to the best professors of rhetoric in Rome.

◇　◇　◇

We are fortunate in possessing some record of Ovid's training and the figure he cut in the stuffy classrooms where rhetoric was taught and practice speeches were recited by professors and students. Seneca the Elder, a connoisseur in oratory, was Ovid's senior by more than ten years but survived him by at least twenty. At the age of about ninety, he composed memoirs of a unique sort. He gave lively portraits of the many rhetors whose classes he had attended in bygone years and illustrated their art and manner by thousands of verbatim quotations; his stupendous memory enabled him to cite freely from orations delivered fifty or sixty years before. In that work, Seneca also speaks of the favorable way in which young Ovid's declamations impressed his fellow students (*Controv.* II, 2, 8). "His talent," Seneca says, "was of a polished, pleasant, and likable nature. Even then his oratory might have been taken for nothing so much as poetry in prose."... At the time, however, people merely thought of him as a good declamator." In other words, a more discerning audience would have been able to see that Ovid's eloquence, even though as yet it was discharged in prose, was of the poetic variety. And indeed, Ovid himself narrates in his autobiography (*Tristia* IV, 10, 23–26) that, while writing out his school orations, he had some trouble in sticking to prose; the words would naturally fall into verse. From Seneca (§8) we learn further that in the course of his studies Ovid changed his preference in rhetorical style and consequently also changed his professors.[4] One of them he admired so greatly that he later inserted into his own poetry, by way of compliment, many of the professor's conceits (*sententiae*).[5] He did not blindly submit to the routine curriculum, but chose the subjects for his declamations according to his own judgment. He would rarely recite a forensic speech of the usual type (*controversia*), because he had no stomach for the arts of proving or disproving the alleged facts of a fictitious case (§12).[6] In that, I think, he showed good sense.[7] The problems assigned to students were woefully lacking in topical detail, and the speaker, in debating the case, was obliged to juggle flimsy generalities and pass them off for solid arguments. Ovid, disdaining the shadowy play of pseudo logic, preferred two other types of oration. One was the so-called *suasoria,*[8] that is, a speech giving advice in a critical situation and recommending a certain course of action. The other was the *controversia ethica,* in which the student was to argue the moral aspects of an action already committed.[9]

In his discussion of one such *controversia ethica,* Seneca writes this (§9): "In the class of Arellius Fuscus, Ovid treated this particular topic, in my opinion, with far more wit [than the professor himself], except that he rambled through the points of view with no certain order. I remember these passages from his oration...," and now Seneca goes on to quote some salient parts from Ovid's treatment of the case in hand. The theme was as follows. Suppose that a certain man and his wife, in the frenzy of their mutual attachment, had made a compact that neither would survive the other. The husband went on a journey and from abroad sent home intelligence of his own death.[10] The wife tried to commit suicide, but failed and recovered. Her incensed father then ordered her to leave her husband, and repudiated her when she disobeyed his order. The court had either to uphold or annul the father's act of repudiation.[11] It was a fantastic story on which the issue hinged, but no more fantastic than was common for the school exercises; the teachers tried to appeal to the romantic vein in their youthful students. Ovid was pleading for the foolish lovers against the father, and, according to Seneca's recollection (§ 10), this is some of what he had to say about the parental meddling with marital eccentricity: "It is easier to kill, than to tame, a lover's passion.[12] Do you presume, sir [addressing the father], that you can induce the couple to respect such limits as you determine for them, and to take no action without due deliberation, and to make promises in the manner of legal stipulations only, and to weigh their every word on the scales of reason and conscience? It is the old gentlemen who love after such a fashion."[13]

Seneca concludes his chapter on Ovid with some critical remarks on his poetical style. It is worth while to follow the genial writer on the path of this digression (§ 12): "[In his rhetorical exercises,] Ovid took no liberties with the diction, as he did in his poetry. In his verse he was not ignorant of his own faults, but fond of them. This is apparent from what once happened when some of his friends asked him to destroy three out of all the lines he had written, and he in turn requested the right to select three lines which were to be immune. They thought the condition was fair; in private they put down the lines they wished to see taken out, and he those he wanted to remain safe; and the same lines appeared in both lists.[14] . . . Hence it is clear that Ovid, a man of supreme talent, was lacking not in judgment but in inclination when he failed to restrain the liberties of his poetry. He used to say that sometimes a face would be rendered more attractive by the presence of some mole."[15] Seneca's authority for the charming anecdote was a man reputed as a most accomplished storyteller,[16] and of course there is more fiction than fact in it. But, like other good anecdotes, it is truer than the truth; and the rest of our quotation has likewise a convincing ring. Other ancient critics of Ovid's art make the same charges as Seneca does;[17] and the poet himself chimes in and declares that he does not care if his writings "are marked by their characteristic color and set off, perhaps, by their faults" (*Po.* IV, 13, 13–16).[18] It is obvious that actually, just as the anecdote presupposes, problems of this sort were aired in animated discussions between Ovid and his literary friends, but the poet would stubbornly stick to his own manner even if it was not in perfect taste. Defiant of conventions, Ovid preferred native individuality to drab academic correctness. For that matter, his views were similar to those expressed shortly afterward in the treatise on the Sublime.

Seneca's recollections may easily have been tinged, for better or for worse, by the reputation Ovid had earned for himself in the meantime by his poetry. In any case, the verdicts which Seneca passes on Ovid's youthful rhetorical endeavors can be applied to his literary works as well. Any reader of Ovid's poetry will agree that "his talent was of a polished, pleasant, and likable nature"; and he will also deplore that the author too often "neglects to observe some definite order." We shall likewise assent when in another passage Seneca quotes a critic of Ovid's poetry who brands the writer as "incapable of relinquishing a point after it once had been well made" (*Controv.* IX, 5, 17). Instead, Ovid would more than once repeat the idea, turning it this way and that. Each variation may be good enough in itself, but they lose their force in the accumulation.[19]

◇   ◇   ◇

When he had completed his studies in Rome, Ovid traveled to Athens, as was customary, to put the finishing touches on his education, and probably stayed there for some time.[20] After his return, he began his political career with the administration of some minor offices. A little later, however, when his quaestorship was due and with it his rise to senatorial rank was imminent, he made up his mind and determined to spend his life in the service of the Muses rather than of the state.[21] He was then about twenty-three. The reasons for his decision he indicated thirty years later in these words:

The burden would have been too heavy for my strength;
neither was my body equal to the strain nor my mind suited for toil.
    I disliked the restless struggle for prestige,
and the Muses urged me to seek the peace
    of retirement (*otium*), which my heart had always loved.
                                        (*Tr.* IV, 10, 36 ff.)

The lines sound as if Ovid had preferred poetry in order to escape hard work. But before we accept his declaration at its face value, let us remember that Roman society strangely misconceived the nature of poetry and invariably associated it with idleness. It was an established dogma that only three types of activity could be considered as serious business (*negotium*): the making of money, the acquisition of power in peace or war, and the exercise of authority in peace or war. All the rest was classified as play and not work, and it was assigned to leisure (*otium*) and not to the business of life. In Greece, a poet would by virtue of his calling command the respect of his community, and the nation at large would look upon him as one of its spiritual leaders.[22] In Rome, poetry had no proper standing because the spirit had none.[23] The study and production of poetry ranked among the amusements and hobbies; moreover, it was a recognized school subject for children. Apart from its value for recreation and education, poetry was not thought of as a power in its own right, but rather as a convenient tool for the promotion of political and social prestige, and great poets were time and again obliged politely to decline an invitation to celebrate and perpetuate the exploits of an important man.[24] At best, poetry would be called upon to glorify the nation and to propagandize its true virtues. Any poet whose work was unrelated to practical purposes because it was exclusively devoted to the concerns of the mind and heart, saw the fruits of his earnest endeavors classified as playthings and relegated to some quaint limbo beyond the pale of consequential reality.[25] Thus he established for his creations a setting of their own, apart from normalcy. He constructed, for instance, an imaginary pastoral way of life congenial to the delicate feelings to which his verse was dedicated;[26] or he romanticized the farmer's way of life so as to represent at its best unadulterated nature in man, beast, and plant; or he played on the incredible miracles of myth and legend; or he plunged into the state of love, frantic or playful, which entitled him to many sorts of sentiments and illusions. A very considerable part of the great Augustan poetry is erotic, and the reason is that the lover's world, while it offered a suitable habitat for free poetry to thrive in, yet at the same time was situated not without, but within, the Roman actualities. Amorous adventures, although they were not accorded any serious dignity, were still rated as standard features of real life.[27]

The degradation of poetry in public opinion was bound, moreover, to undermine the legitimate self-respect of a born poet. Horace stood up well under the severe strain because he was possessed of a rare measure of poise and tact; but others became, as the case might be, reserved and retiring, or ironic, or apologetic, or arrogant; for they were confused and hardly knew, themselves, where they belonged. Ovid's utterances on the place he assigned to his verse are contradictory and sometimes evasive. Of his own free will he shut himself out from the business side of life and positively enjoyed having nothing to do with it; but in the context from which we have been quoting he dared not bluntly say that the personal and emotional and human side of life was just as real and, after all, more important. We shall soon see, however, that at other times he spoke out and indicated how he felt in his heart of hearts.

3. THE "AMORES"

AFTER YOUNG Ovid had made his own choice, he looked up with more veneration than ever to the great masters of Roman verse who were still living. He was eager to make their personal acquaintance and to hear them recite their own poems (*Tr.* IV, 10, 41–55). But they were soon to leave the scene. Of those men whom we are accustomed to call the poets of the Augustan age, Ovid was by far the youngest. He was only twenty-four years old when Vergil and Tibullus died, in 19 B.C. On the death of Tibullus he wrote an elegy which bears testimony to the most sympathetic intimacy with Tibullus' writings (*Am.* III, 9). Sometime after 15 B.C., Propertius passed away, and in 8 B.C., Horace.

Very soon Ovid established his own reputation as a writer of elegy. He did not have to wait for fame until his first book was published and on sale in the bookshops. At the time, it was the custom to have the manuscripts of single poems circulate among those who were interested, and to recite to a group of invited guests a number of one's own compositions as soon as they had been put into their final shape. Ovid started giving recitations, as he tells us, after "he had had his beard trimmed once or twice" (*Tr.* IV, 10, 57 f.).[1] Valerius Messalla Corvinus, a man of high rank and a friend of the Muses, recognized Ovid's talent and encouraged him to make his work public (*Po.* I, 27–28; II, 3, 75–78; *Tr.* IV, 4, 27–32). The first collection of poems he published bore the title *Amores* and was in five books. We possess the second edition, which the author had reduced to three volumes by eliminating material he thought less valuable. The number of elegies is fifty or fifty-one. Most of the *Amores* seems to have been written while he was in his twenties.[2]

When we open a book of love poetry, we expect to find in it the expression of that particular author's individual experiences. A Roman collection of erotic elegies is broader in scope and less closely bound to reality. No doubt the Roman writer would actually be in love with someone when he composed a love poem, and he would speak as if he were, at the moment of his writing, involved in the situation he describes; yet his ambition was to ignore the accidental limitations of his own personal adventures. He was trying to picture, not one person's emotions, but any true lover's love (cf. *Am.* II, 1, 7–10). His subject was *The Story of Love,* and that, after all, is what the title *Amores* means. The *Story* is told by Ovid in terms of various specific experiences, real or imaginary, of the author. Not only was the poet entitled to improve on the crude facts; it was beside the point to ask how much of what he said was actually true as long as all of it was potentially true; not even strict consistency throughout the book was required.[3] By a number of concrete examples the poet tried to present a comprehensive image of what a young man's existence is like when it is dominated by a passionate attachment.[4] Of the lover's existence he would draw an ideal picture which boldly challenged comparison with the lives of nonlovers.

◇ ◇ ◇

Life under the lodestar of Love was contrasted by Ovid with the merciless toil under the harsh light of the day in a fine elegy on *The Dawn* (*Am.* I, 13), a poem which seems to have had a remarkable success in influencing posterity. It probably inspired, twelve centuries after it had been written, a whole genre of medieval verse: the

---

[1] For notes to chapter 3, see pages 175–190.

Provençal *alba,* the French *aubade,* and the German *Tageliet.* The subject of the medieval songs is the parting at daybreak of the lovers who cannot risk being found out by the lady's husband or his helpers. The motif of an imminent danger is absent from Ovid's elegy,[5] but there is some drama in it as well. Its structure is original. Only the first and the last couplet are of a narrative character,[6] the first announcing that Aurora, the dawn, is bringing the day, and the last describing the arrival of the day.[7] Both couplets end on the same decisive word "day." The body of the poem is thus set in the few moments of transition, and it is made up of a futile address to Aurora, in which the poet attempts to avert the inevitable.

The opening distich is dignified and solemn, and so is the first couplet in which Ovid speaks to Aurora. Ovid is appealing to her affection for a son lost long ago. Aurora the mother of Memnon, and Aurora the dawn, are both addressed at once. Classical Greek poetry had taken care to keep the personal and private life of the gods apart from their function in the phenomena of nature, but the Hellenistic period had taken special delight in merging the two sides. Ovid took up the Hellenistic line and carried it to its culmination in the *Metamorphoses.*

Two delightful couplets explain to Aurora why she ought to tarry. The first describes the profound happiness of the lovers united, not in the raptures of passion, but in the tranquil felicity of their rest side by side; the other distich mentions the sweet depth of sleep in the wonderful hour of dawn, the bracing freshness of the air, and the music of the awakening birds:

> This is the hour when I delight to rest in the tender arms of my lady;
>   now, if ever, is she close to my side.
> This is the hour when slumber is rich, and cool the air,
>   and clear the chant from the soft throats of birds.
>   (I, 13, 5 ff.)

A new expostulation to Aurora is rather sharp in its tone, but the pentameter reverts to measured dignity. Aurora was reviled as "unwelcome to both men and girls," and presently the scope of the accusation widens. Dawn is charged with inflicting misery upon all mankind, and one class of people after another is shown on the point of being thrown out of blissful night and into the throes of day.[8]

Dawn robs the sailor of the helpful guidance of his stars and makes him drift in a desolate vastness which bears no markings:

> Before you [Dawn] rise, the sailor scans his stars
> and is not lost, bewildered, amid the waters.
>
> (11 f.)

The distich is unusually fine even for Ovid; and, although couched in simple and lucid words, it lends itself to a broader interpretation. The sailor's day, spent amid a shapeless, restless, and confusing waste, might represent every man's distracted, unoriented workaday life as it will be illustrated in the next six couplets; and the sailor's night, when "his" stars shed their steady light upon him, might serve as an image for the collected serenity of a lover who both knows and has what he desires, as it had been described in two preceding distichs. Ovid, to be sure, does not in explicit words indicate so wide a purport. It was not given to him to deal in abstract generalities; he rather drew concrete pictures. His pictures, however, do sometimes carry a transcending meaning; and I believe this to be so here, since the argument manifestly trends toward it, and there are a number of parallels to support such an interpretation.[9]

After the seafarer, the traveler on land is mentioned; and after the peaceful itinerant, the soldier who at dawn readies himself for a new day of hateful slaughter:

> When you appear, the weary wanderer rises,
> and the warrior fits to weapons his brutal hands.
>
> (13 f.)

In Roman love-poetry, travels on land and sea and the bloody calling of the soldier, all of them motivated by the lust for wealth, are often referred to as the antithesis of a lover's concerns. Next, the hard life of the farmer is described in a distich depicting the weight of his tools and the heavy gait of his oxen.[10] The likeness is very different from the usual idealization, which turns into an idyl the peasant's laborious quest for his daily bread. Another couplet is given to the young children who hate to go to school and be beaten by the teacher;[11] one more to the greedy man of business who performs precarious transactions, saddling himself with worries and the dread of ruin; and one to the jurists and pleaders who serve the relentless machinery of ever-renewed strife. This accounts for all fields of masculine life;[12] a concluding couplet adds the toil to which womanhood is subjected.

At this juncture, the point of view changes. Ovid begins to complain of Dawn's unswerving punctuality. Nature ought to be accommodating and oblige a person who wants to fulfill man's higher destinies; but, instead, its cold unbending mechanism enforces upon us its own blind laws. If Aurora were not an inanimate phenomenon but, as mythology contends her to be, a woman riding a chariot, might not for once something happen to thwart her power or interrupt her drive?

> How often have I wished, Night would not yield to you,
>   the Stars would not stir and flee your sight.
> How often have I wished, a storm would break your axle,
>   or your horse would founder in a thick cloud.
>   (27 ff.)

There is ingenious humor in the way Ovid elaborates the circumstances of the imaginary accidents;[13] of course he has been conscious all along of the fact that his protests are utterly futile.

Yet it is a relief to vent one's anger. Ovid is growing bitter and heaps abuse on Aurora. Her son Memnon is mentioned again, but not in the same strain as when the poet was trying to ingratiate himself with the goddess. Memnon happened to be a Negro, although both his parents had a white exterior; from this Ovid infers that his mother's inside was black. A "black" heart might mean several things,[14] one of them that "she is not free from the flaw of adultery" (*Am.* III, 5, 43 f.), and thus the poet starts to hint at Aurora's scandalous affairs,[15] of which poor Tithonus in his helpless dotage does not dare to tell. Mentioning Aurora's aged husband, the poet tries a new way to explain Dawn's unwelcome haste. Lovers are monomaniacs and apt to interpret everything in terms of their own preoccupation. Obviously, Ovid supposes, Aurora is in a hurry to get on the skies because she loathes to stay with Tithonus any longer. But if she were holding in her arms[16] some young and handsome gallant, she would act as Ovid is doing and ask Night to linger on.[17] It does not seem fair for her to penalize a happy lover because her own marriage is giving her no comfort. It was not Ovid who had arranged the unsuccessful match. She should remember what Luna had done for Endymion's sake.[18] There is another precedent also: once upon a time, the Lord of the Universe himself doubled the night and kept Aurora out, the longer to enjoy Alcmena's love. Here the speech ends.

The hexameter of the concluding distich caps and outdoes the sportive fancy of the quips that precede it. Ostensibly, Ovid had tried to make Aurora feel ashamed of herself; and, lo and behold, he seems to have succeeded. "You would imagine she heard me: she blushed." With this joke, which results from a facetious merging of the two natures in Aurora,[19] the last vestige of make-believe is blown away in a burst of laughter. Aurora, alas, has but one nature; and the last line acknowledges in dry and sober words the defeat of a pleasant but unreasonable dream:

and yet no later than it was wont to come, there rose the day.[20]

(48)

Does the elegy on *The Dawn* deserve the title of an original creation? If we attend to the subject matter only, and if moreover we break down the train of thought into its individual constituents, we have to state that not one of the ideas was novel, with the possible exception of the detailed comparison between day and night.[21] For the main theme Ovid may have been inspired by two Greek epigrams written about two generations before by Meleager of Gadara (*Anthol. Palat.* 5, 171 and 172 Stadtmüller = 5, 172 and 173 Dübner). In the first, Meleager scolds the morning star for appearing too soon and complains that he has hardly had the time to warm himself at the bosom of his beloved Demo; so he asks the star to reverse his course and turn into the evening star, as he had done once before in order to double the length of the night for Juppiter and Alcmene. The second epigram reproaches the morning star for his slowness in appearing, while Demo is caressing the poet's rival. The two epigrams are meant to form a pair, and together they illustrate the fact that the same event may affect us in opposite ways, just as the same heavenly body serves to usher in both day and night. Beyond that, they have neither significance nor poetic value; but as epigrams they are tolerably good.

On the same level is an epigram by Antipater of Thessalonice, a contemporary of Ovid (*Anthol. Palat.* 5, 2 Stadtmüller = 5, 3 Dübner). It consists of three distichs. In the first couplet, Antipater addresses his mistress and tells her that the cock is ushering in "grudging" (φθονερή, cf. *invida* in Ovid) Aurora; in the second, he curses the rooster, "most grudging of birds,"[22] for chasing him from home and forcing him into the company of chatting young men;[23] in the third, he says: "You are growing old, Tithonus, else you would not drive away so soon your bedfellow Aurora." The epigram is hardly more than a product of wit, and the morose way in which grudging Aurora, the grudging rooster, and aging Tithonus are blamed one after another for ending the night, is a far cry from Ovid's sustained attack on Dawn.

A comparison of Ovid's poem with the epigrams makes it obvious that he has not inflated an epigram, but composed a genuine elegy, rich with poetical stuff in every one of its couplets, lively in its changing moods and the continuous flow of ideas, and yet firmly organized and neatly framed. There is considerable force in it, and we need not wonder that for its own part it has provided the inspiration for scores of medieval songs.

It is not for us, however, to ask what the Middle Ages may have found in the elegy; we want to find out wherefrom Ovid's poem, as a product of its own time, derives its force. And we see at once that its power springs from its substance rather than from its perfect form, or from the genial humor that animates it. The elegy evidently has substance; the fugitive flight of an artist's fancy does not account for all that is in it. If this is so, it will be possible to cull from it some of the broader ideas underlying Ovid's poetry. When we use the few lines we have yet read for the illustration of rather general concepts, we shall perhaps seem to carry our exploitation of the one specimen poem too far. The procedure, however, is convenient; the alternative would be to analyze dozens of pages and spread thin the exposition of crucial points.

Thus we set aside for the moment the lighter aspects of the elegy on *The Dawn*. We forget the sportive element present in the whole elegy and the boisterous joke at the end, and we lend the ideas, as indicated or implied in it, all their potential weight. In the first half, the concerns of a feeling heart were set against those of a calculating mind. On one side, there were quiet, tender delights; on the other, the stark exigencies of practical life; on one side, leisure (*otium*), represented by a lover, with its wealth of sentimental values; on the other, business (*negotium*), represented by people of all sorts and professions, with its quest for material values. It may be noted that the clash is not between reality and imagination, but between two different sets of values—although both sides will contend that the values which the other group prizes are largely fictitious. There can be no doubt which side a poet will take; he will assert that it is only the finer emotions that make life worth living.

In the second half of the poem the main idea is that of the mechanical course of nature versus the mythological interpretation of nature and legend in general. The one is, as Ovid knew very well,[24] a fact and the other nothing but an illusion, and yet the poet will again prefer the more sentimental views. Ovid welcomes mythology and legend as a perfect medium for the representation and clarification of the whole range of human experience. And indeed, it is an unsurpassed means for such purposes; the Western world made use of it in that sense down to the 18th century, when its function was taken over by the novel. Stories upon stories had been invented by the Greeks; they had been developed in the course of many centuries by penetrating Greek thought and creative Greek imagination, they had been connected so as to coalesce into an intricate structure; and the result was a very complete system of examples which could be invoked and would answer the call of any man's emotions in any of the vicissitudes of life. The system was to receive its final polish from the hands of Ovid; and yet, when he composed his *Metamorphoses,* he did it with the mental reservation that he was describing the world not as it is, but as it ought to be on the strength of the heart's logic. It was while the sun was setting on Greek myth that its skies glowed in the most gorgeous colors.

We shall find Ovid haunted by the problem of reality, and of the different planes of reality, throughout all periods of his career.

◇　◇　◇

In Ovid's time, when people were too enlightened to believe in myth but had as yet no substitute for it, the sense of reality was shaken. But other fundamentals as well were upset under the stress of a crisis in the spiritual history of mankind. Views of long standing were shattered and fixed habits of behavior overthrown; and while the ancient system of ideas was breaking down, experiences of a novel sort became possible. Striking evidence of this fact can be found in a certain elegy from Ovid's *Amores;* but before we approach the crucial point, we shall analyze the remarkable poem in its entirety.

The elegy, which may be named *The Contrite Lover* (I, 7), has so strange a subject that a few words of introduction will be in order. As Roman love-poetry is more comprehensive than ours and tends to present any and all essential phases of a passionate love affair, it also includes the love quarrels. We must not forget that we have to do with Southerners. In their opinion, "Error" and "Folly" were inseparable from Love (*Am.* I, 2, 35), and tiffs between the lovers, mostly caused by jealousy, were part and parcel of the adventure. Since they arose from high-strung sensibility and were fostered by a distorted sense of values, they seemed to testify to the intensity of a lover's affection. Without them, the relationship would have been considered a lukewarm and insipid affair; *amantium irae amoris integratio est,* says Terence (*Andria* 555). Without such an occasional outbreak on the part of her lover, the girl might feel slighted. Lucian has one of his female characters dryly remark: "If a man is neither jealous nor angry, and never beats you or cuts off your hair or tears the dress open on your body, is that man still a lover?"[25]

Ovid's elegy has such an act of intemperate violence for its background. The subject does not particularly appeal to our taste; but if for the time being we set aside our legitimate objections, we shall appreciate the fine qualities of the poem and the genuine sentiment behind it. It expresses the poet's emotions immediately after the excess, with frantic anger giving way to remorse no less inordinate. As he looks back upon what he has done, his deed is exaggerated beyond all due proportion, and in the abandon of his repentance he penetrates to an unusual depth of feeling.

The elegy opens with the poet stretching out his arms and calling for somebody to chain them until his madness will have completely subsided—his madness which impelled him to raise his hands against his mistress and has made her cry. He reflects on the enormity of his crime, which appears to him as nothing short of sacrilege. In the traditional code of ethics, the first commandments were: Worship the gods, and honor thy parents; what he had done was like attacking one's parents or the gods. Was there ever such insanity before? Yes, there are examples to be found in that treasure house of human experience, Greek legend and Greek drama. Ajax raged against meek and harmless animals (and woke up to feel as Ovid now feels: Sophocles' *Ajax*); Orestes killed his mother and, harried by the pangs of conscience, tried to fight goddesses (Euripides' *Orestes* 268-276). In his madness, the poet has torn the hair of his mistress. (Now at last we learn what had happened). And, with her loose flowing hair, she looked more lovely than ever. She was a beauty unadorned like Atalante,[26] the huntress in the wilderness. Like Ariadne on Naxos, she was attractive in the careless simplicity of her attire and pathetic in her grief for a lover who had lost his affection. She was like another Cassandra, the sacred priestess who was dragged from the temple with her hair disheveled,[27] her place of refuge violated by sacrilegious hands.[28] And the gentle creature was too frightened to utter one word of reproach. But her countenance made a silent complaint, and her tears rendered a mute indictment. The culprit pleads guilty. His arms played him false; he used his strength for his own undoing; his hands deserve chains for a punishment, if not as a precaution. Others are being punished for an assault on some lowly wretch, while he has harmed his own mistress whose slave he is (*domina*); Diomede had laid hands on a goddess, Venus herself, but then, he met her as an enemy in battle, on the Trojan plain, while Ovid, harming his goddess,[29] hurt the one whom he professed to love. Following up the preposterous idea of a lover's war on his lady, Ovid imagines an abominable triumph to celebrate his shameful victory; and in the procession his mistress is led captive, bearing the marks not of love but of hatred, the very marks which he had actually inflicted upon her. Then he goes on to muse over her ignominious condition and sets off the impropriety by a double foil: how, instead, she ought to have been treated (41-42), and how, at the very worst, she could have been treated short of a sin against the essence of love (43-48).[30] The thought of the limit which should have been observed brings about a final admission of how far Ovid had gone beyond it: he had not only torn the lady's hair, but had also scratched her cheeks (49 f., cf. also 39). Her reaction on his profane outrage is now shown by an exquisite series of similes. Stunned by his incomprehensible behavior, she froze to resemble the pale beauty of a marble statue, cold and lifeless like the mountains from which the stone had been cut. Then a shudder ran over her body, as when a wind plays on the sensitive foliage of a poplar tree, the trunk remaining unmoved; next, her body began to shake like a reed in the wind; returning consciousness again animated her features as when the surface of water is ruffled by a warm breeze. Thus gradually cold terror yielded to the warmth of trembling life, and just as snow on the ground thaws into running water, so her icy rigidity melted and tears began to flow.[31] By the sympathetic communion of love, the poet's anger likewise melted away at the sight of her tears and yielded to bitter remorse. He fell down before his mistress and lifted his hands in supplication for her pardon; but she, still fearing them, pushed his arms away. By now, however, the time is ripe for a conciliation. The retrospective monologue ends and Ovid begins to speak to his lady. He asks her to soften her anguish by retaliating the outrage; anger will lend strength to her hands. The circle is thus closed; it is no longer his hands, but hers, on which we are looking. Naturally, they will do nothing harsh and unkind, and his invitation to chastise him bodily was hardly serious. The extravagance is subsiding. Normalcy is definitely restored when in the concluding couplet[32] the poet suggests: "Let us do away with the somber marks of my crime; please put your hair back in order." The half-humorous touch in this thoughtful proposal goes far to redeem the heaviness of the poem's subject, and the elegy ends on a more cheerful note.

⬦ ⬦ ⬦

In the rich and well-organized imagery of the poem, two things stand out forcefully, both of them mentioned close together three times: his raised hands and her tears (1–4; 22–28; 57–62). He lifts his hands, to have them shackled; and to revile them for what they had committed; and to implore his lady to forgive him. In his mortification, he apostrophizes his hands with these words (27): "What have I to do with you, servants of murder and crime?"—speaking to his own limbs as if they were something apart from himself, slaves[33] perhaps, because he feels estranged from his own self of a moment before. His identity is broken up.[34] The other image is her tears: the tears into which she eventually burst; those tears which reproached him when she was still too frightened to speak; those same tears which converted him from furious anger to ecstatic tenderness. It was then, as he saw her tears streaming, that he realized his guilt (59); but something else also came to pass at the moment. To express it in our terms, her anguish flashed over to his own soul, and he was one with her in a sudden unison of emotion. Ovid, to describe the occurrence, has coined one of the most astounding lines to come out of pagan antiquity:

sanguis erat lacrimae quas dabat illa meus.

(60)

"The tears she shed were my blood." He had said before (27) that his crime was equivalent to bloody murder, but it is his, not her, blood which he now feels flowing in her tears.[35] The identities of the two lovers have been merged in a mystic union.

Experiences of this sort do not seem extraordinary to us. But it was an unheard-of novelty for the ancients that a person should no longer feel securely identical with his own self[36] or should become identical with some other self temporarily. There is no sign of a previous emergence of these possibilities; Ovid took them for granted and used them freely in his poetry.[37] Whether we like or dislike the notion of dubious or fluid identity,[38] it is one of his characteristic themes, and the reader who fails to respond to it misses much of what the poet is trying to convey. We shall discuss later a number of examples from the *Metamorphoses;*[39] for the moment, be it enough to state that, with the self losing its solid unity and being able half to detach itself from its bearer, a fundamental shift had taken place in the history of the human mind.

◇   ◇   ◇

From the point we have reached, we now take one further bold step. It stands to reason that a shift of this sort makes possible a new kind of sympathy between fellow human beings, that kind which

we justly are accustomed to associate with Christianity. If we have
broken with the habit of sticking to our identity, and have learned
to transfer ourselves into our neighbor's self, then any relationship
between persons can assume a different character. We are no longer
isolated from one another as people had been, for instance, in Attic
tragedy. In tragedy, every individual was pent up in his own self,
and the great personalities more so than the rest. They were clad, as
it were, in the armor of an unbreakable loneliness. This is one of the
things that make for the sublime and stern definiteness of Sophoclean drama. Man could help or harm man, love or hate him, be
loyal or treacherous; he could very well appreciate some other's joys
or sorrows; but nobody would have been able to fuse his own and
the other's experiences and, to use the Christian term, to bear his
neighbor's cross. That situation we find radically changing in
Ovid's poetry; and to our knowledge, rather suddenly so, although
Menander's gracious plays, to mention one example, already show
signs of a more gentle spirit; and so does Epicurean philosophy,
while the Stoics tended in the opposite direction and consequently
had pains to smuggle into their gospel of self-salvation a justification for concern with the welfare of others. That Ovid, in that
respect, was the first to take his stand on our side of the fence is
apparent everywhere, but it is most obvious in his behavior in love.
It is easy to see, but would take a long time to demonstrate, how his
attitude toward women differs from that taken by his immediate
predecessors Propertius and Tibullus. They would desire to possess
their mistress and have her near them like some very precious object,
as dear to them as their very life; while Ovid is able to see everything
with the eyes of the woman with whom he is in love. He may be lax
and weak, but he is also kind; and fond, thoughtful, understanding
kindliness is a quality for which nothing else can substitute: no flat-
tering admiration, no fervor of desire, no pride of ownership, and
no magnanimous sacrifice. The new element of comprehending
kindliness, be it unselfish kindliness or kindliness as a stratagem in
the warfare of love[40] or kindliness as a commodity in the give-and-
take of love, was probably a major factor in the great success of
Ovid's love poetry. But the change in attitude is not confined to the
relation between lovers.[41]

Probably Ovid was not aware that he saw human relations in a different light; it was in his nature, and he knew no better than feeling and reacting as he did. Nevertheless, he was leaving behind him Antiquity as we know it and traveling on the path to a new age of mankind.[42] His poetry reveals that he was giving up many things that had been highly prized before. He ceased, for instance, to uphold the proud tenet of unshakable personal identity. With naïve unconcern, he candidly voiced his experiences in the same modern spirit in which he lived through them, ignoring established traditions and the code of wary discretion. The Emperor Augustus, who tried to revive the old Roman conventions and the old Roman frame of mind, eventually crushed Ovid. Augustus knew what he wanted; he may instinctively have felt, better than the poet himself did, what the real issue was. Ovid has never been able to comprehend what was objectionable or dangerous in his own poetry, and why he was persecuted and exiled for the rest of his days to a place where he was cruelly cut off from the one thing most necessary to him: an intimate intercourse with fellow human beings.

◇ ◇ ◇

One short line has taken us far afield. Let us now return to the text of the *Amores* and examine another example of blended identities. The elegy which can be named *The Chariot Race* (*Am*. III, 2) is far less emotional than those we analyzed before; in fact, it is meant to be superficial and flippant, but at the same time it is very pleasant and felicitous. Like the poem on *The Dawn* (*Am*. I, 13) it consists of an address to a partner who never says a word. The author is sitting in the circus next to an attractive lady and tries to enter on a flirtation. While the audience is waiting for the show to begin, he opens a one-sided conversation with his neighbor and explains:

> I am not here out of interest for noble steeds
>   (although I pray for the victory of the driver whom you favor);
> rather I have come to talk with you and sit with you
>   and have you know of the love you inspire.
> You watch the race and I watch you; let us both do
>   what our hearts desire, and both feast our eyes.

The reader will here wonder whether the admirer can be satisfied with so little; on the other hand, what can he do when the two have no interest in common? In this quandary, Ovid uses an ingenious trick to establish a sentimental bond between the girl and himself. No doubt one of the drivers is her favorite, although he has yet to discover which one it is (cf. 67). Thus he exclaims: "Would that I could attract your attention in the same manner as he does! If I were in his place, I should do my utmost to win for your sake . . . ," and soon the poet proceeds to elaborate the fanciful story of a charioteer with whom he identifies himself. Thus he makes us forget both that the race means little to the real Ovid and that the girl means nothing to the real driver, who in all probability does not even know of her existence. The result is an imaginary Ovid who is valiantly to drive a chariot in the coming race, and is at the same time very fond of Ovid's pretty neighbor, while she returns his affection and wants him, her hero, to win. That composite person is now compared to a hero of legend: Pelops, the man who once upon a time engaged in a frightful chariot race, staking his very life against the hand of fair Hippodamia, who was in love with Pelops and helped him to win the contest. There are more things in the elegy than we can mention in this context; but later in the poem, when after a complication the race has eventually come out as the lady desired it, Ovid makes it appear that the driver's victory implies the success of his own suit, and forthwith he claims his prize from his beloved. The logic in fact convinces the girl: "She smiled and there was a promise in her eloquent eyes"; and so the elegy ends with a happy prospect. Ovid has conquered his lady by understanding her concerns and insinuating himself into her wishes and projecting his own self into that man for whom she happens to care.

◇   ◇   ◇

We have so far analyzed a few individual poems from Ovid's *Amores,* and have pondered certain particular ideas in these poems. Our next step will be to look to *The Story of Love* as a whole, under broader considerations, and to formulate the set of general notions underlying the entire collection of elegies.

The main assumption of the poet is this: Love is no mere inci-

dental event, flavoring an otherwise normal life; it is a preoccupation which molds the whole being of its victim into a new and
specific shape and places him, as it were, in a new and peculiar
sphere apart from the rest of mankind, with a different horizon,
climate, and atmosphere. The kind of love the Roman elegists have
in mind is neither purely sensual nor predominantly sentimental;
rather, they glorify a passionate state of mind which fails to dis-
criminate between the two sides. The lovers, of course, are not married to one another, nor do they want to formalize their friendship;
a proposal of marriage has no place in this kind of poetry or in this
romantic frame of mind. A marriage, as a rule, was preceded in
Rome not by a courtship but by negotiations between the respective
families; and the contentment of domestic and family life would
never be admitted as a subject for literary treatment.[43] Thus the
lovers in the elegies are united by no legal ties, and their relationship
is dependent on their affection alone. Society did not object to irregu-
lar connections of that sort, as far as the young man was concerned;
and the young woman would supposedly not belong to society, but
be free to follow her inclination. The lady is assumed to live by
herself or with some other man of her choice;[44] beyond that, her
position is left rather indefinite.[45] It is made plain, however, that the
concerns of the heart rather than material considerations ought to
determine her attitude toward the admirer. He would, it is true, try
to brighten her life with such presents as he could afford; this, however, was an accessory only. No doubt there were in Rome very
many independent young women to answer the specifications (*Ars
Amat.* I, 55–66), and with one or another of them a union would
be formed which, after all, was not to last forever and yet gave the
attractive prospect of a more than momentary engrossment for both
the partners. It is axiomatic for Ovid that the woman should be on
an equal footing with the man and should be looking for the same
kind of benefits from their association; a fundamental divergence
of objectives would spoil everything for him.[46]

The atmosphere of Ovid's *Amores* is by no means blissfully en-
trancing and balmy with May-day fragrance; rather, the emotional
weather is brisk and subject to moody shifts like April storms and
sunshine. *The Story of Love* consists of a series of dramatic incidents

and crises, and more especially so since the relationship is not on a secure and permanent basis. Hope and fear sway hither and thither the mind of the adventurous lover, and he does not want to miss the thrills of either hope or fear. Continually he is haunted by jealousy, and yet his pleasure is heightened by the constant threat of a rival, real or imaginary. The existence of an eager competitor proves that his mistress is desirable, and his own successes are the more valuable as they are precarious. Nothing is stable and final. The lover will sometimes swear eternal allegiance to his lady and perhaps at the moment actually mean what he says, but in fact there is no bond which cannot be severed, just as there is no break which cannot be mended.

This erratic state of affairs is reflected in the incoherent character of a work like Ovid's *Amores*. There is little continuity in the volumes of Roman erotic poetry, and scholars who have tried to piece together the history of one individual affair have lost their labor. The order in which the elegies are arranged is willful and confusing,[47] and it is an exception when one poem begins where the previous one left off.[48] Each elegy is to be seen in its own light, and taken all together they give a composite picture of a lover's life and world. In twelve of Ovid's elegies the lady is given the pseudonym Corinna; but even in one of those twelve it is made abundantly clear that no one woman was able to monopolize the poet's attentions. It also happened that Ovid was unable to make up his mind which one of two lovely girls he preferred, with the result that he devoted himself to both with equal ardor (II, 10). All that can be expected is that there was one to occupy the first place in his heart for most of the time, and she was presumably identical with the so-called Corinna (II, 17, 33–34). Thus the situation became never quite dull and stationary, and the man as well as the woman offered their partner ample opportunities for jealousy. Exuberance rated more highly than loyalty.   ◇   ◇   ◇

The modern reader, however historically minded, is likely to have moments when he frowns on that sort of exuberance and feels that, even if people did indulge in such practices, there was no need to waste good poetry on them. It may therefore be remarked in passing that a Roman young man of feeling had little choice in his quest for a worthy pursuit to employ his leisure. Where should he look for something to engage his youthful enthusiasm? He belonged to a nation which was none too imaginative and was not given to spiritual, theoretical, and impractical pursuits; and he was a member of a snobbish and prejudiced society. Roman religion made no appeal to the emotions; it was more of an institution than an inspiration. Not a few people at that time were won over to Oriental beliefs and cults which gave a more satisfactory outlet to fervid piety; but fervid piety was outlandish and wholly against the spirit of Roman traditions. There was, of course, philosophy which tried to appeal both to the heart and the intellect. But the philosophies of the age were past their fresh and creative stage; all schools were annoyingly contentious; their teachings had an air of quaint unreality; and, worst of all for our young man, they opposed any and all strong emotions and professed to lead their adepts to a calm and mellow serenity. There might have been science and scholarship; but the Romans had a natural gift for only two special fields: antiquarian history and the development, if not the theory, of law.[49] Furthermore, the idea seemed insufferable that a better-class Roman should bend all his energies to research for its own sake. He was not supposed to do more than round out his general education and equip himself with a smattering of the current views and theories; or, at most, make a hobby of reading or writing books on material already familiar to experts. There was art; but if one wished to retain his standing in the world of fashion he could indulge in a passionate artistic interest only by collecting expensive objects or feverishly building mansions and villas, two lines which for an obvious reason were not open to the average young man. There was the wide-open world to be explored; and one could, and did, travel and see the old centers of civilization. There was literature. The study of literature and the writing of poetry, indeed, were taken up by many Romans of the time, young and old, with almost fanatical zest.[50] And there were, finally, friendship and its far more emotional counterpart, love. Love and literature were combined in Roman erotic poetry. Here then was a field of literature congenial to the typical young Roman because it originated from personal experience and pointed the way to practical experience; just as, on a very different level, a mature statesman would be engrossed in books of history because he had his hand in the making of history.

◇   ◇   ◇

Love as an autonomous occupation is frequently contrasted by Ovid to other pursuits, as we saw it done in the poem on *The Dawn*. War with its strenuous exertions is the direct opposite of love with its languid sentimentality; nevertheless, that truism challenged ingenuity to invent reasons why they should not rather be considered as similar (*Am*. I, 9; II, 12).[51] Once, in the elation of his first triumph over Corinna's heart, Ovid makes a clever remark to the effect that love is a kind of one man's war upon the enemy in which teamwork is out of the question and chance plays no part (*Am*. II, 12, 9–16); which is a facetious way of saying that love is a very personal kind of activity. There, it is each man for himself, and the effort, the achievement, the prize, and the glory are all his own.[52] In earnest, of course, Ovid would never match himself against a soldier. His tender heart abhorred the cruelty of war, and his liberal mind despised the sordid greed which animated most professional soldiers. Doubly odious were ruthless soldiering and base avarice[53] to Ovid when they desecrated the sublime sphere of love. As a horrible example for everything love should not be, Ovid once pictures his lady in the arms of a soldier (*Am*. III, 8). As he puts it, the intruder had made a fortune by hiring out his body for the loot to be gained in war (line 20); and the poet's mistress had yielded to that man in the same mercenary spirit.[54] In this connection, Ovid again rehearses the worldly pursuits of mankind: bloody war; trespassing in ships on the ocean; stirring up the soil with the plow; and the other occupations that human ingenuity devised and perfected to the debasement of the human soul, all of them motivated or corrupted by avarice. Wealth alone, he says, gives access to the senate, and it is wealth which lifts a man to equestrian rank and invests him with the authority of a judge.[55] "Be it so; let them[56] lay their grasping hands upon everything, let them sway elections and lawsuits, if only they leave one thing—it is all we ask—to the poor man" (*Am*. III, 8, 35–60). In another characteristic elegy (*Am*. I, 10), a slight lack of delicacy on the lady's part is enough to make the excitable lover complain in bitter indignation. "You ask why I have changed? 'Tis because you demand gifts from me." Chafing, he explains that he used to love her both body and soul; but now[57] the blemish on her character has tarnished the brilliance of her beauty, so that it dazzles him no more; his madness is over, his mind once again clear and sober. (We wonder how coolheaded he may be with his offended feelings.) Then he proceeds to lecture his mistress as if she had actually begun to sell, instead of giving, him her favors. The lecture goes on for a long time (too long a time, in fact), until the poet suddenly relents (this is typical of Ovid) and says:

> There is no harm, of course, in demanding a reward from a
>   rich man....
> But the poor pays with his service, his devotion, and his loyalty.
>   Let each man give his mistress what he happens to possess.
> A deserving woman can also be celebrated in poetry.
>   That endowment is mine; I make known her whom I select.
> Dresses will rend, jewels and gold will crumble;
>   but the glory which poetry bestows will live on through time.
>   (I, 10, 53; 57 ff.)

This sententious prophecy would have made a resounding finale, in good conventional style, for the elegy; but Ovid adds a gentle postscript,[58] as it were:

> It is not my giving but your demand which hurts and repels me.
>   You ask for a thing, and I refuse; cease to want it, and I shall give.

The comprehending lover is ready for a liberal compromise; he will soon make up for his diatribe with a surprise gift.

These examples show how the spirit of love, as conceived by Ovid, sets up its own code of propriety, and how it enjoys the fight for its own preservation, waging a jolly war on enemies both from without and within. There are many things the lover has to contend or put up with, but I shall not, and indeed should not care to, offer a complete list of them.

✧   ✧   ✧

In Ovid's erotic elegies the struggling passion is dramatically depicted with all its reasonings and imaginings. Some of the lover's notions change with his moods; others are inherent to his condition. Invariably he will feel that the concerns of the heart are of prime importance and that everything else must give way to them. He tries to ignore any facts that contradict his sentiment (cf. III, 14, 45–50). Out of his own emotions and what they reveal and demand, the lover builds an exclusive system in which he wishes and labors to believe; all the rest of knowledge and experience is pushed back out of sight, to a secondary plane of reality, shadowy and unsubstantial by comparison.

As a consequence, in this poetry delusion and self-deception are considered as meritorious whenever they satisfy the feeling and invigorate the emotion. "I often mistake what could be for what is," says Ovid (II, 13, 6),[59] boasting no doubt of the independence of his active mind. The possibility to which he is referring in the context makes the anguish of a pathetic situation more poignant and more personal for him. Another time, he indulges in jealous suspicions which are obviously unfounded (II, 5).[60] While trying to convict his mistress of a breach of faith, he sadly overrates the stringency of his arguments; but his gratuitous reproaches show how highly he treasures the integrity of their association. In his heart of hearts, however, he knows very well her profound devotion to him, and with a delightful couplet (51–52) he half recants his incriminations. More frequently, breezy imagination travels in the opposite direction, looking for pleasant dreams to blot out unwelcome realities. More than once Ovid tells his mistress to dissemble and steadfastly deny whatever transgression she may have committed (I, 4, 69–70). One elegy begins with this couplet:

> I own that your beauty gives you the right to sin;[61]
> but I refuse to have the wretched truth forced upon me.[62]
> (III, 14, 1 f.)

Thus the poet exhorts his lady to develop a double personality; he wants her to appear modest under ordinary circumstances, and only in the most private moments of their relationship to cast off all her reserve. Her frank admission of faithlessness has given him a cruel shock:

> I am out of my mind and dying, whenever you confess to have sinned,
> and the blood in my veins flows cold.

That makes me love, makes me hate—in vain, for I cannot help loving;
    it makes me yearn to be dead—but together with you.
I shall not ask questions, nor search into that
    which you are hiding. Deceit I shall accept as a bounty.

(37 ff.)

These forceful lines are unusual,[63] penetrating as they do deep into a maze of strange and painful emotions.[64] The poet sees no way out of it except by embracing the part of a dupe. In default of what he really craves for, he invites thoughtful cant.

Time and again we find Ovid bent on concealing from his own eyes a disagreeable fact; but he also sees to it that the cloak is transparent. The bitter-sweet passion of love, as he conceived it, fed upon the incongruity between things as they are and as they ought to be. There is some degree of realism, after all, in a game where you know that an illusion is an illusion.

◇   ◇   ◇

The make-believe in Ovid's erotic verse frees the lover's soul and allows his sentiments to range far and wide, deep and high, unhampered. But there is no artificial disguise; the lovers are not garbed in a pastoral costume or put into fictitious pastoral surroundings. The ladies are represented as real ladies of real Rome, and yet the poet's love invests them, in earnest or in sport, with extraordinary qualities and powers. In an ecstasy of veneration he deifies his mistress (I, 7, 32), or ranks her with the divine beings because like the almighty gods she can make or mar his happiness. In fact, the goddess in the flesh can do more for him than the dubious beings in faraway heaven.[65] Ovid once prays to Venus to give him victory over the heart of his fair neighbor on the circus bench, and he pretends to have seen the image of the deity nod assent; immediately, however, he asks the lady personally to confirm the promise:

May Venus pardon me: you will be a greater goddess.

(III, 2, 60)

In the following elegy he says that "beauty possesses a divine majesty" (*forma numen habet,* III, 3, 12), so that the gods themselves bow to its authority and ignore a girl's false oath, if she is pretty enough.

Poetry likewise is considered as divine:

> We poets are called sacred and favorites of the gods;
> some even believe that we possess divine power.
>
> (III, 9, 17 f.)

We are quoting from the poem on the death of Tibullus, the revered master of erotic elegy. When Tibullus' body was burned on the pyre, Ovid was shocked by the experience that death was permitted profanely to lay his "dark hands" upon the prophet of the Muses (19–20).

To write poetry means, among other things, to transform reality, lifting it to a level where it can satisfy man's finer thoughts and nobler sentiments. Love performs a similar feat by means of a similar inspired madness. Small wonder, then, that Ovid wove his poetry and his love into one and the same texture. He indicates that he would enter on an amorous affair with an artist's eye on converting it into verse (I, 1, 19–24, and I, 3, 19). Seen in this light, erotic poetry was more realistic and substantial than either drama or epic; here alone, the author composed his own life and lived his own verse. It was, however, a universal dogma that drama and epic, with their lofty and virile themes, ranked far above erotic verse.[66] Ovid had no reason to question this view so far as style and treatment were concerned; his talent did not tend toward sustained grandeur, and it was the most natural thing for him to keep his *Amores* on a moderate level, with only momentary excursions into the sublime. On the other hand, he was convinced that the emotional experiences of people of feeling, as exemplified in his own person, deserved to be represented in poetry just as well as the fables of myth, the figments of legend, or the exploits of the great; and he happened to be a past master in giving voice to the events going on in the human soul. Thus he must have resented the tenet that erotic poetry was the lowest variety of the art, undignified and inconsequential.[67] In his many utterings on the objectives and merits of his erotic elegiacs, he wavered between an apologetic attitude and a defiant one, or else hid his confusion behind playful irony. Now he would submit to the general view (I, 1; II, 18), and now scoff at the idea of his writing elevated hexameters about the legendary war between the gods and the giants. I was describing that cosmic battle, he says,[68] and in my verse was brandishing Juppiter's thunderbolt, when my mistress locked me out; immediately I dropped the bolt and forgot Juppiter:

> Forgive me, O Jove, but your weapon availed me nothing,
>   for the thunderbolt of a locked door is more formidable than yours.
> So I took up once more my own weapons, blandishment and elegy:
>   mild words softened the hard door.
>
> (II, 1, 19 ff.)

This kind of poetry, then, was practical; its ingratiating charm helped the lover to persuade a woman, and its glory held out for her the coveted honor of being made known all over the world (I, 10, 60; II, 17, 28; *Ars Am.* III, 535–538). And passion, in turn, provided the writer with congenial subjects and with the proper frame of mind for composing his spirited verse; it had aroused his talent (III, 12, 15–16):

> I was lazy and born to sluggish leisure,
>   couch and shade had made my mind soft,
> when my care for a fair lady woke me from sloth
>   and ordered me to serve Love as his soldier.
>
> (I, 9, 41 ff.)

Thus it seemed well worth while to Ovid to sing of that which filled his life and heart, and he felt that he was accomplishing more than if, as the conquering and debating Romans of old used to do, he should

> kick up the dust to hunt for the prizes of war,
> or memorize long-winded laws,[69] or hire out
>   my voice to the thankless forum.
>
> (I, 15, 4 ff.)

Exultantly he defies his detractors who say that he is wasting his youthful strength in sterile idleness (1–3). He knows that he is engaged in a work which will not die with him:

> Even when the flame of the pyre will have consumed one part of me,
>   shall I live and much of my self survive.
>
> (41 f.)

Thus it was art for life's sake, and life for art's sake; the pattern of reciprocity seemed impregnable. Nevertheless the charmed circle was once breached by a peculiar complication. Ovid tells the story of the annoying disturbance in one of his most amusing and reveal-

ing elegies (III, 12), with which we shall wind up our discussion
of the *Amores*. The poem begins with the baffled author wondering
what the cause of the misfortune was: an unlucky day, perhaps?
a bad omen? a hostile star? or the wrath of a god? Finally we learn
what is troubling him. Ovid is afraid he has begun to share with a
crowd the favors of his Corinna; and no one but he is to blame for it.
In his elegies he has advertised Corinna's perfections so persuasively
that now his readers are flocking to her, in order to secure for themselves such delights as his verses depict.[70] Ovid had always felt that
poetry should be personal, and now his personal poetry has played
him false. He might have written, instead, on innocuous subjects,
the Trojan War, for instance, or the deeds of the Emperor; and yet
it was Corinna alone who had stirred up his talent. In his predicament, Ovid gives away an arcanum of poetry. There is no such
Corinna in the flesh as appears in his verse, and Ovid's rivals are
pursuing a phantom:

> Poets do not want to be heard like witnesses in court;
>   I would rather that my words had no weight with you.
>   (III, 12, 19 f.)

We writers, Ovid explains, boldly fashion our own material so as
to fit our story. Where a superwarrior is required, we invent a giant
with a thousand arms; a fabulous hero's horse is fitted by us with
wings; thanks to us will Jove, the arch-lover, take on any shape that
best serves his purpose; and Orpheus with his lyre, a singer like ourselves, will set the very rocks in motion:

> A poet's rich caprice knows no bounds,
>   it does not tie its word to the truth of fact.
> You should have known that my praise of her was false.
>   I suffer now because you are too simple.
>   (41 ff.)

Here the elegy ends, but in another passage Ovid points out a better
way to read his elegies:

> A youth, wounded by the same arrow which made me what I now am,
>   may recognize the familiar tokens of his own fire,
> and, marveling long, he will exclaim: What telltale taught
>   that writer to set in verse all that happened to me?
>   (II, 1, 7 ff.)

It will be well for us to keep in mind, for the *Heroides* and *Meta-morphoses,* that Ovid requests us to translate his writings into terms of our personal experience.

❖   ❖   ❖

Although not given to theoretical reasoning, Ovid saw clearly some essential facts of his own calling. He understood that poetry lives on its own plane of reality and that we commit a blunder when we confuse the different planes. He also saw that our ideals are not to be found in life as it is, but are to be projected by us into our individual lives. And indeed, the higher we set our human standards, the more we must create what we shall worship. To that truth Ovid was to give the final and consummate expression in the Pygmalion story of the *Metamorphoses,* a story which we shall examine later on.

We have referred to the *Metamorphoses* before we come to it, for several reasons. First, we would indicate the consistency of Ovid's thinking all through the different periods of his life. Secondly, we wanted to show that we have not been exaggerating the significance of the ideas implied in his erotic elegies. If Ovid later followed up one or another of those ideas and developed its full import, then we can conclude that the sportive play of his earliest work also has a more serious side. And lastly, it may be interesting to throw a fleeting glance at the finished form of a thought while we are still studying its first emergence and still remember the conditions under which it arose. The *Amores* gives a vivid picture of the decadence of Ovid's age, and it shows how the poet, far from being a radical reformer, enjoyed and promoted those trends which could make life more tenderly emotional.[11] But he did more than merely select what he wanted and ignore the rest. With loving zeal he embellished whatever seemed defective, and substituted fine illusions for offensive facts. Pygmalion, as Ovid will tell his tale in the *Metamorphoses,* was shocked into creative idealism by the depravity he witnessed in actual life. The ferment of disintegration set free all sorts of forces; and some of them were, after all, constructive and progressive.

4. THE "HEROIDES"

OVID DID not wait for his *Amores* to be completed before he undertook another work in the same elegiac meter. The title is *Heroides,* which means *Women of Legend;* and the book consists of fifteen letters supposedly written by as many women of legendary fame. The reader, as soon as he saw the names of the correspondents, would recall their adventures and misfortunes, and he would often also be reminded of some previous poem or drama on the same subject. Each letter is supposed to have been composed by the lady at a critical moment of her life, and it is directed not to some confidant but to the very man of her destiny. All are love letters. The lady will, for instance, entreat her beloved at long last to return to her; or to let her go back to him; or to reciprocate her affection; or to take good care of himself in the dreadful perils of war.

◇   ◇   ◇

The critics, when they introduce us to the study of Ovid's *Heroides,* seldom fail to direct our attention to the fact that in his college years the author had practiced the rhetorical *suasoria,* which by definition is a speech advising a certain person to do a certain thing. Persistently, the *Heroides* is styled a collection of "*suasoriae* in verse." The label, however, sheds little light on the actual content of Ovid's work.[1] Perhaps we can find a more helpful analogy. When we read through the fifteen verse letters, we come here and there upon a passage the like of which we ourselves meant to write in some crisis of our own life. I say that we meant to, and not that we did, because I am thinking of a special kind of letter, the kind which in actual fact we rarely put down on paper and would hardly ever drop in the mailbox. Nevertheless we did carefully prepare that letter in our own mind, silently arguing out the issue with our remote and unwitting partner, perhaps for hours on end; anticipating his objections and thwarting his evasions; and with each repetition we improved on the clarity of our reasoning and the moral force of our appeal, until eventually we had perfected our unwritten letter so as to render it, on its own merits, irresistibly convincing. Unfor-

---

[1] For notes to chapter 4, see pages 190–193.

tunately, we had no means of communicating with the person we were thus addressing; or, if he were to receive such a letter, he would not be greatly impressed, because he was already prejudiced in the matter; or he would not open it, because he was not interested in anything we had to say; or, perhaps, it was not proper for us to tell him how we felt, for tact and pride and shame forbade it. For one or another of these reasons, our letter never materialized; and yet for our own sake we worked it out mentally.

Now Ovid's *Heroides* are very nearly letters of this kind—thought letters, as we may call them. It is true that they pretend to be material letters in black and white; but their tenor is so peculiar that it makes little difference whether or not they were written out and dispatched and delivered.

The main characteristic of the series is that the epistles, with possibly two exceptions,[2] are invariably unavailing, and the reader, familiar as he is with the stories, is expected immediately to recognize their futility. The reasons why the letters are devoid of any practical consequence vary. Two of the epistles, those of Penelope and Briseis (I and III), are unnecessary because the course of events is independently moving in the desired direction. In this case, the irony of a useless appeal is of a friendly and humorous kind. Nevertheless there is some bitterness in store even for Briseis: she implores Achilles to make her come back to him; he will do so, but in his own time and for reasons of his own. As a rule, however, the impending frustration of the writer is of a grim and tragic sort. Protesilaus will pay no heed to the letter warning him to be prudent in the war, or perhaps he will not even have a chance to see it before he dies (XIII). Hercules is already fatally ill because of his wife's mistake and Deianira learns of the fact before she has completed her epistle to him; thus she decides to commit suicide, and the last lines she puts down are a farewell to her husband and to life (IX). Other letters are written with no hope of realization from the beginning. Dido acknowledges in her first lines that she despairs of influencing Aeneas in her favor and that the epistle is meant to be her swan song (VII); and so is Phyllis certain of her own doom (II). Some of the writers, to be sure, indulge in the illusion that the letter may accomplish its purpose, but their actual chances are absurdly slim. The first of the series is from Penelope to Odysseus, who has not been heard of for the last ten years and whose whereabouts is utterly unknown; and yet Penelope will hand her letter to some sailor who may at some time and somewhere happen to run into her husband. Thus it is much more a matter of pleading one's own cause and unburdening one's own emotions than of achieving something, and the writer may well be aware of this futility even when she does not say so directly.[3] When Phaedra (IV) begins by contending that it will not harm Hippolytus if he reads her lines through, she is evidently aware that he will not even trouble to glance at them;[4] and when she goes on to say that it is not uncommon to put into writing the most dreadful secrets, she half admits that in actual fact the letter ought never have been written.[5] The emotions as the writers set them forth are genuine, but the medium which they choose for expressing themselves has no proper place in solid reality. Ovid was doubtless aware of the improbabilities which his theme involved, but, unconcerned as he was with that kind of realism, he set aside the pedantic objections. Since a letter seemed to him the obvious medium for a request to a distant person, he pretended that the epistles had originally existed in pen and ink, just as they were in pen and ink in his volume of elegies.[6] Once, however, he supersedes that fiction. Ariadne has been deserted by Theseus; while she was asleep, he sailed away and left her on a solitary island. Now the woman, sitting on the shore in dread of the unknown perils of the wilderness, writes her epistle to Theseus and concludes it thus:

> If by some miracle you should see me from the high deck of your
>   ship,
>   the sight of my sad figure would prevail on you.
> So then look upon me, as indeed you can, with your mind's eyes;[7]
>   behold me hugging a cliff pounded by restless waves . . .
> Then alter your sail and course, Theseus, and float back to me;
>   if I die before you reach me, you will yet recover my body.
>   (X, 133 ff.; 151 f.)

Thus she tries, just as we do in our thought letters, to commune with her distant lover and draw him to her by means of a spiritual contact; Ovid has, for the moment at least, discarded the notion of a material letter, which is more than usually incongruous here. If it were sent off from the island (but how?), it would reach Theseus (if ever) not before he arrived at Athens, when it would be too late for him to turn back and rescue the marooned lady. And yet in the middle of the pathetic appeal across the waters the poet refers to the physical act of writing (140): "Behold [says Ariadne] how the letters totter, drawn with a shaking wrist."

◇　◇　◇

The fact that the epistles are cognate to thought letters gives them a rare intimacy. We are permitted to read the mind of a lonely woman in distress and to watch its passionate arguing, anxious searching, pensive musing, and wishful daydreaming. There are, for instance, the letters of Penelope and Laodamia to their husbands who have gone far away, and the wives can do nothing but in blank ignorance wait for "the slow days" (I, 8) to go by. Odysseus has not returned for another ten years after the conclusion of the Trojan War, and Penelope writes:

> It is true, Troy lies low, the city execrated by Greek womanhood;
> hardly was Priam worth so much suffering, nor entire Troy ...
> For the others Pergam is destroyed, for me alone it still stands.
> (I, 3 f.; 51)

And then she loses herself in the thought that her husband alone survived the war but has never been heard of since:

> It were better if the walls built by Apollon were standing even now
> (I hate myself for so disloyal a wish);
> then I were certain where you fought and I feared only the war,
> and shared my sorrow with many another.
> I know not what it is I dread, but in madness I dread everything;
> wide open is the field for my anxiety.
> (67 ff.)

Laodamia's situation is different: she is a young bride; her husband has just left her and is still on his way to Troy. But her emotions are similar. She envies the wives of the enemy, who will be able to see the battles and be near their men in whatever happens to them,

> while we are in doubt, and our alarm compels us
> to take what can be for what is.
> (XIII, 149 f.)

The very place names of Troy land,

> Ilion, Tenedus, Simois, Xanthus, and Ida,
>   these names frighten almost by their mere sound.
>   (53 f.)

For us who know what is in store for her, it is touching to see how
her apprehensive mind misreads the chart of destiny. She thinks
that Paris, who had caused the war by raping Helen, will be a
powerful and dangerous foe for Protesilaus (55–56), while her husband, in her opinion,

> is far more gallant in love than in battle;
>   let others wage war, and Protesilaus love.
>   (83 f.)

Actually, the seducer Paris proved an indifferent warrior, while
Protesilaus was the first eagerly to jump on the hostile shore and
met his death before any other man had disembarked. The same
epistle also gives a fine example of the way in which frequently the
writer's mind is swayed hither and thither by blind anxiety and
expectancy, with her moods and thoughts helplessly adrift:

> Of all the thousand ships, let yours be the thousandth,
>   let it as the hindmost plow the worn-out flood.
> Also I warn you to be the last in disembarking;
>   it is not the paternal soil to which you hasten.
> But, coming home, urge on your boat with both oar and sail
>   and swiftly set foot on your own shore!
> Whether the sun be hidden or high above our earth,
>   join me swiftly, by daytime or at night!
> But rather at night than by daytime . . .[8]
>   (97 ff.)

Then she speaks of her lonesome yearning for his company, but also
tells him of the nightmares that visit her, when his image appears,
pallid and lamenting. Now again she anticipates the bliss of his
homecoming, and how he will tell her of all his adventurous exploits; but once more her imagination turns to his present doings
and his voyage to Troy:

> When I remember Troy, I think of storms and sea;
>   fond hope breaks down, felled by alarm.
>   (123 f.)

She has learned that adverse winds are keeping the fleet in port, and she is quick to surmise that the gods do not favor the expedition; may the leaders heed the warning! Then she recants:

> But how? Dare I call them back? Far be the omen of calling back,
> may a friendly breeze help them through calm water.
>
> (135 f.)

Although some of the elegies have a rather delicate subject, they are all more restrained and dignified than the *Amores;* this time it is the ladies who do the talking, and legendary ladies at that. The writers, on the other hand, in spite of their title as *Heroides* which is misleading to the modern mind, are no damsels and matrons solemnly draped in the stiff and dusty pomp of antiquity; they are just so many women in love, wise or foolish. Too many, perhaps, they are. When we read the epistles one after another, at times they sound monotonous, and we feel reminded of Amelia's love letters in *Vanity Fair:* "She wasn't a heroine. Her letters were full of repetition" (Vol. I, chap. 12). But it is our own mistake if we read elegies in bulk, and there is in the volume as much variety of case, character, and treatment as was possible, given the common theme. In order to appreciate the range of variation, we shall briefly examine two more examples, the epistles of Phyllis to Demophon and of Briseis to Achilles.

◇   ◇   ◇

In contrast to most of the other epistles, the subject of the Phyllis letter (II) was taken from some rather obscure source. But the tradition from which it came is irrelevant, because the story is essentially an everyday occurrence and it is treated in a simple, direct, and unaffected manner. True enough, since here we are in the province of legend, Phyllis is a princess and her lover a son of Theseus, king of Athens; nevertheless, the royal station of the characters is only incidental and does not detract from the typical nature of the situation. The Thracian girl Phyllis, an artless young orphan, has hospitably received young Demophon, who had been shipwrecked off the coast of her land. She put him up in her house, fell in love with him and gave him her all, on the promise that he would come back within a month and live happily with her ever after. The letter is written four months after Demophon's departure, when Phyllis has little hope left for his eventual return and is soon to commit suicide. I quote two passages:

> If you count the time that has elapsed, and we lovers do count it,
>   you will see that my complaint does not come too soon.
> Even so was my hope laggard; one is slow to give credence
>   to that which brings pain, and still my love refuses to be hurt by you.
> Often I lied to myself for you, often I saw
>   a stormy south wind driving your sails back to port;
> often I cursed your father for not letting you go—
>   and perhaps it is not your father who keeps you away.
> Sometimes I feared that on your voyage to Thrace
>   your ship had been swallowed by white breakers;
> often I kneeled before the gods and burned incense
>   on the altar, praying for you, knave, to be safe;
> often, when I saw the winds to be favorable on the skies and the sea,
>   I said to myself: If he is safe, he is coming.
> My faithful love fancied every obstacle to your eagerness
>   and my imagination was busy to excuse you.
> Nevertheless you are laggard . . .
>   (II, 7 ff.)

The other passage intimates that the writer's life is wrecked beyond repair. But Phyllis does not describe her situation in tragic terms; she merely states that, together with her honor (60), she has also lost the prospect of another husband:

> The Thracians whom I scorned shrink from marrying me,
>   because I preferred a stranger to my own people.
> They will remark: "It is high time for her to go to clever Athens;
>   we will find someone else to rule over warlike Thrace."
>   (81 ff.)

And now she grows impatient with those who measure the value of any action by the yardstick of practical usefulness:

> "The result justifies the act," says the proverb. I wish no success
>   to him who would judge deeds by their outcome.
> Let only the sea near our shore be whipped to foam by your oars,
>   and they will own that I was wise for myself and my people.
> I was not wise; nor will you, Demophon, feel moved to live
>   in my palace, or bathe your weary limbs in Thracian waters.[10]
>   (85 ff.)

She means to indicate[11] that she has not been calculating her chances, but wants to be reproached or commended for her trusting love alone:

> Tell me, what have I done? If I was imprudent in my love,
>   my sin could have earned me the right to claim you.[12]
>
> (27 f.)

The Briseis epistle (III) diverges from that of Phyllis in more than one respect. The characters differ widely; the plot is complex and circumstantial, this time; and in a delectable fashion the tenor of the letter constantly challenges comparison with its literary model.

The epistle is set against the most illustrious of backgrounds, for the subject is taken from the main plot of Homer's *Iliad*. In consequence of a quarrel between the leaders, Agamemnon robbed Achilles of a slave woman by the name of Briseis. Briseis had been captured by Achilles when he conquered her native city and slew its king, her father, her three brothers, and her husband; and he had taken her for his concubine. Then Agamemnon changed his mind and tried to make amends. He sent messengers to Achilles and offered not only to restore Briseis to Achilles, but also to give him his own daughter in wedlock and to present gifts amounting to a huge fortune. But Achilles, in the stubborn pride of his indignation, refused to accept the offer, and even hinted that he might leave for home the next morning. That same night Ovid's letter purports to be written.

As soon as we read the first lines and the rising curtain uncovers before our mind's eye fair Briseis spelling out in a tongue foreign to her an eloquent love letter to Achilles—at that moment we realize that a very familiar story has acquired a surprisingly fresh appearance by a radical reversal of perspective, and that a most monumental story now assumes the hue of fond tenderness through the different light by which the stage is flooded. The perspective is changed by causing the glorious events to be seen from the point of view of a mere accessory, a person who in the ancient epic played only a minor and passive part; in the *Iliad,* Briseis had nothing to say and was no more than an object of transactions between the great kings. And the lighting is new because she is a very feminine woman, whereas the *Iliad* was the most masculine of epics and

Achilles its most masculine character. Moreover, the epistle is replete with reminiscences from the text of the *Iliad* which the reader will greet with almost a smile, seeing how iridescent they become when Briseis, of all people, sets them down. This way of quoting would border on parody were it not for the fact that the lady has a perfect title to discuss any of the events affecting her own vital interests. Ovid, in transposing views and words from the factual and heroic epic into personal and sentimental elegy, puts forth an intriguing play of good-natured banter.[13]

Unlike the sweet provincial girl Phyllis, Briseis is a woman who had been married before and is experienced in the ways of menfolk. Intellectually she is probably superior to the rash fighter and lover Achilles. Seizing upon his immense pride, she tries to rouse him to action by taunts of which she does not mean one word seriously (113–124). No other epistle is artful in such a style. And yet her stratagems will fail because, blinded by her own love, she overrates Achilles' attachment to her when the scales are weighted on the opposite side by his self-assertion. She feels sure that it was a mistake on Agamemnon's part to dispatch mere male messengers to Achilles; if she had been sent instead, her personal presence would have stood a far better chance of prevailing upon her lover than all the eloquence of Phoenix or Odysseus, not to mention awkward Ajax (127–134). In her own soul, affection outweighs pride. She ought to be deeply offended by the slight she had received, but knowing what kind of man Achilles is, she understates her grievances and proffers them with a touch of humor (*pauca queror* 5–6; 8–14; 21–42; 111–114, etc.). Her genuine devotion comes into the open in a passage where she tells of the cruel shock she received when she learned that Achilles had threatened to sail the next morning. Rather would she be dead than stay behind. She implores him to take her with him; but she has seen too much of life to aspire to more than she can hope for:

> If you have decided for a return to your ancestral mansion,
>   I am no heavy burden for your fleet;
> I shall go as a captive with her conqueror, not as a wife with her
>   husband;
>   my hands are trained to work the wool.

The very fairest among the Grecian ladies will enter
  —and may she enter—your chamber to be your queen,
a worthy daughter-in-law to your father, grandson of Jove and Aegina,
  and to your mother, daughter of Nereus:
I shall humbly do the task assigned to your slave
  and spin out my own thread from a full distaff.
Only I wish your wife would not harass me,
  for she will not be fair to me for whatever reason;
and you must not let her tear my hair while you are there,
  nor must you say lightly: That one also I have possessed.
Or even, you may let her do so, as long as I am not scorned and left
  behind.
  This is the dread which, alas, shakes my wretched frame.
(III, 67 ff.)

For scenes like the one anticipated by Briseis, a woman slave mistreated by the housewife, and the husband casually referring to the pleasures the girl had given him in times bygone—for scenes like this Ovid could find his models in the world in which he lived. It happens often in the book *Heroides* that the reader is permitted to forget the legendary setting of the stories. For Ovid does not stress the mythical features of the plots. Rarely does he mention miracles, nor ever, in the Hellenistic style, paradoxically combine the fabulous with the natural. He rather keeps up an even and balanced manner, midway between dignified antiquity and commonplace modernity.

◇   ◇   ◇

In Ovid's *Heroides,* legendary figures come to life as in a drama, but it is a lyric monodrama condensed into a single monologue. The circumstantial facts of the plot form merely the background for the lone character on the stage, and there is no action in the play except for the stream of thoughts and sentiments that flow through her tender soul, and for her eloquent protest against things she has no power to alter. Emotionally, much is going on; substantially, nothing happens as long as the scene lasts. The real events are all in the past and in the future, and the partner whom she is addressing is beyond her reach. Thus we find Ovid's art once more moving on a plane different from ordinary reality,[14] and different in a peculiar way. The idea of verse epistles of this sort was new, and Ovid felt justly proud of his originality.[15] A letter is, according to an ancient definition, a halved dialogue, and the *Heroides,* moreover, are only half letters. Poetic exploitation of a twilight existence was in line with Ovid's particular gift.

5. THE "MEDEA"

WHEN OVID published the book of fifteen epistles and, a little later, the first edition of his *Amores,* he was probably still in his late twenties or, at most, not far beyond his thirtieth year.[1] His next work was to be a tragedy.[2] The new project was far more ambitious than those in which he had been engaged before. Ovid knew well what was involved in his transition to the province of tragedy, and, communicative as he was, he announced to his readers the step he was taking and explained it in detail. Even while he was still rounding out his collection of erotic elegies, so he reports, "the nobler task was presenting itself and pressing for attention" (*Am.* III, 1, 70). He realized that he had been dallying too long (*Am.* III, 1, 16). The theme of languid love (*Am.* II, 18, 3–4) was keeping his talent from rising to its full stature; now it was high time for him to write on virile subjects (*Am.* III, 1, 23–25). His juvenile pursuits had outlived their usefulness. True enough, his passion for Corinna had activated his latent genius (*Am.* II, 17, 34; *Tr.* IV, 10, 59–60); the erotic writing had trained his ability and matured his artistry (*Am.* III, 1, 59–60); it had already secured for him a standing as a poet of distinction (*Am.* I, 15; III, 15); but now he was impatient to accomplish a work of a higher order. Thus he began to experiment with dramatic writings, and a tragedy was taking shape under his hands.[3] The attempt satisfied him that he was possessed of the power and vigor necessary for such an undertaking (*Am.* II, 18, 13–14; III, 1, 30). And yet he was loath to part with his previous genre, he was still, as he puts it, too much of a lover; and thus he was shaken time and again in his resolution (II, 18).—It was never easy for Ovid to make up his mind clearly and definitely.—After some wavering (II, 18; cf. also II, 9a and 9b), he settled down to a compromise. He consented to obey the call of Dame Tragedy, but bargained for a

---

[1] For notes to chapter 5, see pages 193–195.

short delay (III, 1, 67-70). Thus he continued for a while to write love poetry, but finally his lingering hesitancy came to an end. In the concluding poem of the *Amores* (III, 15), he bade farewell forever to love and elegy, resolved upon attending to tragedy for the rest of his life (III, 1, 68).

Ovid did complete the one tragedy (*Tr.* II, 553); and thereafter he was to go back both to love and to elegy.

At the time when Ovid decided to embark on his new venture and compose tragedies, he saw himself as the future singer of "manly deeds" (*facta virorum, Am.* III, 1, 25). Broadly speaking, the term "manly deeds" covers well enough the themes for ancient tragedies. Ovid's first play, however, which was also to be his last, dealt with the deeds not of men but of a woman, and its theme was once more love and jealousy, though now on a heroic scale. Its heroine was Medea, the exotic sorceress who sacrificed everything to her passion for Jason, only to see herself deserted by him; and then she killed her lover's bride on the day of the nuptials, and slew her own children to punish their father. How closely Ovid's play paralleled Euripides' celebrated drama we cannot tell, because his *Medea* is lost. Tacitus (*Dial.* 12) rated it as one of the greatest Roman tragedies, and Quintilian (*Inst. Orat.* X, 1, 98) says that it shows what Ovid was able to accomplish when he chose to command his talent rather than yield to it.

With the publication of the *Medea* a very busy time came to an end for Ovid. In the last few years he had been simultaneously completing the *Amores,* composing the *Heroides,* and trying out his talent for tragedy; he had been torn between two widely different styles of writing; then he gave up the one with which he was familiar and worked hard to master the other; and no doubt he felt some apprehension over how his new aspirations were to succeed. The strain can hardly have subsided before the *Medea* had been completed, published, and favorably accepted. Ovid was then probably between thirty and thirty-five years old. He did not undertake any other important task for about five to nine years. He could afford to rest on his laurels for some time. His love poetry had become so popular that his elegies were acted on the stage, after the fashion of those days, with the Emperor in the audience.*

6. MORE EPISTLES OF FAMOUS LOVERS

IT MAY have been in that period of repose, when Ovid had no major literary project on his mind, or perhaps rather at some later date, that he added six poetic epistles to the fifteen he had published before.[1] The *Women of Legend* had proved successful, and he could not resist the temptation to augment the series; he never acquired the knack of wisely dropping a theme some time before all its possibilities had been exhausted. The additional letters, however, are not of the same type. For one thing, they come not singly but in pairs, the man writing first[2] and the woman replying. Paris, who dwells in Helen's palace as her guest, wooes his hostess in a note transmitted by a servant, and she answers by the same means; Leander and Hero correspond across the Hellespont; and Acontius exchanges letters with Cydippe. Moreover, it is only in the second pair that catastrophe looms on the horizon; in the last, a happy ending is in sight; and the first two correspondents, gay and carefree, are not greatly perturbed at the thought of causing a Trojan War.

When in his younger days the poet was composing the *Heroides,* a certain friend of his, Sabinus, immediately reciprocated the gift of advance copies by writing replies to six of them. Ovid was evidently delighted by the quick response, because otherwise he would not have told the world about it in one of the *Amores* elegies (II, 18, 27–34). His craving for a friendly hearing must have blinded him to the lack of taste on the part of Sabinus. It was far better to leave alone that shadow of futility which hovers over the original letters; there was no use in giving it a material body and formulating replies to the effect that the gentleman, to his profound regret, was unable to accede to the wish of the lady for such-and-such reasons.[3] Whether the answering epistles were serious or playful, well written or otherwise, it is a blessing that they have not survived. Nevertheless, a scholar of the Renascence who happened to bear the name Angelo Sabino substituted poems of his own composition for three of the lost Sabinus letters.

Perhaps it was the original Sabinus letters which gave Ovid the idea of pairing his new epistles, and probably it appeared to the poet

---

[1] For notes to chapter 6, see pages 195–199.

as an advancement over the single epistles of the first collection. While in his beginnings he loved to leave much to the imagination of the reader and to present in a *clair-obscure* light fragmentary bits of plot and circumstance, in his maturer years he tended somewhat more toward rounding out his stories and balancing his artistic effects.

◇   ◇   ◇

The letters supposed to have been exchanged by Paris and Helen before they sailed for Troy together are executed in the spirit of the *Art of Love,* and they can very well serve as paradigms for directions given there. In the *Art* (I, 437–486) the admirer is advised to test the going by correspondence before declaring his love face to face. The woman, in turn, is counseled to reply in such a manner that her lover is kept in suspense between hope and fear (III, 467–478), and this is exactly what Helen does: she both rebukes and encourages the advances of Paris.[4] This pair of letters is amusing, but nothing more.

◇   ◇   ◇

The second pair, that of Leander and Hero, is excellent though not flawless poetry. The story on which the letters are based was not derived from the body of legendary tradition; it was an isolated incident which perhaps had actually taken place in comparatively recent times. Leander and Hero, living at opposite sides of the Hellespont, were not permitted to marry, but they succeeded in wresting sparse hours of bliss from the adverse circumstances. Leander used secretly to swim the narrows at night and return home in the same fashion. The arduous venture was too often repeated, and Leander was drowned on a night when it was stormy. When Hero found his body, she took her own life. The story had been treated in a Hellenistic poem which is lost to us, but we can still perceive that Ovid adopted from his model a number of such features as were congenial to his own art.[5] In spite of these borrowings, the two epistles are thoroughly Ovidian.[6] Before the eyes of the knowing reader, a stirring picture of fondest love is set against a background of impending disaster. But the youthful correspondents themselves are too much engrossed in their passion to be deterred by the heavy odds. Of the two, Hero is the more tender, Leander the more spirited. It is he who has dared the hazard before, and he is eager to do it again. At the moment, the weather is too forbidding, but his impatience may soon cause him to challenge the vicious waves. Pained by his separation from Hero, he evokes the memory of their first intimacy. His affection is everything to him, and he is proud of the self-sufficiency of love. His love requires nothing outside itself for bringing about its own consummation; it turns him into boat, sailor and passenger at once (XVII, 148);[7] it keeps him warm in the cold flood (89-90); it gives him the strength to endure the ordeal (83-94); and like a lodestar it guides his course over the sea, in the shape of the light Hero had set up at her window (149-168). She is the light of his life (85-86), and his goddess (66-74).[8] With all his enthusiasm, Leander remains natural and human; he admits that he is afraid before he goes into the water,[9] but his fear subsides in the moment he lays aside his clothes (57).[10] But we shall not try to transcribe the fine poem.

Hero's reply is still finer. In moving words she expresses her ardent yearning for his presence:

> Forgive me if I confess it: I have no control over my love.
> We burn both with equal flame, but my strength is not equal to yours.
> I suppose that men have a greater power of mind.
> (XVIII, 4 ff.)

You men, she goes on to write, have so many distractions in your various activities,

> I am kept out of those. Even if my ardor were less great than it is,
>   nothing were left for me to do but to love.
> And I am doing that which is left to me, and I love you, my only joy,
>   more than you can ever pay me back.
> (15 ff.)

Then she tells Leander how again and again, in her thoughts and dreams, she lives vicariously through all the stages of his adventurous journey across the narrows, and how in a tempestuous night she upbraids the inclement sea "almost in his name" (22). In a confusion of wishes, she exhorts him to brave the elements and warns him not to risk his life; she suspects that he failed to come because he had transferred his affection to another woman and yet she feels sure of his steadfast love. In the last part of the epistle (121 ff.), the rising fury of the storm at the time of Hero's writing portends Leander's imminent death in the waves; the artistic effect is like that of an aria, half confident and half fearful, accompanied with threatening accords by the orchestra. Hero herself grows more and more apprehensive. She prays to the gods for the safety of her lover; she repeats what her nurse had said to give her comfort, but the words have a sinister second meaning;[11] and she tells Leander of a dream she had, not knowing that it indicates his destruction.[12]

⋄ ⋄ ⋄

The third, and last, pair of epistles is again light and playful in subject and treatment. It is based on the Hellenistic story of Acontius and Cydippe. Acontius of Ceos fell in love at first sight with Cydippe of Naxos when both were visiting on the island of Delus and admiring its ornate sanctuaries; and he tricked her into binding herself to him before they had as much as talked with each other. This is what he did. He scratched upon an apple[13] the words: "By Artemis I swear that I shall marry Acontius," and in the temple of Artemis he threw the apple so that it rolled before Cydippe's feet. The young woman read the writing aloud, as was the custom in antiquity,[14] and when she realized what was involved, she had taken the oath already. Shocked and bewildered, she hoped that the incident would remain without consequences and kept it secret. After her return to Naxus, a date was set for her marriage to the man her parents had selected for her; but as soon as a preliminary ceremony was performed, she fell seriously ill and the wedding had to be postponed. When the same coincidence twice repeated itself, her father sent to Delphi for an oracle; Apollo revealed what had happened, and Cydippe was married to Acontius. The tale of Acontius and Cydippe was widely known because Callimachus had told it in a celebrated passage of his *Aetia.*[15] A sizable part of that passage has recently come to light on a papyrus (frag. 9, 1–49 Pfeiffer), and we are thus in a position to compare Ovid's two epistles with their model. Callimachus narrates the sequence of events, as is his wont, with the air of a detached but discreetly amused reporter; the presentation combines, in an inimitable blending, neat precision with casual informality. In a word, Callimachus treats the story as an anecdote. Ovid's letters, on the other hand, are half dramatic and half lyric; they reflect the various facts, thoughts, and sentiments as Acontius and Cydippe themselves live through them up to the moment of their writing, which is the moment before the oracle becomes known. There is another characteristic difference also. Callimachus is dryly factual with respect to Cydippe; siding with Acontius, he tells the story from the man's point of view, describes how he acted in his infatuation (frags. 9 f and 9 g, p. 31), and at the end "surmises" that Acontius was as happy as a king when at last he took Cydippe into his arms (9, 44-49). Ovid is less interested in the sentimental condition of the suitor,[16] and elaborates rather the character of his fair victim. Ovid's Acontius is a pallid figure, and his letter is airy; but Cydippe and the epistle she writes are endowed by the poet with color, contour, and circumstance. Acontius has already shot his bolt and knows that it struck home; thus, in his letter, he apologizes for his stratagem but at once glories in its cleverness,[17] and he follows it up with more arguments why Cydippe should marry him. The lady, by contrast, describes the details of her embarrassing position. Hellenistic poetry loved to picture plain, ordinary people embroiled in extraordinary circumstances. Callimachus had not taken this line in his own narrative; but Ovid represents Cydippe as a lovely but rather bourgeois female who is shocked to be put in a questionable situation and would have preferred a more conventional (XX, 127) and less dynamic courtship. She is portrayed as a young girl who at Delus had nothing on her mind but the excitement of sightseeing when the strange occurrence changed her whole life. She resents being caught in a trap[18] and is understandably annoyed by the ailment and the jeopardy of her very life her lover brought upon her time after time. Nevertheless she appreciates his romantic maneuver as a tribute to her charms (33-38), and the poet gives us to understand that by now she is warming up to Acontius and that their marriage will turn out an unlimited success. The other man, the one to whom her parents had engaged her, is already receiving hints from Cydippe that she does not care for him (193-202). It is he, and not one of the main characters, who will see his hopes blighted.

In this last pair, just as in the first, there is little to remind us of thought letters. It was different in the epistles of Leander and Hero; moreover, they did not so much argue a case as, under the shadow of doom, vent the emotions of mutual passion.

7. THE "ARS AMATORIA," BOOKS I AND II

WHEN HIS fallow years were over, Ovid was gripped by another creative spell and began to write and publish one work after another in rapid succession. The first of them was *The Art of Love,* in two books, composed in the years 2 and 1 B.C. Ovid was then in his early forties. It is little wonder that he was no longer quite the same person he had been in his twenties, and that his attitude toward love had noticeably changed.[1] It will be worth while to exemplify the nature of the shift before we proceed to a short examination of the work and its purport.

The contrast in the views of the young and the mature poet is most striking when the identical experience appears in a different light. In the Second Book of the *Art of Love,* Ovid uses for the illustration of his directions an incident which he had treated before in the *Amores.* In the context of his didactic work, Ovid has remarked that he is not writing for the instruction of a wealthy lover; one who can give rich presents needs no preceptor; it is the man of modest means, like the writer himself, who requires the author's advice. Then he goes on to say:

A poor man must love guardedly and fear to scold the lady;
    he must endure a great deal the rich man need not.
I remember, once, in anger, I mussed my mistress' hair:
    that act of temper robbed me of many a day's happiness.
I do not believe, nor did I notice then, that I rent her dress,
    but since she said I did, I paid for a new one.
So you be wise: shun the mistakes of your master
    and beware of such losses as my folly caused for me.
There may be war with the Parthians, but with your elegant mistress
    let there be peace
    and frolic and all that leads to love.[2]
             (II, 167 ff.)

---

[1] For notes to chapter 7, see pages 199–203.

Ovid is reminding his readers of the elegy on *The Contrite Lover* which we have discussed previously.[3] But now he gives the old story a new complexion and remodels it to suit his present purpose. In the elegy, the poet was mortified to have committed a brutality little short of sacrilege; in the *Art of Love,* the divine lady has turned into a clever lass who was quick to take advantage of her foolish lover's remorse and confusion,[4] and what now looms largest in the picture is that allegedly she tricked him into spending more than he could afford. Ovid glories in the progress he has made since the days of his *Amores;* experience has enlightened him, and his readers are invited to profit from the author's dearly bought wisdom. In his present mood, he reinterprets in practical terms one of his deepest and most moving elegies, and pokes fun at his own juvenile ardor and reverent devotion. On passionate excesses like "scratching the girl's cheeks, rending one's own or her dress, and tearing her hair" he now looks down with mild benevolence, and terms them as "becoming to boys hot with youth and love" (*Ars* III, 568–571). The poet himself has long ago outgrown that stage; he is no longer a servant of love but its master, and is proud of his dignity. It is in that spirit that the *Art of Love* is conceived.

⋄   ⋄   ⋄

The delightful preface to the *Ars Amatoria* makes the intention of the work quite clear. When the author explains his own qualifications for the task he has set for himself, he says he will not falsely assert that Apollo or the Muses inspired him:

> From practice this book springs; hearken to the experienced bard![5]
> The tale I shall tell is true; smile on my work, O Mother of Love!
> (I, 29 f.)

Ovid announces that Venus, Amor's mother, has appointed the poet to be her son's tutor (I, 7); after what he himself has formerly suffered from Cupid's darts, he will now the better be able to take his revenge on the urchin (I, 23–24). "Young Love is fierce and exuberant, but all boys are easy to manage. The fierce Achilles, while he was still small, respected his master Chiron and was taught by him to play the lyre; music soothed his temper" (I, 9–21). Thus Ovid indicates that he intends to substitute, as it were, pleasant and melodious tunes for the tumult of inordinate passion. This is to be accomplished by a methodical training of the raw lover, or prospective lover.[6]

The *Ars Amatoria* is a didactic poem in the elegiac meter, the first of three such poems which Ovid was to compose during his second period of swift and continuous production. Didactic poems were a fad at the time; a poet might offer instruction on any subject. Aemilius Macer, a friend of Ovid, wrote in hexameters on snake venoms and medicinal drugs; others gave, for instance, poetic directions for different games and sports, or taught how to take care of house guests and how to arrange dinner parties (*Tr.* II, 471–492). The *Ars Amatoria* is in a way cognate to those because, ostensibly, it deals with love as a kind of sport or game and social entertainment; and as to the snakebites and medicines, Ovid was later to write another poem on the *Remedies for Love*. Love, it is true, does not appear at first sight to lend itself easily to a systematic discussion, but we remember that in Rome erotic poetry had from the outset a touch of the didactic[7] and methodical, in that even a collection of disconnected elegies was designed to represent all the main phases and aspects of the passion in their ideal and most satisfactory form.[8] This, then, is the historical background.[9] But the *Ars Amatoria* needs no outside justification; its graceful charm will at once conquer the reader. The Ovid of the *Art* plays his instrument with consummate ease; his touch is light and his notes are clear. The critic who tries to interpret the work feels more than ever conscious of his own clumsy fingers.

◇   ◇   ◇

Ovid begins his exposition with outlining his program.[10] The First Book will teach the adept how to find and win a mistress; the Second, how to hold her. The theme for the Second Book shows that Ovid thinks not so much of momentary pleasure as of a connection which will last a long time.[11] For this reason, he recommends a careful selection of the partner, and warns the young man not to fall rashly for a girl at a banquet, when the wine and poor lighting will impair his judgment of her qualities (I, 243–252). He will have to keep his eyes open and go hunting at the proper places. She will

not be wafted into his lap from the skies (I, 43), but if he knows
how to go about it he will find that Rome can supply women of
all descriptions. The benches of the theater, for instance, are a good
hunting ground; and whoever attends a show with such an object
in mind can vindicate his intent with an illustrious precedent (133–
134). No less an authority than Romulus, the founder of the City,
organized the rape of the Sabine women in the theater. This point
gives Ovid his occasion for telling the old legend, and he tells it
very well. More than once in the *Art of Love* he illuminates his
lesson with a picturesque story from legend, as if he were already
training himself for the *Metamorphoses* and *Fasti*.[12] Mentioning
then the circus as another likely place, he exploits his own elegy on
The Chariot Race (III, 2) from the *Amores* to the point of repeating
an occasional line from it.

◇ ◇ ◇

The material of the *Art of Love* is in large measure taken from
Ovid's earlier elegies. But whereas in the *Amores* the incidents
which inspired each emotional outburst were merely implied, the
poet now sketches the individual stories and adds his explanatory
comment. He pictures typical situations; he describes how the man
will act, and predicts how the woman will be likely to react; he
weighs chances against risks, and advantages against drawbacks;
and he recommends to the intelligent lover some tactical maneuvers,
but cautions him against others. The *Ars Amatoria* is perhaps the
most lucid of Ovid's works. Since the author assumes an air of knowing superiority, he remains all the time clearheaded and does not
allow his reason to be clouded by emotion. The perfect lover, as
Ovid now sees him, is no romantic dreamer, nor is he lost in the
wilderness of passion; in this book there is no place for wavering
indecision and nebulous sentiment. Clarity of vision and argument
rather than profundity of feeling is indeed one of the main virtues
of the *Ars Amatoria*. Here the author displays at its best that rational
and objective spirit which so significantly distinguishes the literature of the Greeks and Romans. The excellence of the work mani-
fests itself mainly along traditional lines, and here those novel
trends which mark Ovid as a precursor of the coming age are not

conspicuous.[13] Only one of his more modern qualities is given free range in the *Art:* his gift for sympathetic understanding of the concerns of others. That trait somewhat mellows the crudities in the advice which the author dispenses, and makes the reader more willing to take the poet's worldly wisdom in good part.

◇   ◇   ◇

In fact, Ovid had his own moral scruples while he was composing the book; but he did not allow them to get the upper hand. At the outset he warns his audience to leave respectable ladies alone; he has in mind only such women as are fair game for his pupils (I, 31–34).[14] Once, he tells the lover astutely to ingratiate himself with his rival, in order to deceive him the better, but immediately he recants the dirty scheme (I, 579–588).[15] Sometimes he goes to the trouble of justifying his methods, and he is never at a loss to find a graceful excuse for them. For instance, he gives the lukewarm admirer this advice:

> You must play the lover; words of tongue must simulate wounds of
>   heart.
>   By whatever means, induce her to trust in your affection.
> It takes little to make her believe it, for any woman thinks herself
>   attractive;
>   no matter how poor her figure, she is pleased with her looks.
> And then, he who pretends to love often falls in love
>   and lapses into the condition he affected.
>   (I, 611 ff.)

The implication is that thus the falsehood is subsequently remedied. Or Ovid asserts, and we take it with a grain of salt, that the majority of women are "an unholy lot," deceivers who deserve to be deceived (I, 643–658). Not much later, when Ovid will be instructing no longer the men but the women, he will reverse his contention and say that the men are more wicked (III, 7–40); but for all practical purposes the conclusion remains the same: no matter who was the first to use tricks, there is no real harm in the artful game so long as it is played well and delights all those who take part in it. And this seems to be his basic vindication. Ovid is convinced that, after all, both partners will find their happiness if his directions are carried out (I, 269–342; 665–714;[16] 767–770[17]), and he is anxious to see both of them benefit in like manner from the success of their connection, or else love will lose all its charm (cf. II, 682–688). It is always understood that the art the master is teaching is one of mutual enjoyment and mutual satisfaction, and in that respect Ovid is superior to both Tibullus and Propertius, who think only of themselves. Although Ovid's amazing candor often seems more cynical than their discretion, he is less of an egoist than they were. And it is gratifying to hear Ovid, in the Second Book (II, 601–640), inveigh against those who, desecrating the mysteries of Venus, boast of their successes instead of keeping them to themselves. Some even go so far, he complains, as to conquer girls merely for the sake of the record, or to slander a lady by bragging of favors they have actually never received.

There is not much violence (I, 669 ff.) in the rules of the game as Ovid decrees them, and no sudden and stormy surprise of an unsuspecting victim, but a great deal of insinuating finesse, careful application, and steadfast forbearance. Characteristic is a casual remark to the effect that the great adventure should not be approached in the spirit of a reckless gambler (I, 381), and another which warns the wooer not to lose patience but rather allow the girl's response to develop in its own good time (I, 482). The lover should send her one letter after another; a constant trickle will wear down the hardest rock. He should see to it that she reads his notes, but should never force her to reply; she will eventually do so of her own free will.   ◇   ◇   ◇

In this context (I, 459–486) Ovid solemnly admonishes Roman youth to study the liberal arts—that is, rhetoric,—which can be as useful for love letters as in the courts of law:

> But keep your powers hidden and do not show your eloquence;
>   your style must shun phrases that annoy.
> Who but a fool sends a composition to his gentle friend?
>   A brilliant letter has often caused dislike.[18]
> Address her in a plausible manner and with words homely
>   but fond, so that you seem to speak to her while you write.
>   (I, 463 ff.)

Those critics who are impatient of what they call rhetoric in Ovid's style may take note that at least in theory he understood how irritating set patterns and elaborate artifices can be.[19] In another passage, Ovid, encouraging a beginner who should now make his first declaration but is bashful and confused,[20] emboldens him thus:

> There are no rules I can give you to shape your speech.
> Only crave her favors, and eloquence will come of itself.
> (I, 609 f.)

No rules, indeed! For once, love is left on its own, with no tutor meddling. For once, the wise master is disavowing himself and stirring up the question which has been on our mind all the time: In what sense can Ovid, after all, believe in an art of love? We shall try to glean our answer from the Second Book.

<> <> <>

The Second Book, which has for its theme the preservation of love, is less dramatic but more subtle and personal than the First. To use Ovid's own words: While conquest is in part subject to chance,[21] the holding of a woman's affection is a matter for art alone (II, 14). We are more puzzled than ever. The opposite seems more nearly correct. Clever stratagems may sometimes be of service in winning a lady's love, but for the man who wants to keep her attached to him for a long time the prime requisite is most certainly a well-disposed heart. We wonder what place, if any, will be assigned by Ovid to the heart, and what to craft? Looking, then, closely into the actual directions and suggestions of the Second Book, we find that essentially they add up to a recommendation of constant loving care and thoughtful, patient, humble[22] devotion; and yet, under the pretense that a war game is being taught, natural and spontaneous tenderness is presented in the garb of cunning shrewdness.[23] Three examples[24] will illustrate this amusing disguise.

In autumntime, Ovid explains (II, 315–336), the girl's health may be affected by rapid shifts of hot and cold weather. The lover will comfort her as best he can, and assist her as much as she lets him. He will not mind her sickly moods, but will bear with her feverish condition; and he will offer his cheek for her kiss, so that

> her dry lips drink up his tears.

Nothing could be more affectionate than such a scene, or more delicate than the subsequent caution against annoying her with too much ado. But then, lest the Mephistophelian touch be missing, Ovid concludes with this warning:

> Do not prescribe her a diet, nor offer her a cup
>   with bitter medicine; your rival may mix that drink.

Another suggestion is this (II, 287–294): "If you are about to set free a slave, or to let off a servant from punishment, cause him to apply to your mistress, and then do it on her request." The idea is, of course, that she will feel proud and happy in the illusion that she has done a service to a wretched human being; and certainly that idea could spring only from a gentle and loving disposition. On this aspect, however, Ovid does not waste a word, but rather wraps his thoughtful little stratagem up in strictly selfish reasoning, stressing the deceit involved and the advantage to be gained by the maneuver. This is the way he puts it: "Whenever you have made up your mind anyway to do a certain thing in your own interest, be sure it is your mistress who asks you for it"; and at the end he explains: "It will then cost you nothing to oblige her[25] and make her think that you obey her orders."

Our third example (II, 295–314) mentions art specifically. The teacher is exhorting his pupil to show himself overwhelmed by the good looks of his lady, no matter what she is wearing:

> She comes in gold brocade? To you she will be more precious than
>   any gold ...
> She stands in a tunic only? Cry out: You kindle a devastating fire,
>   but add, with concern in your voice: Take care not to catch cold.

After these, and many other, illustrations of enthusiastic approval, Ovid winds up with this warning:

> But do not let her find you out when you are merely pretending,
>   nor allow your face to belie your words.
> Art is useful only when hidden ...
>   (311 ff.)

"Art is useful only when hidden"—this is true enough for the practice of love; but for theoretical instruction in love the maxim

can be reversed. More often than not, the Second Book of Ovid's
Art of Love sets up a screen of art to hide warm sentiment[26] and
understanding thoughtfulness. All the time, the adept is supposed
to anticipate the thoughts and wishes of his girl and to go out of
his way to live up to them. It is true that he will not always exactly
feel the same way as he is acting, but then he may dissemble his
indifference or vexation for no other reason than because he is a
well-mannered, tactful, and indulgent friend. Ovid, however, in
deference to the playful fiction that love can be studied like a school
subject, represents the lover as somewhat of a crafty hypocrite,
methodically cajoling and humoring his mistress.

⋄ ⋄ ⋄

Nevertheless, the instructor is once compelled to admit that the
position he has assumed is untenable. He has recommended com-
plaisance to the point of tolerating and ignoring a successful rival:

> I confess, in this art I am not accomplished.
> I cannot help it; my own advice is too arduous for me.
> (II, 547 f.)

The ideal student whom he has in mind should prove himself
"more learned" (553), that is, more cool and self-controlled, than
his master.

Another time, the teacher forgets his professorial aloofness and
goes into raptures of personal delight in a very unorthodox fashion.
He is describing the lady as frantic because she has been told that
her lover has been unfaithful:

> Happy four times over and many more times than I can tell
>   is he for whom his mistress grieves in anguish.
> To her ears, unwilling to believe, comes the tale of his villainy:
>   straightway she faints—poor girl, voice and color fail her.
> I want to be he whose hair she tears in fury,
>   I want to be he whose cheeks her fingernails assail,
> on whom she looks in tears, he whom she beholds with blazing eyes,
>   without whom she cannot live, wishing she could.
> (II, 447 ff.)

Thus Ovid does not throughout sustain the part of the level-
headed, scientific master of love. Everybody understands anyway

that he is only giving himself airs, and that consummate love amounts to something more than a bag of tricks.

And, indeed, in a passage at the very beginning of the Second Book a far broader view of love prevails, the widest even that can be conceived. In the context, Ovid is posing the question: How can your mistress be prevented from losing her interest in you? One answer that suggests itself is at once rejected (II, 99 ff.). Magic and philters were a favorite theme of ancient love poetry, but Ovid disdains the use of means so base and mechanical: "Such practices [he exclaims] are ineffective, or else they harm the mind and bring on madness; far be from us any abomination."[27] Then follows a positive recommendation of the most sweeping character: To be loved, be lovable (*ut ameris, amabilis esto*);

> and your face and figure are not enough to make you so . . .
> To hold your mistress, and spare yourself from being forsaken and
>   bewildered,
>   add gifts of mind to charms of body.
> Beauty is not a lasting possession . . .
> Mold in time your soul to fit up your beauty;
>   the soul alone remains with you to your last day.[28]
>   (II, 107 ff.)

Plato had praised homosexual love as a powerful agent for perfecting the soul; Ovid now sees in the same light the love of a man for a woman. Another passage in the Second Book elaborates this notion. Ovid speaks of the first emergence of mankind, when the primordial chaos had given way to our world, and continues as follows:

> At that age, man was lost in a lonely wilderness,[29]
>   and he was nought but mere strength and uncouth body.
> The forest had been his home; herbs, his food; leaves, his bed;
>   and for a long time each one knew nothing of the others.
> But then it is said that fond pleasure softened their souls.
>   (II, 473 ff.)

This amounts to proposing that it was love which gave man a feeling soul in addition to his body, and that it was sexual love which taught him to know and understand and like his fellow human beings, so that he would build up a society.[30] Later, in the *Fasti* (IV,

107–114), Ovid added that love was the prime mover for the development of higher civilization. There he explains that the first poetry was erotic (it is certainly true for Ovid's first poetry); that eloquence was invented by those who wooed a woman,

> and a thousand arts sprang from love; the will to please
> caused man to discover many things hidden before.

This notion is the background against which the *Art of Love* and, indeed, the entire body of Ovid's erotic verse want to be seen.[31] Even that sort of love made Ovid discover many things hidden before.

8. THE "MEDICAMINA FACIEI"

OVID WAS NOT content with his two volumes of advice for lovers, but wrote on and on around the theme. Following a fashion of his age which produced, for instance, poems on dyes for dresses[1] or on clays for making wine cups, he even stooped to compose a booklet with the title *Medicamina Faciei,*[2] that is, *Face Cosmetics.*[3] From this work only fifty couplets have survived, and we have probably no reason to regret the loss of the rest. The remnants show that Ovid versified the actual recipes and included the figures governing the quantities of the ingredients. The subject seemed harmless from a moral point of view, and thus the author implies that this time he hopes to have respectable ladies for his readers.[4] In fact, he makes a point of proving that it is not below the dignity of any woman to use cosmetics. He reasons that even men have taken to them recently, and that the practice itself is innocuous:

> What matters is only for whom a lady adorns herself, and whose love
> she seeks. Daintiness deserves no blame.[5]
> (27 f.)

Even in a solitude, he contends, a woman will try to look her best, and even chaste maidens take pride in their appearance.[6]

The poem begins with a eulogy on *cultus,* that is, culture and refinement. *"Cultus,"* so Ovid proclaims, "helps the earth to produce grain instead of weeds; it improves the taste of fruits; it gives a pleasant appearance to things that surround us. Houses are built

---

[1] For notes to chapter 8, see pages 203–204.

lofty, the ceiling is covered with gold, and the ground is hidden under marble; wooden implements are encrusted with imported ivory. It is true that in olden times women concerned themselves more with the culture of fields than with their own and worked hard in their rural households. But our ladies are delicate, and they cover their dresses with gold, they wear gems from foreign lands ..." Thus, by speaking of cultured embellishments to amend the natural fabric of things, the author aptly introduces his topic.

9. THE "ARS AMATORIA," BOOK III

THE CONTRAST of modern ways with the boorish simplicity of early Rome is a favorite theme with Ovid, but nowhere does he dwell on it in so personal a manner as in the preface to another work:

> Let others take pleasure in antiquity; I am happy that I was born
> in this age which suits my own nature ...
> because now *cultus* prevails.

The phrase "let others take pleasure in antiquity" is no mere figure of speech. At the time of Augustus, a powerful movement was under way which tried to reverse the development of civilization and to revive the ideals and virtues of the past. The reformers wanted the people of Rome once more to become a nation of modest and laborious farmers, brave and strenuous soldiers, and exemplary statesmen. Private life was to be governed again by the old, stern standards; the religion of the forefathers was to be restored; and the taste in art, language, and literature was to orient itself toward models from former times.[1] The age was certainly not ignorant of its own decadence; in fact, for a long time writers had been lamenting that the political and economic expansion of the Empire had brought in its train a steady decline in morality, discipline, and firmness of character. Augustus was the chief exponent of the reformatory tendencies, and he promoted them with all the powerful means at his disposal, including legislation. And yet, in the lines we quoted, Ovid naïvely publicized his own indifference toward a trend sanctioned by the Emperor. He was made to approve of modernity and

---

[1] For notes to chapter 9, see pages 204–206.

give eloquent expression to modern views. He enjoyed drifting in the current of his own age and had no understanding whatever of people who tried to build a dam, stem the flood, and turn its course backward. He was to pay dearly for his lack of subordination to the supreme worldly authority.

In one respect, however, Ovid was a true Augustan. The passage from which we just quoted a few lines testifies that with Horace and many others he shared a scorn for the senseless extravagance of those wealthy people who built their villas out into the very waters of the sea and bought up mountains of marble to stuff their mansions with statuary. He liked to have things neat, pleasant, and diversified, but not pompous, sumptuous, and obtrusive. This is what he meant by *cultus*.

✧ ✧ ✧

The passage is to be found in the Third Book of the *Art of Love* (III, 121–128), and in its context it serves once more to extol the importance of *cultus* for modern womanhood. The master lover had hardly completed his textbook on love for young men when he felt that the young ladies also should have the benefit of his guidance. Thus, as an afterthought, he added a third volume to the two he had written before. He declared that it was not fair to leave one sex uninstructed when its opponent in the perennial warfare had received expert directions (III, 1–4); and besides, he probably could not resist the urge to go on in the same manner. Whichever his real motive was, already the next year[2] found him busy with the supplement, the *Art of Love* for women.

All things considered, there is remarkably little repetition from the first two volumes in the third. One reason for this is that none of the more aggressive stratagems has a place in a book dedicated to the training of the ladies. More significant, however, seems a change in the author's own attitude. Even where similar subjects are treated, the tone is different. In vain shall we look in this volume for clues to the open secret that the proficient lover is animated by a spirited devotion. The previous examples of tenderness in disguise have no more than one counterpart here, and a feeble one at that as far as the tenderness is concerned.[3] Rarely, if ever, does the author betray personal emotion.[4] Technical advice holds the field unchallenged. It appears that the cool aloofness which Ovid had often affected in the first books has by now actually taken hold of him. The poet has written so much about love that the underlying sentiment has been used up in the process, at least for the time being.

In line with this change in attitude, the standards and requirements for perfect love have been scaled down considerably. There is no longer a question of the soul to be refined for the sake of love and through the experience of love. The author proceeds on the assumption that the lover is not interested in the personal character of his mistress;[5] in fact, he takes it for granted that her actual character is not an asset but a liability and for this reason remains better hidden.[6] Whereas in the Second Book the young man was encouraged to cultivate his mind so as to become a fascinating talker (II, 121–144), the young women are directed to entertain their partners not by their conversation, but by singing, dancing, playing games with them, or, at best, reading poetry to them.[7] The ideal woman as Ovid pictures her here is attractive in her looks, her attire, carriage, and deportment; she has command of one or another social accomplishment; she is amiable, cheerful, and sprightly (509–524); she flatters her lover by pretending that she is under the spell of his charm (667–686); she keeps her wooer in suspense, and her gallant on tenterhooks (473–478; 593–610); she knows how to deal with a young and fiery admirer, or with a mature and steady friend (555–576); and she puts all her lovers to good use according to their individual abilities:

> Let the rich man make presents, the jurist give legal advice,
>   let the orator often plead the case of her who is under his protection,
> and let us who write verse, send her nought but our verse!
>   Our guild is better fitted for love than others.
> We spread far and wide the fame of our chosen beauty . . .
>   many people wonder who my Corinna is.
> And then, we sacred bards are free from guile,
>   our art ennobles even our characters . . .
>   (531 ff.; 538 ff.)

and so forth. The poet, of course, is a hallowed being:

> A god dwells in us, we have dealings with heaven,
>   (549)

but the women of the Third Book are by no means divine.[8] There is nothing in it to remind us that twenty years before the author had been looking up to his mistress as if she were a goddess, and the name of Corinna sounds out of place when we hear it mentioned in this context.

The first half of the book is well organized, but the presentation becomes later somewhat erratic and the transitions are no longer elaborated.[9] When he is nearing the end, Ovid frankly indicates his impatience to be done with the poem.[10] For the second time we find him tired of his own genre.

10. THE "REMEDIA AMORIS"

OVID WAS NOW forty-three, and he had been writing on love for the better part of the past twenty-five years. No wonder that the subject had worn thin for him. We remember how he had relinquished the writing of erotic elegiacs once before, in order to become a playwright. At that time, he was very vocal about his step and anxious to impress the world with the effort it took him to part with so enchanting a theme, and so endearing a preoccupation, as love. Now, when he had completed the Third Book of his *Ars Amatoria,* he was again unable to quit the subject at once and in silence. This time, however, he did not bid his farewell to love in personal terms; rather, he gave it an objective turn and wrote one more didactic poem, the subject of which was withdrawal from love. The title of this poem is *Remedies for Love,* and the book offers advice to those who tackle the painful task of fighting and defeating a sentimental attachment.

There was some confusion in Ovid's mind about the character of his own work. It occurred to him that it would brand him as a renegade, but he was unwilling to admit the inference. He insists that he is not renouncing love as such, but only instructing those who are put to misery by a misplaced or frustrated affection (1–74); and he denies that his new work "robs Amor of his darts, puts out the god's torch, clips his wings, and unstrings the sacred bow" (699–702).[1] But his protestations are futile; the mental reservation fails

---

[1] For notes to chapter 10, see pages 207–208.

to prevail over the substance of the work, which is such as to subvert love on every one of its pages, with no discrimination concerning the nature of the liaison. The proviso of limited application remains immaterial because the author hardly ever troubles to refer to the reason why an individual affair deserves to be broken up; nor does he differentiate his advice and suggest that the soft spots, those circumstances which render the particular relationship offensive, should be singled out for breaching the mancipation.[2] Broad and general as his directions are, they militate against the very spirit of love.[3]

These preliminary observations do not bode well for the quality of Ovid's new work; moreover, the reader is by now likewise tired of the theme. Ovid, however, always has surprises in store for those who study him, some for the better and some otherwise. One of the pleasant surprises is that little more than a third of the precepts against love merely reverse previous instructions for love.[4] On the other hand, a section of the *Remedia* is repulsive like nothing else that Ovid wrote; it is that in which he professes to sow "seeds of hate" (308) by teaching the lover how to contrive disgust with the girl to whom he is bound all too closely (299-440). This hideous passage is out of character for the poet and inconsistent with the rest of the work. In general, the author tries to induce indifference rather than aversion, and the measures by which the sufferer is to be cured are of a gentle and indulgent nature. Ovid does not imagine his patient as a superman who will "once and for all deliver himself from pain, breaking the shackles that chafe his mind" (293-294). There is no high-pitched drama in the fight against love, and no violent clash between raging passion and stern resolve. Ovid does not believe in a radical therapy:

> Try to calm the flames while they are fresh and weak,
>   or when they have exhausted their own strength;
> but while fury is on its way, give way to fury.
> (117 ff.)

And he says:

> Let love vanish by stealth and go up in thin air,
>   let it die out by gentle degrees.
> (653 f.)

The termination should likewise be lenient, moderate, and quiet:

> It is a crime to hate a girl whom you recently liked;
>   such a finish fits brutal natures.
> It is enough if you no longer care for her. He who ends love by rancor[5]
>   is either still in love, or his cure is as bad as his ailment was.
>   (655 ff.)

The healer understands the disease full well. From personal experience of long standing he is familiar with the subterfuges by which the infatuation is likely to evade the treatment:

> Love tries ever to outwit you; to keep alive, it invents delays.
>   (95)

When the lover is going abroad to flee from the dangerous woman, the passion, in order to draw its victim back, will disguise itself as honorable homesickness,

>   screening your guilt with specious words.
>   (240)

Therefore the author recommends to combat fraud with fraud and cheat one's own self:

> Hide from yourself what you are designing, do not keep before your
>   eyes
>   the undoing of your affection; often a horse fights the curb.
>   (513 f.)

Indirect means of defeating the inclination play a larger part than a frontal attack on it, and the author is aware how important contributory factors are. He cautions against whatever promotes a disposition for love. Leisure, he says, is to be avoided because it induces and feeds passion (138); solitude is also likely to pamper morose propensities (579–608). It is not conducive to health either to see erotic scenes enacted in the theater or to read love poetry, including the author's own works, which, as he humorously admits, "have some such tones in them" (751–766); and if he associates with people that are in love, the bystander is likely to catch the disease from them (609–626).

Ovid deals at length with the delicate condition of the convalescent (609–794), who must be on his guard against a relapse. Among other things, he is warned not to reread the lady's love letters (715–

722); nor must be brood over the causes of their separation, or justify it by complaining of her:

> I would have you hold your peace rather than boast that you put an
>   end to it.
> Whoever announces too often: I am not in love, is.
>
> (647 f.)

It happens rarely in the *Remedia* that a concrete scene is pictured or the outward shape of things described; the author concentrates more than before on mental conditions. Moreover, there is often a certain touch in the setting and phrasing of his instruction which turns mere knowledge into mellow wisdom. Ovid's style has ripened.

At the same time, the purview of his writing widens. In order to break Cupid's tyranny over his servant, the counselor suggests a diversion to some other pursuit. Thus we see Ovid recommending a number of such occupations as he had ignored or spurned in his earlier works. We shall not, however, jump to the conclusion that the poet has undergone a radical change of heart. Most of the pursuits are listed in a perfunctory and conventional fashion, and it is obvious that Ovid advocates them merely for the sake of the argument. Their number includes the professions of the pleader and jurist, soldiering, and politics (151–168); furthermore, hunting, bird catching, and fishing (199–212).° But the tone becomes really warm when Ovid speaks of traveling; here one couplet at least has an arresting ring:

> Once you have left, a hundred comforts for your grief are provided
>   by the open country and your companions and the long road.
>
> (241 f.)

And with full and genuine enthusiasm does the poet portray the delights which life in the open country has in store for the gentleman farmer:

> When that pleasure has once begun to caress your mind,
>   Amor looses his power and flies away with feeble wings.
>
> (197 f.)

The description which Ovid here gives of rural activities (169–196) is fine enough to challenge anything written on the subject by other Roman poets. In my opinion, it improves on that given by Horace in the Second Epode; and where Ovid refers to the cycle of seasonal joys and labors (187–196), the few lines duplicate some of the charm emanating from Vergil's *Georgics*. Even at the early time when he was writing the *Amores,* Ovid had twice broken the tepid monotony of love by an elegy which let in the bracing air of rural life.[7]

⬦ ⬦ ⬦

One last passage from the *Remedia* may be mentioned because it is revealing in several respects. When the instructor is about to give advice of a very intimate sort, he interrupts his argument to justify in advance the frankness of his discussion. In this digression (359–398) he says that his *Art of Love*—completed in the same year or the year before—was censured for its indelicacy. Ovid treats his critics with scorn and thinks he is refuting them when he points out that the particular playful genre of poetry in which he excels requires such liberties. His argument, of course, is wide off the mark. No matter what we think a certain style demands, the dictates of discretion are paramount, and the latitude we permit ourselves can and must be subordinated to them. Ovid, however, was evidently unable to comprehend the objection because his own nature was devoid of that particular sensitivity. He was naïve and ignorant in that respect, rather than bold. This can be inferred from the fact that his most daring passages are never sultry;[8] obviously, he breathed freely where others would perceive the tenseness of a sweltering atmosphere. For that reason, he could not grasp what his warners were talking about. Cocksure of himself like a bad child, he turned a deaf ear to them and persisted in his bland unconcern for the offense he was giving. He may have thought, moreover, that he owed it to his pupils to inform them on whatever had a bearing on the problems for which they would consult their wise master. There was to come a time when he would bitterly regret his misguided sense of objectivity and appropriateness.

As yet, however, he had no inkling (*Tr.* V, 12, 67) of the gravity of his mistake, and with a light heart defied his opponents:

> Provided my writings find favor as they are, and are recited all over
> the world,
> the one or the other may blame my work at will.
>
> (363 f.)

His own explanation of the criticism is that his detractors are only motivated by the envy with which they view his literary success. Under this assumption, he concludes the digression with the following proud reply:

> Burst, O nagging malice! Great is the name I have,
>   but it will be still greater if only I can keep up my stride.
> You try to stop me too soon. If life be given me, you will be hurt more.
>   My spirited mind holds many new songs.
> It delights me, and with my growing fame ambition too has grown.
>   My steed has just begun to climb where it aspires to go,
> and already elegy is as much indebted to me
>   as glorious epic is to Vergil.
>   (389 ff.)

Thus the poet announces that he has a loftier task in mind for the future; probably he was thinking of the *Metamorphoses*. His new project may have distracted him even while he was still working on his didactic books, and for that reason he perhaps did not give them his undivided attention. Be that as it may, he was not saying too much when he promised that his literary career would soon soar to an unexpected new height.

11. THE "METAMORPHOSES"

THE FATE OF his life allowed Ovid seven more years of normal working conditions, up to the age of fifty, and this short span sufficed him for the composition of the fifteen volumes of the *Metamorphoses,* with only the final revision lacking. In addition, he wrote six books of the *Fasti;* for again he started a new undertaking before he had laid the last hand on his current work. The *Metamorphoses* is his masterpiece, and it is one of the finest poems handed down to us from Antiquity. Moreover, it is one of the most original and personal, and for that reason it is rather intriguing. Its value cannot be gauged by conventional standards, nor will its peculiar import reveal itself to the casual reader. Its very luster is baffling. The brilliant surface causes us to wonder how much, or how little, may lie hidden beneath. If we do probe and bore through we shall not always come upon a substantial core. We must not, however, give up after one or another disappointment. A long and entertaining book cannot and must not be overloaded with serious import. And besides, we remember that Ovid's writings are never even in their content, because the author lacked severity of self-criticism and failed to eliminate the insignificant. But if we are patient and curious enough to search on with a mind responsive to anything, unexpected as it may be, then we shall be rewarded by startling finds. They cannot be very conspicuous at the surface because, as we already know, it was not possible for Ovid to formulate with neat precision the novel things he had to say. One reason is that they were not easy to express for anyone, because the language had not yet developed terms for such phenomena as, for instance, wavering identity; nor had theoretical thought devised roads by which facts of that order could be methodically approached. The other reason is that Ovid, for one, had no command of abstract thought and in fact only dimly understood, himself, what he was doing. Thus he was not the man to invent a specific parlance for the new notions and to designate them in a direct and distinctive fashion. Poet as he was, all he could do was apply to his purposes the common medium of poetic art and cloak his discoveries in the garb of his legendary stories; and this he has achieved very well indeed. He has done his part; and if now we do ours, I am convinced that the implications of some of his fables can be clearly demonstrated, as things of this sort go, and be proved to be real treasures.

We shall give only a few examples in the course of our discussion of the *Metamorphoses,* but the rest will then, I hope, follow of itself.   ◇   ◇   ◇

The writing of the *Metamorphoses* meant a new departure for Ovid in more than one respect, and his powers were to be exercised in fields in which he had little previous practice. For one thing, his poetry had moved, so far, only in the given and natural world, and he was now to conquer the province of the fabulous and miraculous. He took to it as if he were finally coming into his own. The same is true for his mastery of the narrative on a large scale. In his previous works, he had been expressing emotional experiences and formulating general rules and observations; specific events had come in only incidentally and by way of illustration. It was the reverse now. For the *Metamorphoses,* the poet had to cultivate concreteness. Hundreds of definite characters had to be portrayed, and their stories had to be told appropriately; settings and sceneries had to be devised and elaborated to fit the plots; graphic descriptions were needed in large numbers. That test, too, was met by Ovid to perfection; his command of invention and presentation was more than equal to the new task. Then there was the epic style to be handled by an author who had been writing elegiacs all the time. There was more to it than merely the shift from the pulsating beat of couplets to the even and steady flow of hexameters. The greater dignity and seriousness of the epic also involved a new adjustment with respect to the selection and construction of stories, the nature and shading of sentiments, the display of detail,[1] and the choice of words. Ovid complied with the demands of the epic style as successfully as he had handled elegiacs before. To observe so many and so subtle distinctions[2] would have been an impossible feat, were it not for the fact that ancient poets worked out their works aloud, reciting them as they wrote, just as a composer will create his music more at the piano than at the writing desk. No reading or writing was done mutely, and for this reason both the authors and the public were well trained in the proper tone and modulation for each genre of poetry. With the change in the mode of recital, a corresponding change in subject matter and presentation would come with natural ease.

And finally, Ovid had somehow to overcome a serious defect of his intellect, his inability to order his material systematically and to develop his ideas consistently. Handicapped by this grave deficiency, how could he venture to organize fifteen long books of stories which were not to admit a single break in continuity? By a stroke of genius he turned his weakness into an undisputed triumph.[3] He made up for his constitutional infirmity with an inexhaustible ingenuity in improvisation, blandly muddling through the entire vast expanse of his huge epic, as it were, with all sorts of random expedients so felicitous as to enrapture his admirers and compel the respect

---

[1] For notes to chapter 11, see pages 208–228.

of his most bitter detractors. There is never a moment of uncertain hesitancy. Constantly Ovid is luring on the reader from one story to the next, and yet he is always arresting him with the present tale.

◇ ◇ ◇

Ovid had been taught that an epic poem ought not to begin with a lengthy and heavy preface,[4] and thus he used no more than four lines to start the reader on his ramble over a course of twelve thousand hexameters. In terse wording the author announces that he intends to sing, in a continuous narrative, about shapes changed into new bodies from the beginning of the world down to his own days. Actually, the principle of historical sequence makes itself distinctly felt only for a shorter stretch at the beginning of the epic and for a longer one at its end (in Books 1-2 and 11-15). In most of the work, the writer gives an impression of moving about at will in the legendary past.

The first few pages aspire to that sublimity of subject and treatment which is often associated with the idea of epic art.[5] Ovid begins with the greatest of all metamorphoses, the gradual formation of the Universe out of the primordial confusion which he terms 'chaos,'[6] and then goes on to relate the emergence of life, the birth of mankind, and the progressive depravation of man from age to age. Finally, the giants attacked the very seat of the gods; their revolt was smashed by Juppiter, but out of their blood was born a race more violent and wanton than those who preceded it. The stage is thus set for the deluge to blot out the past and make room for a new and more temperate humanity to populate the earth. Juppiter now proceeded to close one era and initiate the next.

While recounting these somber and grandiose events, Ovid covertly suggests an anology (cf. 176): in a similar manner, out of the chaos of the late republic the well-organized monarchy of Caesar and Augustus had arisen. Finally, the author makes the parallel explicit and directly addresses the god-emperor (204) who had imposed law, order, and peace on a world in uproar, wickedness, and confusion. Likening Augustus to Juppiter, Ovid thus pays his homage to the ruler of the Empire within the first chapter of his epic and after a fashion makes up for the lack of a formal preface. Throughout the first three hundred lines the progress of the narrative is swift and sometimes hasty;[7] the presentation is skillful, but none too personal. Ovid's artistry was by that time mature enough to deal with any subject, even though his heart was never in things spectacular, majestic, and ponderous.[8]

◇   ◇   ◇

Immediately after this, however, when he is telling the tale of Deucalion and Pyrrha (1, 313–415), Ovid displays at its best the genteel delicacy which was his. According to a crude, ancient legend, the deluge which exterminated all life on earth was survived by one man and one woman. Themis gave the couple an oracle which ordered them to throw over their heads behind them "the bones of their great mother." They understood that by 'mother' was meant Mother Earth, and out of the rocks which they threw over their heads a new race of men grew. Ovid renders the story in a melodious but dignified style; his narrative is lucid and full, and at the same time it is imbued with a sentiment of simple piety. Deucalion and Pyrrha, in contrast to the ruthless and overbearing race of men which had deserved to be destroyed, are pictured not as spirited fighters for what is right and honorable, but as demure, modest, and kindly people. They clung to each other with a marital affection strangely accentuated by their lot, each being the other's only available companion, helper, and comfort in the midst of complete desolation. They were still shaken by the catastrophe from which they had escaped, and apprehensive of what might yet be coming; and they felt lost and lonesome in an empty and silent world. Yearning for fellow human beings to come into existence, they prayed to Themis, asking her to indicate some device by which the damage could be repaired. Their prayer was answered; they were chosen to create a new humanity, with earth and stone for their material. "Hence we are a tough race with a heart for toil (*experiens laborum*), bearing witness to the stuff from which we sprang" (1, 414 f.).

The two progenitors are treated by Ovid with a good-natured humor wholly his own. When they found themselves to be the only extant specimens of mankind and the only links between its past and its potential future (365–366), they were perplexed by their fate and responsibility, but they did not feel helpless. They approached the goddess with fearful awe, but also with trusting hope. Since the oracle which they received seemingly commanded them to dese-crate the bones of their mother, it taxed their piety and threw them into more perplexity. After some searching, they saw a possible solution but were still doubtful; wondering whether or not their idea would work, they decided that there could be no harm in try-ing. And thus the miracle they were allowed to perform came to them as half a surprise. The reader vicariously experiences their feeling of relief and quiet happiness at the result, even though Ovid's art is restrained enough to be silent about it. Ovid never makes the mistake of spoiling the happy ending of a story by saying too much.

One more thing remains to be mentioned before we go on. All over Ovid's continuous narrative in the *Metamorphoses* we find echo-like recurrences to which it is worth while to give ear. These repetitions do more than merely inject another element of musi-cality into the flow of verses and images. They connect the tales with one another, or connect distant parts of the same tale;[9] they accentuate certain aspects of the fables which otherwise may be lost in the swift succession of details;[10] and they sometimes point toward the deeper significance below the running sequence of events. In our story, before Deucalion and Pyrrha by their devout touch cause the *soil* (*terrena* 408) and cold *stone* of Mother Earth to *soften* and *bend,* they kneel down on the *soil,* shyly kiss the cold *stone* of the temple steps (376), and pray that the wrath of the gods may *soften* and *bend* (378). The notions, and indeed the words, repeat themselves,[11] and by this subtle device Ovid ties up the yielding mercy of the relenting (*mitissima* 380) gods with the yield-ing and relenting (*mitior natura* 403) of the elements when the merciful miracle is performed and mankind revived from its mer-ited destruction. Both stubborn anger and stubborn matter are con-quered (*victa* 378) by the pious and loving couple; in the world of fables there is little difference (*parvum discrimen* 10, 242) between mental and physical hardness. Thus Ovid indicates, ever so dis-creetly,[12] that humble and tender believers in the good are able to mollify rigidity and enliven numb coldness. These overtones, which lose much of their soft charm when they are isolated and trumpeted aloud, give the whole fable a transcendent meaning. Through them, the poet has turned a primitive fiction into a symbol for a substantial truth. The maxim that warm devotion melts frigid indifference had also been the *leitmotif* in Ovid's *Art of Love*.

◇   ◇   ◇

It does not take Ovid long to reach the point where he can start his next story. After the flood, so he narrates, animals developed again by spontaneous generation,[13] and the world seethed once more with fresh life. Monsters too came into being, and Apollo killed one of the monsters. "His first love was Daphne," the poet goes on to say (1, 452) with casual abruptness, as if it were a matter of course that in his epic the theme of love was to rank second only to that of metamorphosis. A great many stories begin with a person falling in love and end with some metamorphosis, such as that of Daphne who was changed into a laurel tree; the Greek name of the laurel was *daphne*. The laurel was, according to Greek ideas, the queen of trees,[14] and sacred to Apollo. Ovid stresses the programmatic character of his first love tale by the invention that Amor engineered the affair in order to prove his supremacy over all other powers on earth and in heaven. He inflicted desire on Apollo, and upon the nymph Daphne an abhorrence of love.[15] Thus the young woman, who by her beauty was bound to inspire tender emotions, was incapable of sharing them (488–489); she was like a fine but frigid plant, we might say. The incongruity was mended by her transformation into an actual plant, and thus the miraculous metamorphosis remedied a defect (547) which could never be healed in the natural world. The fabulous nature of the *Metamorphoses* made it possible to offer half-satisfactory solutions for situations which were entirely hopeless otherwise. Daphne's lover Apollo was likewise only half-frustrated: he chose the laurel tree for his personal plant and has ever since been wearing a branch of it on his head. Thus Daphne was, in a way, wedded to the god after all. Ovid makes the ambiguous character of the ending obvious when he says that friends who came to call on Daphne's father after the event were in doubt whether they should condole or congratulate him (578). This is characteristic; Ovid had a natural propensity to undecisive compromises.

◇   ◇   ◇

The next metamorphosis differs in that the change does not heal a breach, but creates one. This time, however, the transformation is later reversed and thus a pleasing outcome is effected. The victim is the nymph Io, whom Juppiter ravished. When his jealous wife was about to surprise the lovers, the god turned his mistress into a cow. Stricken with madness, Io wandered restlessly from land to land. When she finally reached Egypt, her human form was given back to her, and under the name of Isis she was elevated to the rank of a goddess.

Ovid believed in the ancient fable no more than we do, but he elaborated it in his own way. He dwells on Io's bewilderment and anguish when she found herself to be a cow:[16]

> She sought to lament, and out of her mouth came a lowing;
> the sound frightened her, her own voice struck her with dread.
> When she came to the river Inachus where she had often played
> and, standing on the bank, saw mirrored in the water
> her new horns, they frightened her and in frenzy she shrank
>   back from her own self.
>   (I, 637 ff.)

Here, then, is another case of confused and divided identity. Ovid had described Io's strange predicament before in the *Heroides*,[17] and there he reinterpreted the madness that drove her over lands and seas as a frantic flight from herself.[18] In the epistle, the writer sympathetically addresses the raging Io as if she could help her to come to her senses:[19]

> What is the reason for your flight? Why do you wander over wide
>   oceans?
> You will never escape from your own face.
> Child of Inachus, whither do you hasten? You are the same who both
>   pursues and flees.
> It is you who lead yourself, and you go where you lead.
>   (*Her.* 14, 103 ff.)

Why is it that, in spite of the fantastic plot, we are moved by Ovid's
tale and feel concern for the cow-woman? It is, I think, because we
have lived through similar experiences ourselves, although a miracle
has never come our way. We understand all too well what it means
to try to escape from our own self. And we also remember the shock
we received when, in our adolescence, we were standing before the
mirror and for the first time with an adult perception realized how
plain and homely we looked to others; or when we were speaking
and it happened that our voice sounded wrong and hideous, utterly
incapable of conveying what we felt; or when, growing old, we discovered that we were no longer the person we meant to be. There is
much in Ovid's metamorphosis fables which can easily be divested
of the miraculous element and translated into some everyday occurrence.[20]

With a peculiar but attractive mixture of the grotesque and the
pathetic, Ovid's transformation stories often evoke such minor
tragedies of inadequacy, inhibition, and frustration as may visit us
in our own lives. Take the story of Callisto (2, 409–507), another of
the many women who had the rather trying honor of incurring
Juppiter's favor. Callisto was turned into a bear, and in the bear the
combination of human and animal traits is more convincing than
it was in the case of Io the cow. Ovid must often have seen bears
perform in the hunting spectacles of the circus. There he could
watch their erect posture and their deft but awkward-looking ges-
ticulations, and he could hear their voices which sound threatening
and sorrowful at the same time.[21] Ovid's narrative makes good use
of these ambiguities when he pictures how Callisto tried in vain to
express her human concerns in bear language. The transformed
woman wants meekly to pray for mercy and release from her animal
shape (cf. 482), but

> her voice issues from a coarse throat
> with an angry, menacing, dread-inspiring tone.
> And yet her mind remains the same even in a bear's frame.
> She utters her pains in ceaseless moans,
> lifts up her arms—they were not quite arms—to the stars and sky
> and, as she cannot say it, thinks that Jove was ungrateful.
> (2, 483 ff.)

The incongruity of Callisto's condition comes to a dramatic climax later when her son Arcas, a boy of fifteen who roams the woods hunting, happens to come upon the she-bear who is his mother:

> When she saw him, she stopped
> and appeared like one who recognizes; he shrank back.
> He knew not why her eyes stared upon him endlessly
> unswerving; it frightened him; and as she eagerly approached,
> he was on the point of piercing her breast with his wounding spear.
> The Almighty prevented it and whisked away them and the impending
> crime. Snatching mother and son through the void in a whirlwind,
> he set them up in the heavens and made them neighboring
> constellations. (2, 500 ff.)

That is: Callisto and Arcas were given an eternal existence in the form of the Great Bear and Arctophylax (or Bootes).[22]

◇　◇　◇

In general, the character of the *Metamorphoses* is romantic and sentimental, and the stories of Io the cow and Callisto the bear are typical examples of that spirit. For once, however, Ovid treats the subject of a cleavage in identity on a very different basis, applying to theological speculation the notion of two natures within one self. The passage is notable because it prefigures the dogma of two natures in Christ. In the Ninth Book, Ovid tells of Hercules' death and deification (9, 229–273). Hercules—"the redeemer of the world," as the poet calls him (241)—was a son of the Lord who rules in heaven and beneath, while his mother was a mortal woman. When he was dying on the pyre he had himself erected, his divine father said, according to Ovid:

> He, who conquered all things, will conquer these flames which
> you see.
> He will feel Vulcan's might only with his motherly
> part. That which he drew from me is eternal, free
> from death, and safe; no fire can subdue it.
> (9, 250 ff.)

And then the poet speaks of Hercules' ascent to full divinity thus:

> Meanwhile the fire had taken away whatever it had
> power to ravage. The remaining shape could no longer

be recognized as that of Hercules: nothing was left in him that
   stemmed
from his mother's image, only Jove's imprint did he keep.[23]
Even as a snake which has rid itself of its skin and old age
thrives with new youth and gleams forth in fresh scales,
thus, when the Tirynthian emerged from his mortal frame,
grew he strong with his better part, and larger waxed
his form; awesome became his majestic dignity.

(262 ff.)

These untranslatable lines were written between the years 2 and 8
of the Christian era.[24] It took two hundred years until Tertullian
found the same formula for Christ and for the first time spoke of
his "double status, not merged but combined in one person: God
and Man."[25] The idea of two natures combined in Hercules' person[26]
was certainly not of Ovid's own invention,[27] but he was able to give
it so exquisite an expression[28] because it was in line with the novel
tendencies of his age[29] and congenial to his own mind.

◇   ◇   ◇

   Interplay between otherness and sameness, either within one self
or between two persons, is a theme capable of infinite variation.
Ovid explored this new frontier of experience in a great number of
stories. In most of them the confusion is brought about by a metamorphosis, but there are some in which the tangle has nothing to
do with a change in body. This is the case in one of his best stories,
the tale of the narcissus flower who once upon a time was a young
man and of the echo who was a young woman (3, 339–510). As
Ovid tells the fable, Narcissus was a lovely boy, the son of a river
god and a brook nymph. When he was born, his parents consulted
a soothsayer and inquired whether the child

was to see long years of ripe old age;
and the fate-telling prophet spoke: "Unless he know himself."[30]

(3, 347 f.)

At the age of sixteen, between boyhood and manhood, Narcissus
aroused the love of both men and girls, but, tender though his
beauty was, it made him arrogant and hard; his heart remained

unmoved.[31] One of his unlucky admirers[32] called down upon him just retribution with this curse:

> May he love even so, and even so be frustrated.
>
> (405)

His punishment was not slow in coming, and it took the most fitting form: self-seeker that he was, he found himself.[33] In the secluded solitude of a lush meadow deep in the woods[34] he lay down at the bank of a pond to drink, and the calm water mirrored his shape:

> While he tries to quench his thirst, another thirst arises,
> and while he drinks, an image of beauty takes possession of him:
> he loves a bodyless lure, mistaking a shadow for a body.
>
> (415 ff.)

Ovid describes at length the strange deception and the enchantment with which Narcissus "unwittingly desires himself"; then he breaks the progress of his narrative with a direct address. The poet, like an excited child in the theater who tries to help the hero on the stage and calls out loud to warn him of a trap into which he is about to fall, forgets his supposed aloofness and talks to his character[35] in order to extricate him from his error:

> You simple boy, why do you vainly hunt a fleeting appearance?
> What you pursue is nowhere; turn away, and you will undo that
>   which you love.
> You are looking at the shadow of a reflected image;
> it is nothing in itself: with you it came and stays,
> and with you it will leave—if only you could leave.
>
> (432 ff.)

Finally the truth dawns on Narcissus: "He is I":

> What can I do? Am I to be wooed or the wooer? And what shall
>   I hope for?
> What I desire is with me, affluence is my starvation.
>
> (465 f.)

Inopem me copia fecit: the perfect wording defies translation.

The Ovid of the *Metamorphoses* is far from composing parables or preaching sermons; he merely tells fascinating stories; and yet, in so doing, he furnishes material for many a sermon. The medieval *Ovide moralisé* is mostly inept, but the idea was not so preposterous as it seems. The words in which Ovid expresses Narcissus' fatal pre-

dicament lead very close to a profound truth. Self-love is headed
for self-destruction. Its thirst can never be quenched, because love
conquers only through a mutual surrender of two selves, and in
self-love there are no two, and no surrender of the self. Narcissus
now longed for nothing but death, and he did waste away in physical (cf. 437–439) and mental starvation; but even his death was
marred by self-pity (472). When he was gone, his beauty was preserved by his metamorphosis into a flower as white and pink as he
used to be[36]—a flower, we may add, as fine and proud, as single and
useless as he used to be.[37]

Have we been reading too much into our text? If proof is wanted
to confirm our interpretation, it can be found in the way in which
the story of Narcissus is interwoven with that of Echo. Echo was a
nymph who loved to talk but could never say anything of her own;
she could only repeat the last words of her interlocutor. She was
gripped by a violent passion for Narcissus and yearned to make
advances to him. Alas,

> her nature balked her
> and did not allow her to begin; but she eagerly waited for that which
> was allowed her:
> to hear such sounds as might be answered in her own words.
>   (376 ff.)

Echo thus becomes a symbol of those pathetic but annoying females
who are extremely responsive but have no initiative or originality
of their own. In Ovid's tale, Echo finally had an opportunity to converse with Narcissus in her own inhibited fashion and to offer him
her heart. Unfortunately, a tragicomedy of errors resulted; they
both used the same words, but meant different things. Mortally disappointed, Echo thinned out and faded into the shy, invisible, in-
corporeal phenomenon of the echo. But when Narcissus died, she
was again at his side, repeating his laments for his other self. Now
she was in real unison with him: both were bewailing the destruction of the same beloved youth (494–501).

It was a masterful invention to combine in one tale the two fables
of futile love, that of Narcissus and that of Echo.[38] While Narcissus
was caught in the net of mere sameness and was touched by nothing
but his own unsubstantial reflection, Echo is mere otherness and is

herself only an unsubstantial reflection.[39] He is too much prepossessed with his own self to share it with others, and she has no self of her own which she might share.[40]

◇   ◇   ◇

Ovid's stories sometimes approach profundity; many are at least serious, and some even tragic. At the same time, his great epic is lighted up by a goodly dose of a priceless humor, distinct though never clamorous. How did it happen that Echo was afflicted with that peculiar combination of loquacity and reticence?[41]

> Juno had made her so because, whenever the goddess might have caught
> her husband sporting with a nymph on some mountain,
> Echo would purposely detain her with endless talk
> until the nymph had fled.
> (3, 362 ff.)

There is no need to say much about the humor in the *Metamorphoses,* because it is one of its most obvious features.[42] But some of it is rather subtle. Argus, a monster with a hundred eyes, was charged by Juno to watch the cow Io, and the wily Mercury was sent by Juppiter to rescue his mistress (1, 668 ff.). Mercury sat down next to Argus and alternately sang and made music for him all day long in order to put the watcher to sleep. One pair of eyes after another closed, but a few were still awake when Mercury began another tale, which is rendered by Ovid. This last tale is fashioned by the poet in such a way that it closely resembles a story which we have read a short time before,[43] so that the reader receives the impression that the epic is aimlessly spiraling round, and he becomes, himself, drowsy. The somnolent spell of recurrences comes to a climax when a previous line is repeated almost verbatim (709 = 678), and the subject of the line is no other than a listener "captivated by novel music and sweet voice." Soon after this verse, the last lids sank down on Argus' hundred eyes, and Mercury immediately proceeded to behead the sleeping monster. The sudden transition from lulling echoes to stern action gives a good dramatic effect.

There is no need, either, to expatiate on Ovid's superb skill in presentation, on the effortless power of his narrative, or the clear con-

creteness of his sceneries. We do have occasion, however, to insist that
his brilliant ornamentation never degenerates into mere decorative
art. Apparent exceptions, if we look into them more closely, will
confirm this statement. When I was a boy of twelve, our Latin
teacher made us memorize the opening lines of the Second Book
(2, 1–30), and they are well worth it. There Ovid draws a detailed
picture of the resplendent palace in which Sol, the sun god, dwells.
Pindar once said (*Oly.* 6, 1–4) that a work of poetry should begin,
as it were, with a far-shining façade and golden columns; and thus
Ovid, when he opens his Second Book, mentions lofty columns and
glittering gold in the first two lines, and then goes on to describe
the reliefs on the walls which rendered those beautiful vistas Sol
beholds when he rises from the ocean (8–14), when he drives across
the skies (17–18), and when he looks down to the earth from the
zenith (15–16). True enough, this is an imposing image; but as
Ovid had no particular liking for the magnificent and pompous,
in architecture or otherwise, it is improbable that he inserted the
splendid picture as a mere showpiece of verbal imagery (*ekphra-
sis*).[44] Actually, the description is part and parcel of the narrative.
This is the story. The boy Phaëthon had never known his father,
but his mother had told him that the great god of the sun was his
parent. A naughty comrade taunted him and hinted that Phaëthon's
mother had invented a specious tale to cover up her own dishonor.
The indignant boy burned to ascertain the truth for himself and to
show the whole world whose son he really was.[45] He traveled to the
rim of the world to see the sun god and ask him to let himself for
once drive the chariot of the sun. It is with the eager eyes of that
boy that the reader is expected to marvel at the wondrous palace
and to take in all the glory to which it testifies. Phaëthon approaches
his father's grandiose home with awe and pride, but also with lingering doubt (2, 20); he hopes now to be coming into his own and,
already "conceiving in his mind the heights of the heavens" (1, 777),
anticipates the delight of seeing those sights that are pictured on
the palace walls. The responsive reader will feel everywhere how
deep Ovid's tales are dyed with sentiment. In the best classical tradition, the *Metamorphoses* keeps descriptive detail strictly within
bounds and subordinates it to the issues of the narrative.[46]

As the Phaëthon story goes on, the youth forced his unwilling father to let him drive the sun chariot for one day, in order to refute the slander against his mother. But he could not manage the spirited horses, and set parts of the world on fire. Juppiter had no choice but to throw his thunderbolt and kill the unfortunate charioteer.

Phaëthon's death has a sequel in Ovid's epic:

> The stricken father covered up his face in his deep
> sorrow, and if we believe what is reported, one
> day passed with no sun shining. But the raging fires gave light ...
> Sun hated light, and himself, and day,
> he buried his soul in grief, and upon grief he piled resentment
> and renounced his service to the world. "Restless enough," he said,
> "has my lot been from the beginning of time."
> I am loath of labors performed with neither end nor honor."
> (2, 329 ff.; 383 ff.)

Juppiter had to coax and threaten him, as tyrants are wont to do, into resuming his duties.

Thus we read of an actual infringement on the laws of nature for personal and emotional reasons. The violation of the rules is of the same order as when Ovid, in one of his early elegies, had desired that Dawn should tarry (*Am.* I, 13). Phaëthon had humanly tampered with the sun's progress and had suffered death for it; and Sun himself was humanly reluctant to restore the ordained course of things. In the *Metamorphoses,* the poet pretends to accept the mythological view, only now and then interposing a slight indication of doubt: "If we believe what is reported." For the sake of his narrative, he acknowledges miracles and indulges abundantly in the human interpretation of nature. For the human interpretation Echo was a delightful example. That the voice of the invisible echo-woman seems to issue from the foliage of bushes and trees at the far end of a meadow or from the depth of a cave, is also explained in personal terms:

> When she was scorned, she hid in the woods and shyly would
>   conceal her face
> behind a curtain of foliage, and ever since she has lived in solitary
>   caves.
> (3, 393 f.)

We cannot expect from a Roman poet of the Augustan age the straight simplicity of artless fairy tales; rather, we may find in the *Metamorphoses* a passage reminding of the dialectical wit of German romantic writers of the early nineteenth century. In such a style Ovid plays upon the double nature of a water nymph who both is and is not identical with the pool she inhabits. The poet imagines the pool and the nymph now as one and the same, now as two and different, and again as two and similar. He pictures the translucent waters of the Salmacis pool as embedded in green meadows (4, 300–301: *perspicuus liquor* and *cinguntur herbis*), and soon afterward he similarly describes the naiad Salmacis as clad in a transparent dress and reclining on soft grass (313–314: *perlucenti amictu* and *incubat herbis*). When Salmacis saw the handsome young Hermaphroditus, who was wandering through the countryside, she at once fell in love with him and without more ado asked him to marry her. Shocked, and flushed the color of the moon in eclipse with embarrassment, he shrank back:

> "Stop, pray," he said, "or else I shall flee both from you and
> from this spot."
> (4, 336)

(Evidently, the youth failed to see that the woman was identical with the spot where he met her, and Salmacis took advantage of it to lure him by a ruse into her arms—that is, her waters:)

> Salmacis was alarmed, and she answered: "I leave this place for
> you to use it,
> O stranger," and she turned about and pretended to walk away,

but she hid among the bushes. Hermaphroditus now believed he was alone and undressed to enjoy a swim in the cool lake. At this point in the narrative, a reader familiar with the conventions of ancient literature expects one of two remarks to be made: either that the dazzling beauty of the naked youth was reflected in the water like the glorious sun or moon (the moon had been mentioned a moment ago); or that, with such a sight before the admiring naiad, hot flames of passion flashed through her eyes into her soul.[48] Since in this case the mirroring water and the eyes of the woman were one, Ovid was able to blend both observations:

Salmacis was on fire, and the eyes of the nymph burned,
even as when the sun, most radiant in a bare sky,
reflects his image in a mirror which faces him.

(347 ff.)

When the youth dove into her pool,

the naiad exclaimed: "I have won, he is mine!" She flung
far away all her garments and leapt into the waves.

(356 f.)

With the water on which the swimmer floated, she clung to his body,[49] and while he was still resisting her, upon her prayer she was united with Hermaphroditus into one being.—As we paraphrased the story, we brought out into the open the pivot of the tale, the half identity of naiad and pool; in the actual text of the poem, however, it is never made explicit, but rather is tucked away in the engrossing progress of the graphic narrative, and thus is lost on careless or prejudiced readers.[50]

◇   ◇   ◇

Not for a moment, of course, would Ovid take water nymphs and miracles for anything but figments of imagination. We have his own word for it that the transformations of his *Metamorphoses* are not to be believed (*Tr.* II, 64), and this goes for the whole body of mythological fables.[51] And yet he gave ancient mythology its unexcelled, final, comprehensive expression. There is no other literary work in which the modern reader can find the pantheon of antiquity represented with equal fidelity and completeness, or with a comparable charm and briskness. Ovid happened to live at the turn of the ages, and that was the last historical moment for achieving what he accomplished. Mythology was by then already doomed and its life was giving out, but still there was some dormant power left in the mythological tradition.

Ovid, if anyone, was the man to animate it in the proper spirit, fired as he was by a romantic yearning for a fanciful world order in which the concerns of the mind and heart held their own, in some measure, against the insipid laws of nature. And all the other requisites, too, were at his command. He possessed, first of all, an abundant imagination; and he had also the faculty of adequate, and

in fact brilliant, expression. He was vocal and articulate; his verse
is pure and fluent. He was able to conjure into words the palpable
shape of things as well as the drama of actions and reactions in their
connected succession, and the wayward flux of emotions coming
and going. He had both wit and a sense of humor. Being an unbe-
liever, he injected into the fables that grain of irony which is just
enough to serve as an antidote for the melodramatic—an overdose
would have led to satire and clownishness. He was far from drawing caricatures, as Lucian did later on; good-natured, responsive,
and kindly as he was, he took his characters for what they purported
to be. His sensitive heart went out with brotherly charity to all creatures, first to the men or those who were like men, but then also to
animals, and sometimes even to plants. He was both worldly-wise
and playful. He took a boyish delight in the fabulous, and was able
blandly to manage miracles so as to make them appear almost natural. Securely and with perfect grace he moved in the in-between
land of half-reality. And lastly, he had worthwhile ideas of his own,
although some of them were none too clear and distinct.

⬦   ⬦   ⬦

Our picture, however, of Ovid's views is not yet complete. We
have still to pose the question of the spiritual fundamentals. On
what religion or metaphysics, on what firm trust or expectancy did
that impressionable man, or did his contemporaries, base their lives
and their ideals? When we envisage the answer, we shudder to see
how shaky the ground was upon which all the splendid glory of
Augustan civilization was resting.

With respect to the gods of ancient religion, Ovid was an agnostic.
In the *Ars Amatoria* he declared (I, 637): "it is useful that there
be gods, and so let us believe in their existence accordingly." The
line is quoted very often, but rarely in its context. If we read on, we
find Ovid saying that it is good for us to believe in gods, provided
we do not think (as the Epicureans did) that in their serene beati-
tude they do not mind what is going on in this our world; let us
rather continue to worship them with modest piety, in the fond, if
forlorn, hope that they reward those who wrong no one. These are
Ovid's words:

> It is useful that there be gods, so let us believe in them as it is useful,
>   let us offer incense and wine on the old altars.
> And they do not keep aloof in quiet unconcern, as if slumbering.
>   Live without doing harm, and divine power will be with you.
> Return to the owner whatever he entrusted to you; abide loyally
>   by your mutual ties;
>   abstain from deceit, and let your hands be clean from murder.

The setting of the passage is sportive,[52] but the few lines themselves rise to a high level. Ovid recites the basic commandments of his own simple creed and indicates that it is hard for us to live up to our obligations toward our fellow men unless we presume that the code is sanctioned and upheld by something above man. And thus he decides to practice without belief, in a mild and tenuous form,[53] the religion of the fathers. As far as persuasion was concerned, he could only arrive at a feeble compromise; there was no other choice.

The religious tradition of Ovid's Rome, broadly speaking, was twofold.[54] There was the native Italian religion, plain and dour; and the fine, mellow Greek religion that had been grafted upon it. What use did Ovid have for such beliefs as had grown wild in his home country? If we earnestly try to put ourselves into his shoes, we are forced to admit that for him and his like, that is, for the average educated Roman, the aboriginal religion must have been stone dead. Rural as that religion had been, it could hardly survive the urbanization of Roman society; superstitious, narrow-minded, and rigidly formalistic, it was bound to collapse under the impact of enlightenment and liberal Greek culture;[55] tribal, clannish, and patriarchal as it had been, it could no longer stand up when Rome had absorbed all Italy and was running a world empire, and when most of the old patrician families were dying out or losing out, while individuals of nondescript origin were assuming positions of power. The Italian religion could therefore only subsist in the shape of rites, customs, and festivals which stood for one knew not what. We shall see later, when we study the *Fasti,* what Ovid attempted to make of that domain.

Greek religion was incomparably more mature, broad, rich, subtle, and profound; but it, too, had already run most of its course. Four hundred and fifty years had gone by since Pindar, Aeschylus, and Sophocles wrote their inspired poetry, and in the meantime scientific philosophy had exploded the myth of personal gods manifesting themselves in the phenomena of nature. The only province left to the gods of tradition was that maze of intangible factors which we call Destiny, Fortune, or Chance, so that the gods would be understood as the agents that determine the turn of events by bending our fates into this or that definite direction. Under this view, the gods would be recognized only by the power they actually exercise over the course of our individual and social life, and thus they would by necessity be associated with worldly might and authority.[56] This was the line which imperial policy took. Augustus was bent on reviving the hereditary Roman-Greek religion for the sake of order, stability, and unbroken continuity; the present was to be firmly tied up with the idealized past. The Emperor restored ancient shrines and built new temples; he celebrated anew half-forgotten festivals, adapting them to timely purposes; he wanted to see the deities honored and worshiped as of old. The ruler himself, Juppiter's vicegerent on earth, was looked upon as "a god in our midst" (*praesens deus*). Thus the official religion was meant to consolidate the reborn nation in one common loyalty. It did not insist upon any dogma or conviction, but doggedly stuck to cult and habit lest organized society should fall to pieces.[57] The gods were allied to the state, and the state to the gods.

Ovid, for one, scorned whatever was senseless and accidental, and took little pride or interest in the Imperial State. Nor was he fitted by his mentality to join one of the philosophical denominations offering its special brand of substitute religion. In progress he could not believe, because no one else did; nor, taken all in all, was there any progress. Unless we misinterpret him, he had two things only in which to believe wholeheartedly: in man, and in art. In man he believed as in an interesting and emotional individual, and, most of all, a being capable of affectionate intercourse with others. Little did he care, on the other hand, for the structure of society, but dispassionately took it for granted such as it was. Business life he probably despised; politics left him cold; but he fervently believed in art because it is liberal, fine, and utopian, reaching out as far as can be toward better men and a better world—just as love does with its

dreamy, cherished illusions. Through the medium of art, but only
within that medium, he also believed in the traditional mythology
and in miracles.

◇   ◇   ◇

These may be the reasons why the Pygmalion fable, a fable of a
miracle, of art, of love, and of a better human being, is the finest
among the many he has told. Like numerous others in the epic, it
must be viewed in its environment.

In the long string of ever-continued narrative, there are often
things that carry over from one part to the next and beyond, and
if we neglect the connections we may miss some of the finer points.
Thus we have now to begin with a few lines preceding the Pygmalion story, ignoble though their subject is.

The scene for the whole passage is laid at Cyprus, the fabled island
where Venus has her home. Among other Cyprian fables, Ovid has
this to tell:

> The foul daughters of Propoetus dared to deny
> that Venus was a goddess. The wrathful deity punished them:
> they are reported to have been the first to lend to any and all their
>   own bodies and beauty (?).
> And as shame faded from their faces and their blood hardened,
> they turned to rigid stone with but slight change.
>
> (10, 238 ff.)

There is perfect logic in the nemesis. When the women refused to
acknowledge that love is divine, the deity of love caused them to
go all the way and practice their unbelief.[58] And again, as women
too obtuse to blush, they were no better than dead rock; so into this
they turned. In the *Metamorphoses* the law of cause and effect
makes sense.

Without introducing the hero of his next story, Ovid goes on thus:

> When he saw how the sisters spent their days
> in guilt, Pygmalion was hurt by the greatness of vice
> which nature has put in the female mind. So he remained for a long
>   time.
> unmarried, with no companion to share his life.
> Meanwhile with wondrous art he carved snowy ivory,
> and happily endowed it with such beauty as can adorn
> no woman born; and he was fired with love for his handiwork.
>
> (243 ff.)

How much there is in so few lines! The sensitive idealist, unable to bear the flaws in the real world, shuts himself up in lonely seclusion for many years. But as an artist, he succeeds in creating out of his own mind that perfection which he can never hope to meet in actual life, only to fall humanly in love with it:

> The face was that of a real maiden, one would think she was alive
> and wanted to move, were it not for her bashfulness.
> So much did art hide behind its own art. Pygmalion gazed in
>   wonder and drew
> into his bosom the flame issuing from the semblance of a woman.[59]

Ancient statues were colored and therefore much more lifelike than the pallid relics we are used to see in our museums with their colors gone. On the other hand, the ancient theory of art was based on the notion of imitation, so that it knew no higher praise for a work of art than to declare that it seemed real except for its immobility. We no longer hold that view; but still this is true, that the consummate work of art shows no more traces of art, but is real and lovable in its own right. Once an idea has been translated into tangible shape, it has an existence independent of its creator. But Pygmalion was no longer content with worshiping the ideal woman; he wanted her for himself in the flesh:

> Often he lays groping hands on his work, to see
> whether it is woman or ivory, and yet does not admit that it is ivory.
> He kisses and feels kissed in turn, he talks, and embraces,
> and believes that the limbs yield to the touch of his fingers
> and fears to bruise her when he presses them.

When the yearly festival of Venus was celebrated all over the island, Pygmalion also sacrificed and stood

> before the altar, and timidly he spoke: "If ye gods have power
>   to give all things,
> then grant me for a wife"—he did not dare to say: "the ivory maiden,"
> but said instead: "one like the ivory maiden."
> As Venus, the golden goddess, was present at her own feast,
> she understood the true meaning of his prayer.
>   (274 ff.)

Thus, in the wonderfully accommodating world of the *Metamorphoses,* Pygmalion's fondest wish was to be fulfilled. The miracle, however, was not performed by the deity directly; Venus left it to the lover to stir life in the image:

> He stooped to kiss the reclining figure: she seemed to be warm.
> Once more his mouth touched hers, his hands tested her breast:
> under the touch the ivory softened, shedding its hardness,
> and beneath his fingers it dipped and yielded, even as Hymettian wax
> under the sun's rays softens and, handled by the thumb, bends
> into any shape; through being used it becomes capable of use.
>
> (281 ff.)

Ipso fit utilis usu. Whoever happens to be in love with an ivory woman may take these words to heart and try out Ovid's directions. The artist's fingers molded the statue into life.[60] The warm sunshine of his affection[61] and the deft touch of his hands melted down frigidity, and, while he was acting upon her as if she would respond, she did finally respond:

> While he was stunned, and half rejoiced half feared to be mistaken,
> while lovingly again and again he fingered his desire:
> it was a woman, the pulse beat when his thumb tried the vein.
> Now the Cyprian pronounced in full solemn words
> his thanks to Venus, and now at last he pressed
> with his mouth a live mouth. The maiden felt the kiss
> and blushed, timidly her eyes opened and met his;
> looking up, she beheld the light both of day and of his love.[62]

It will be noted how accurately the miracle of the preceding story is reversed here. The shameless sisters had frozen into inanimate rock because their sluggish blood would not burst into a blush; while the modest ivory maiden, when thawed to life, woke up with a blush. From this climax Ovid brings his story to a swift and festive conclusion:

> The goddess looked with favor upon her work, the marriage,
> and as soon as the moon had rounded her horns to fullness nine times,
> Paphos was born, for whom the island is named.

The enchanting fable was not only admirably rendered by Ovid; it is quite possible, and in fact likely, that in all relevant respects the invention was his. We possess a report of an earlier version of the Pygmalion legend, and if this was, as it may well have been, all that Ovid had before him, then his crude material was cheap and insignificant by comparison with what he has made of it. That earlier tradition simply told that Pygmalion, an ancient king of Cyprus, fell in love with an ivory statue of the goddess Venus and treated it as if it were a live woman and his mistress.[63] Ovid (if it was he who is to be credited with all the changes) made the statue to be one of a woman, not of the goddess; he made Pygmalion to be a sculptor,[64] not a king; he devised Pygmalion's escape into creative art from the defects of reality; and he originated the idea that the statue came to life under Pygmalion's caressing touch. All these innovations are in line with Ovid's own views. We have seen how intelligently and humorously he wrote about the artist's "boundless liberty" to represent such perfection as nature will never produce;[65] we have found how the characters he had fashioned were to him like actual beings so that he would talk to them with brotherly sympathy;[66] and we have read how feelingly he told of Deucalion and Pyrrha softening and animating cold rock by their touch.[67] In a word, Ovid was enough of a conscious artist to conceive one of the finest apologues on the marvel of creative imagination; and his *Metamorphoses* is, moreover, one of the greatest examples of just such creative imagination. When he composed it, the characters of mythology and legend had already been recognized as beautiful figments, and still he was able, while remolding them, to stir the pulse of warm blood in those ivory statues.

◇   ◇   ◇

Ovid has woven together the Pygmalion story with others into a complicated web of various fleeting relationships. We have seen already how closely it is connected with the one that precedes it. The following legend tells of a kind of nemesis which came upon Pygmalion's house. While he himself had been allowed to marry his spiritual daughter, so to speak,[68] his great-granddaughter Myrrha, in turn, was gripped by an incestuous passion for her real father, the son of Pygmalion's daughter Paphos. The correspondence is obvious, but Ovid, as he very often does, wastes no word on it. On the other hand, there is also a foil for Pygmalion's aversion from womanhood. The Pygmalion legend is put by Ovid into the mouth of Orpheus, who likewise "shied from all love of women" (10, 79),

although for a different reason and with a different result. Again
Ovid fails to make explicit the parallel; nor does he lay his finger
on the similarity that Orpheus too had brought his wife to life
through his powerful art.[69] Other fables in the neighborhood are
connected with that of Pygmalion by the common bond that they
are all exotic in both locale and character, and this feature is stressed
by the poet himself with respect to one of them, at least (10, 304–
310).[70] The closer we look into any one group of stories, the more
cross-connections shall we discover, in addition to the pragmatic
thread which runs through the whole sequence.[71] Certain ideas,
types, moods, or shades persist for a while and then fade out. There
is no point, however, in trying to unravel all the subtle relationships. The reader's mind is most pleasurably enveloped in a complex net and he will hardly care to have it critically ripped to pieces.

Romantic irrationality is a potent element in the *Metamorphoses,*
and it also makes itself felt in the uneven tempo of the narrative
throughout the work. Often the story is pushed forward with great
energy of action and happy conciseness of phrasing; often again,
the progress is measured and deliberate, so that the reader can relish
the details of an arresting situation; there are passages where the
narrator dashes on headlong, and others where he lingers too long
and elaborates too much. The willful changes in tempo made it
possible for the author to pass quietly over such points as his predecessors had treated amply, and to dwell on others. More important,
however, it gave his work that playful freshness which springs from
unpedantic liberty.

◇   ◇   ◇

The main subject of the epic is the transformation into animals,
plants, stones, or constellations of humans or gods. If we rationalize the process by which the concept of metamorphosis had been
evolved, it was performed in two steps. First, things human were
explained in terms of extrahuman nature, and vice versa; then, it
was assumed that transitions were possible between different kingdoms of nature. The first step resulted from the universal urge to
apply identical notions to various provinces of experience, taking
a certain set of ideas from the field in which it was originally developed and having it shed its light on some other field. Human life

stands especially in need of such elucidation. By way of human characters and human behavior, we encounter a far greater variety of
kinds, grades, and combinations than our thought or speech is able
to master. In order to find our way through that bewildering maze,
we want to mark out a number of distinct types to which to look
for our orientation. Such standard types, with definite qualities
and habits familiar to everyone, can easily be found in extrahuman
nature. Thus we speak of "wolfish" or "sheepish" characters, and
clarify what is going on among men by metaphors, similes, or animal fables. If a person is hard and cold, unfeeling and unbending,
so that you hurt yourself when you run up against him, he can be
described, in a word, as "stony." A child, tender, lean, and frolic-
some, may be likened to a kid. The cicada was for the Greeks a
symbol for an old man who looks dry and shrunken but is endowed
with a high, pleasant, powerful voice (*Iliad* 3, 150–152), while the
nightingale reminded them of a woman singing melodious and
melancholy tunes. The comparison inevitably worked both ways:
the woman seemed to complain like a nightingale, and the bird's
call was taken for a woman's musical lament. The next step was
to invent a story according to which Procne (or Philomela) had been
human before she was turned into a nightingale, and legendary
tradition began to explain that she is forever mourning her son
whom she had slain with her own hands for such-and-such reasons. Or, for example, it was told that the goddess Dawn married
a handsome young man and had him made immortal, but forgot to
demand for him eternal youth. Thus, while Tithonus lived in happiness with his divine wife, he became older and older and finally
shriveled into a cicada; so she put him into a cage and had him sing
to her, just as a Greek girl would keep a cicada for her pet. The
notion of a transition from one state to another received support
from various quarters: from the belief that some gods had, or could
assume, the shape of animals; from the widespread theory that
human souls are reincarnated in animals or plants; from the belief
in werewolves (cf. 7, 270–271) and the like; and from ideas akin
to totemism.[73] Once the idea of metamorphosis was accepted, it
could also be used for new purposes. It is, for instance, the typical
nightmare of the hunter that he might become the game and be

hunted in turn; and thus it was told that Actaeon had seen Artemis, the goddess of the hunt and of the wilderness, naked, and for this sin was changed into a stag and killed by his own hounds.

We shall not try to sketch the actual history in Greek art and literature of the concept of metamorphosis. Be it enough to state that, for certain reasons, the theme had been very popular in the Hellenistic age which preceded that of Ovid. Thus he had before him both Greek and Latin books in prose or verse in which metamorphosis fables were told. There was no lack of material which he could use, adapt, and enrich.

Why did Ovid select the theme of metamorphosis for his great epic? The successful way in which he dealt with it proves how congenial to his talent the subject was, and we need not repeat in detail here our previous observations in this respect. One factor was, as we have seen, that the fantastic and utopian character of the stories appealed to him, and that here he could work out a better logic than brutal reality had to offer. Furthermore, the theme gave ample scope for displaying the phenomena of insecure and fleeting identity, of a self divided in itself or spilling over into another self.[73] Once, a metamorphosis is prophesied in these words: "You will be separated from yourself and yet be alive" (10, 566). Separation from the self means normally death, but not in a metamorphosis. This leads to another point. We had occasion to note (see pp. 78 f.) that Ovid's mild disposition shied from a crushing finale, and the device of a transformation offered a compromise for the dilemma between life and death. This is clearly indicated in the Myrrha story. Myrrha could not live on after a hideous sin she had committed:

> She knew not what to desire,
> and between fear of death and loathing of life
> she clung to this prayer: "O ye gods, if there are deities
> who listen to a confessed sinner: I deserve and accept
> harsh punishment. But lest, surviving, I offend the living,
> or, dead, offend the shadows, ban me from both realms,
> change my shape, and deny me both death and life."[74]
>
> (10, 481 ff.)

The anxious question of the contrite woman is answered by the poet in person:

> Yes, there is some deity who listens to a confessed sinner:
> her last wish found its gods.

Again Ovid is not ashamed to intercede in his own narrative and to betray how much it moves him;[75] he feels relieved that Myrrha does not have to die. And when he has reported how she was transformed into the myrrh tree, and how her tears were to be known in all ages to come as precious grains of incense, he even styles the metamorphosis an "honor" rather than a punishment (501). On the confines of life and death the repentant sinner is allowed to rise to a new dignity.

◇ ◇ ◇

It would probably be revealing to muster carefully the range of characters which Ovid portrays in his epic, and to see what qualities are and what are not painted in full, lifelike colors. A militant, fierce, or blustering frame of mind seems hardly to be represented with incisive vigor; wherever there is pride and swagger, it is mostly of the boyish variety; but very many times we are shown devout meekness and humility. The stories abound with instances of passionate desire, but they also contain some of the most delicate instances of marital love in middle and late age. Naïveté can be found everywhere, since Ovid was full of it himself; without it, no man can have vision or be a poet; but he had too much of the precious gift for his own good. Regal dignity and grave authority, Roman style, are rather infrequent, and we would not expect it to be otherwise; once, however, the unpredictable author steeps a passage (7, 456–522) in an animated stateliness which can vie with Vergil's *Aeneid*.[76] Wicked types are rare and unconvincing, except when they can be viewed with humor. There are numerous instances of loquacity;[77] Ovid was certainly a great talker, and that foible was bound to enjoy his sympathy. With sweet understanding he pictures the urge to speak in Hercules' aged mother Alcmene when her great son had died on Mount Oeta and her orphaned grandchildren were being persecuted by a mortal enemy:

> Alcmene, worn down with lifelong worries, turned to Iole
> as one to whom to unburden an old woman's complaints,
> to report her son's labors, witnessed by the world,
> and the tribulations of her own past.
> (9, 275 ff.)

It is a touching sidelight[78] that the mother, when Hercules' career had come to its end, was looking for someone to whom to tell the tale of his labors, no matter how well known they were to all mankind. And Ovid shows, besides, that he comprehends what it means to be the mother of a fearless hero.

◇ ◇ ◇

The *Metamorphoses* is no doubt too long and somewhat repetitious. The range of Ovid's creative imagination was large but not unlimited, and, as usual, the poet overtaxed his ability of variation. When he had composed eleven books, he seems himself to have realized that his themes had grown stale. At that juncture, he might gracefully have brought his biggest and greatest work to a swift conclusion, but once more he was unable to part with what he had under his hands. We know how sorely he lacked the nerve for finality. So he wrote on further, but broke with his previous manner and ventured beyond the circuit in which he had, so far, excelled. On the fresh grounds he still managed to live up to a high standard of technical skill, but with respect to poetical substance he was in general less successful.[79] His genius was slackening even before he was sentenced to a living death. The decline has begun, and yet Ovid's personality does not cease to hold the responsive reader under its spell. The rest of the poet's story makes up in human interest for what it leaves to be desired in the value of his continued literary production.

With the Twelfth Book the epic changes its character.[80] No longer does the author delight us with a bountiful sequence of tender and sentimental fables, most of them short, a few more leisurely than the rest, but all of them moderate in length, intense in feeling, and graceful in presentation. Enchanting caprice gives way to an ambition for grandeur. The writer begins to insert massive compositions, each of them devoted to a single subject. Trying his hand at the truly heroic manner of epic, he now spends three hundred hexameters on a description of Lapiths and Centaurs slaughtering one another (in the Twelfth Book), and four hundred lines on a bitter debate, with tragic consequences, between two great heroes of legend (in the Thirteenth). Competing with the historical epic, he recounts patriotic legends (in Book 14), and in his last book he expounds in full a philosophical doctrine. What, then, has Ovid accomplished in his last four books? And how, in the first place, does the break make itself felt when it occurs?

Ovid, a singularly considerate man, saw to it that the sudden change in his intentions should not come as a shock to his readers. He did not belong to that class of authors who are bent on doing justice to their subject only and forget their audience. He must have been the keenest reader of his own epic, and he had a thousand and one friendly tricks up his sleeve to nurse his reader along and give him what he needed, so as to keep him engrossed but never bewilder him. Where he is leading up to a most unexpected thing, a brutal tale of wounds and deaths by the dozen, he serves notice of what is coming. He is to lay the story in the mouth of old Nestor,[81] and the scene is the tent of Achilles, where the heroes of the Trojan War are being entertained. At this point Ovid says:

> They spent the night in conversation, and valor was the theme
> for their talk. They told of battles; how they had fought them, and
>   how their enemies. . . .
>   What else would Achilles talk about,
> or would men sitting at the table of great Achilles?
>   (12, 159 f.; 162 f.)

Thus Ovid makes it clear in his own sly manner, half apologetically, that for the time being the sway of Venus is terminated and her gallant Mars takes over. Shortly after the lines just quoted,[82] Nestor reports with a wealth of detail the fight that broke out between Centaurs and Lapiths at a wedding celebration. Emphasis is laid on the use of freakish improvised weapons and the ghastly nature of the wounds of which the combatants died.[83] The narrative sounds more like Lucan than Ovid. That Ovid, of all people, Ovid who could not but detest the "gloomy sand" of the gladiatorial arena (*Ars Amat.* I, 164), should have catered to that lurid curiosity for novel kinds of agony, cannot be explained unless we suppose that at present he was willing to buy at any price variety of manner and heroic grimness of subject matter.

His rich talent, however, could also attain genuine sublimity and yet stay in character. Near the end of the book, Achilles' death is mentioned and the hero is eulogized in these fine epigrammatic lines:

> Now he has turned to ashes, and from great Achilles remains
> a small something, hardly filling an urn;
> but his glory lives on and fills the whole world.
> His glory is the measure to fit that man, through it
> Achilles is equal to himself and tastes not the emptiness of Tartarus.
>
> (12, 615 ff.)

Here, then, is a transformation with no power to impair the identity of a great man, a realistic metamorphosis in which the person is destroyed and yet his spiritual entity emerges victorious.

The Thirteenth Book, the longest of all, contains two very extended and elaborate public orations; as speeches of this sort go, they are good and forceful. In the Fourteenth Book, the narrative wanders from Hellenized southern Italy to Latium and Rome; at the same time, the poet takes up legends of native Italian origin and begins to center his attention on the national Roman tradition. This was an incisive change, and Ovid has again clearly marked out the turning point. At the place where the line of the epic swerves into the new direction (14, 320–326), the author sets the "Ausonian lands" and the "mountains of Latium" over against "Grecian Elis"; he mentions a host of place and stream names from Latium and populates the countryside near Rome with nymphs in the Greek style (326 ff.). It is as if he were erecting a portal and inscribing it with the words "Introite, nam et hic dei sunt. Even our own land is full of deities and can be made to resound with mythological lore, just as Greece has done from of old." We are not surprised, then, when soon afterward he foists a Greek etymology on the name of the Italian god Janus (334).

Ovid's interest in Italian tradition was at that time so lively that, without waiting for his *Metamorphoses* to be completed, he embarked on another literary project, which dealt with Italian religion and history. But we cannot enter now on a discussion of the *Fasti*.

✧   ✧   ✧

It is a truism that a story improves any time it is retold by a gifted narrator. Those legends which had been handed down through a long line of Greek tradition were already beautifully shaped when Ovid took them over. By the same token, most of the aboriginal lore of Italy must have been a poor material for him to start with, raw and uncouth as it was by comparison with the poetic legacy of Greece. Ovid was obliged to draw more heavily upon his own ingenuity for the construction of plots, to say nothing of the finer elaboration. Surely he understood what was involved, and it is evident that he bestowed great care on the first story of the series, that of Picus and his wife Canens (14, 308–434). It can therefore serve us as a test case for those specific qualities which he cherished at that period of his writing.[84]

The name Picus means 'woodpecker,'[85] and that bird was held sacred in the indigenous Italian tradition. Thus the legendary Picus personified a bird; at the same time, in a blending which has its parallels in primitive belief the world over, Picus was also thought of as mythical king of Latium and, thirdly, as a deity of the woods, endowed with prophetic wisdom. In adapting this particular legend for his epic, Ovid had not to start from scratch, because Picus had at least once before figured in a poem of transformations.[86] We know nothing about the form in which the tale was told there, but Vergil mentions in the *Aeneid* (7, 189–191) that Picus was changed into a bird by Circe because of her passion for him.[87] Of Canens nothing is known; perhaps the character was of Ovid's own invention. Thus much are we able to state about Ovid's material.

For one thing, he worked out a sentimental background for Circe's revenge on the man she was unable to win. In his theory of love, the poet had emphatically declared that magic has no place in love, and that no witchcraft can force the beloved to return the affection; the sorceress Medea who proved unable to hold Jason, and the sorceress Circe who had to surrender Odysseus to his wife, had served as examples for the validity of the contention (*Ars Amat.* II, 103). In the *Metamorphoses,* Circe is pictured as a woman doomed to unrequited love:

> No other lady had a mind more quickly
> kindled by such flames, be it that the cause rested within herself,
> or that Venus had made her so, offended by the tattling of Circe's
> father.   (14, 25 ff.)

Thus Circe could use her awful might only to wreak vengeance after a defeat. She fell in love with Glaucus and transformed by her magic the woman he loved (14, 8 ff.); she fell in love with Picus, and transformed him. In this fashion, Ovid made Circe into a pathetic character of a type which recurs in his poetry: one who is fated to suffer the same misfortune time after time. To this he chose to add another moving touch. Taking his clue from Vergil's story of Dido (*Aen.* 4, 457–459),[88] he invented the point that Circe had built a shrine and erected in it a marble statue of Picus which showed him in all his youthful glory, and the likeness was decorated with many wreaths (312–315). The reader infers that Circe kept worshiping like a god the Picus that was, even after she had savagely robbed him of his human shape and beauty. Thus Ovid both secularized and sentimentalized the primitive figure of the god, king, and prophet Woodpecker.[89] Furthermore, he gave Circe a foil in Picus' wife Canens, for whose sake he disdained the advances of the sorceress. The name Canens means 'Singing Lady,' and the wife's sweet, spellbinding melodies (337–340) were meant to contrast with Circe's weird incantations.[90] In picturing Circe's black magic and the ghostly atmosphere around it, Ovid went to unnecessary lengths, using that element with cheap operatic profusion—a mistake he had never made before.[91] He was aware of his own change in taste, for he proffers an excuse for it. The whole story is supposed to be told by a maidservant of Circe's; being partly initiated herself, the girl was, as Ovid indicates (311; 318–319), proud of the formidable powers which her mistress wielded, and thus she was apt to make the most of it. The setting is likewise elaborate; the fable is given as a confidential (310) narrative within a narrative within Ovid's own narrative. For all that, the result does not correspond to the pains the author took. To my feeling, the story falls flat, except for the really stirring lines at the end, where the grief and death of Canens are narrated (416–434). In the Fourteenth Book of the *Metamorphoses*, the force of the typical themes was giving out.

⋄ ⋄ ⋄

This does not mean, however, that from now on everything went wrong with Ovid's writing. Far from it; although the quality of his poetry was, on the whole, declining, it would on occasions soar to a high level. Take for instance the very next full-scale fable, with real Italian characters who bear the real Latin names of Pomona and Vertumnus (14, 622–771). That story is a sheer delight, and it happens to be, in contrast to the Picus legend, a very simple tale, steeped in the homely spirit of Italian countryfolk. Little use though Ovid had for the pastoral tone, he was possessed of a lively sense for actual country life, and he loved to work in his own garden and orchard (*Po.* I, 8, 45–48). But he rarely had a chance to prove his worth as a writer in that province; his love poetry was urban in subject, and the Greek legendary tradition was devoid of themes drawn from the peasant's point of view.[92]

In Roman religion, Vertumnus seems to have been a god of the changing seasons by which fruits reach maturity, and therefore he was believed to possess the faculty of changing his appearance, while Pomona was the goddess of garden fruits. Ovid again humanized the two figures, but he Hellenized them only slightly. Applying to Pomona a term from Greek mythology, he introduces her as a "hamadryad," but soon he strips her of the foreign character by making it plain that, unlike Greek Nymphs,[93] and rather like a good Italian farmer's lass, she was interested not in untamed nature, but in gardening, and in gardening only. Around her orchard she built a sturdy fence to shut out thieves and protect herself from the lusty Satyrs and Pans who made eyes at her. Vertumnus tried to win her for his wife, but she would not listen; horticulture meant everything to her, but love nothing. Vertumnus, however, was unable to stay away from her. In order to enjoy the sight of her beauty (653), he approached her again and again in various shapes. Preferably he took on the masks of industrious farmers and came every time in such attire, and with such tools and fresh traces of hard work, as would befit the current season. Finally, he changed himself into an old woman and suggested to Pomona a match with Vertumnus, whom he represented as a substantial landowner and not one of those lighthearted fellows who roam the lands and take a girl wherever they can find one. (As a matter of fact, the very Pans and Satyrs had overrun Italy only as strangers from Greece.) Then, as a horrible example, the hag told Pomona a gruesome Greek story of a haughty girl who despised her ardent lover and caused both his destruction and her own metamorphosis into a lifeless statue. The tale was tinged in the wildest colors and yet it failed to frighten the obstinate Pomona into accepting Vertumnus; but now he put off the disfiguring mummery and, adopting his natural form,

> appeared before her in such wise
> as when the sun in all his shining brilliance
> breaks through the clouds that were in his way and reveals
> himself undimmed....
> The nymph was overwhelmed
> by the beauty of the god and felt the mutual wound.
>
> (14, 767 ff.; 770 f.)

With the indication of Pomona's surrender, the narrative breaks tactfully off.

◇　◇　◇

Looking back from the last four books of the *Metamorphoses* to the eleven that precede them, one realizes the better how homogeneous the main part had been and, concurrently, how very Ovidian it was. When the author, with the Twelfth Book, began adventurously to strike out for new goals, he lost his bearings. Instead of advancing on any one fixed line, he made forays in several directions and erratically experimented with his art in more than one field. There is, however, one thing which all his major new attempts have in common: he was striving for a greater sublimity of subject and treatment.

The Fourteenth Book had been for the most part dedicated to national and patriotic themes, and it was concluded with the apotheosis of Romulus and the Hora Quirini. Italian legends had been worked out, more or less, in Greek style.

The Fifteenth Book has for one of its several themes the Hellenization of barbarian Italy, and most of its longer stories deal with the influx into Italy of Greek men and Greek civilization. In the beginning, Ovid says that King Numa

> was not content to be familiar
> with the rites of the Sabine tribe. His broad mind conceived
> things of a higher order,
>
> (15, 4 ff.)

and thus he made a pilgrimage to Croton to sit at the feet of the Greek sage Pythagoras. Next, the poet tells how Hercules, one of the first Greek heroes to visit the Appennine peninsula, wanted the land where he had enjoyed genial hospitality to receive Greek immigrants. Then follow the tales of Pythagoras, who transplanted from Grecian lands to Italy his profound wisdom, and of Hippolytus the son of Theseus, who found a new home in the new country and became a god there (492–546). These two stories are soon succeeded by a full account of the voyage of the god Aesculapius, who in 292 B.C. migrated from the Peloponnesus to Rome and has ever since been worshiped there (622–745).[94] The underlying idea is that Rome has become the center of the civilized world,[95] and the many place names which the poet enumerates in the course of his narrative (49–59; 699–736) make concrete the transfer of a culture.

All this, however, was not yet enough for Ovid's ambition. He had been following in Vergil's footsteps in the preceding book, and now he wanted also to compete with Lucretius. He filled half of his last book with a long oration of Pythagoras in which a great philosophical theory is set forth. Pythagorean philosophy had in that period been revived from a long slumber, and about the time when Ovid was completing the *Metamorphoses* a Greek philosopher from Alexandria, by the name of Sotion, was preaching in Rome doctrines derived from the Pythagorean tradition. Sotion was admonishing his disciples to live as vegetarians, for three reasons: because nature provided an ample variety of nourishing foods, so that there was no need to resort to bloody slaughter; because the killing of beasts and the devouring of their flesh would inure to cruelty those who practiced it, and could easily lead them on to murder human beings; and lastly, because Pythagoras had revealed that human souls, migrating from one incarnation to many others, are often incorporated in animal bodies, so that the eating of meat falls little short of cannibalism. How forceful an impression Sotion made on Roman youth, we learn from Seneca the Philosopher. As a boy, Seneca studied under Sotion and, as he later wrote, was gripped by "a love for Pythagoras" and became a vegetarian. This happened only a few years[96] after Ovid had put into the mouth of Pythagoras the same doctrine and the same reasoning.[97] It is quite possible that

Ovid, too, heard and admired Sotion,[98] whose humane doctrine was bound particularly to appeal to the poet. But there were also current books in which those doctrines were explained.[99] No matter from what quarter Ovid received the inspiration, it helped him to find his way back to his own compassionate and overly tender nature from the gladiatorial delights in which he had been indulging when he described the fight of the Centaurs and Lapiths. He now writes lines like these:

> Habits how evil is he taking on, how impiously
> does he prepare himself for the shedding of human blood, he who cuts with steel
> a calf's throat, callous to its lowing,
> or he who is able to slay a kid while it is pouring forth
> cries like those of an infant.
> (15, 463 ff.)

And he pleads for fairness toward the ox:

> What has the ox done to deserve this, an animal artless and guileless, harmless and simple, born to laboring toil?[100]
> (120 f.)

The expression of a warm feeling for the dumb creatures fits indeed well enough into the terminal part of an epic in which the poet had made light of the barrier between man and animal.

The plea for vegetarianism, however, makes up only the frame of Pythagoras' sermon (15, 75–142; 453–478). The greater part of the speech (143–452) reproduces at length a Neo-Pythagorean theory[101] according to which everything is subject to constant change of form while the underlying matter remains stable:

> Believe me, in the whole world nothing is ever destroyed,
> things only alter and renew their appearance.
> (254 f.)

One example is the transformation of man from one stage of his life to the next:

> We shall not be tomorrow what we were or now are.
> (215)

Thus the last book of the *Metamorphoses*, delving into philosophical speculation on the nature of things, corresponds to the beginning of the work, where the emergence of the Universe was described. Moreover, the reader cannot help correlating the sermon with the subject and title of the *Metamorphoses*. Whether or not the author meant it so, it seems as if the essay on the universal law of change was to provide the theoretical background for the epic of transformations. But the accord between the doctrine as expounded here and the substance of the entire work is only superficial; in essence, the Pythagoras speech is incongruous to the main theme of the long poem. While the epic is replete with mythological fables "not to be believed," the philosophical exposition stops short of the miracle.[102] It is conceived throughout in a rationalizing spirit, and thus it contradicts rather than clarifies the purport of the stories. This time, the switch from one plane of reality to another does not come off well.

The entire last book is more consistently solemn in its tone[103] and more conventionally religious in its themes than anything the author had published before; Ovid was trying to conform to the ideas of the Emperor when it was too late. At the end of his epic, the poet pays the inevitable tribute to the imperial dynasty.[104] In his last story he tells how Caesar ascended to heaven in the shape of a comet. Then follows a eulogy on Augustus which culminates in the anticipation that he too will become a god upon leaving his exalted station on earth; the Emperor was seventy years old at the time. The long work is finally concluded with the author's personal epilogue; and that epilogue is again, at last, in character. The poet boldly asserts that he himself will prove no less immortal and divine. These are Ovid's words:

> And so I have achieved a work which neither the wrath of Jove,
>   nor fire,
> nor steel, nor gnawing time will be able to undo.
> Let come when it will that day which has power over my frame only,
> and end my uncertain span of years;
> yet in my better part shall I rise to the vault of the heavens
> perennial, and my name will be safe from oblivion.
> Wherever Roman might blankets subject lands,
> I shall be recited by the people; in the memory of all ages to come,
> if there be any truth in poets' prophecies, I shall live.

In these melodious lines there is, beyond the confident pride of a great artist in his undying work, one sharp clarion note of defiance. Ovid challenges not only time and the material forces of destruction, but even "Juppiter's wrath." A few lines back, the lord and father of this world Augustus had been compared, and in fact all but identified, with Juppiter. The Emperor's ire struck Ovid at the moment when the *Metamorphoses* was nearly completed.[105] The poet was banished from his homeland to live and to die at the remotest and dreariest place of seclusion in the wide expanse of the Roman Empire. His musical voice was to be silenced. Ovid dared the supreme worldly power and predicted that the *Metamorphoses* would triumphantly survive. It did.

12. OVID'S BANISHMENT

IT WAS IN the year 8 of the Christian era that the blow fell, when Ovid was exactly fifty years old. He was not sentenced by a court of law, but relegated by imperial decree from which there was no appeal. Perhaps he was never given a chance to defend himself against the charges; cabinet justice was held to no legal procedure.[1] The condemnation was for *maiestas* (*lèse-majesté*); that is, in theory, for having impaired the dignity of the nation. For all practical purposes, it meant that he had acted against the person, the authority, or the policy of the Head of the State.

What had he done to draw upon him the pernicious wrath of the Head of the State? There is no other extant record of his case than what the poet himself says about it. From now on, he speaks time after time of his offense, but always in a veiled manner, so as not to aggravate the Emperor's sensibility, using over and over again certain phrases carefully selected for the purpose. The charges, we learn, were two. One was that his *Art of Love* undermined Roman morality by teaching women how to deceive their husbands (*Tr.* II, 211–212, etc.). The second charge was more specific, but for us it remains a mystery. We are only allowed furtive glances at this or that aspect of the complex incident. The following fragmentary picture can be drawn from Ovid's references to the affair.[2]

---

[1] For notes to chapter 12, see pages 228–229.

Ovid had made a foolish mistake, but had committed no crime. Rather, he had seen someone else commit a crime (*Tr.* III, 5, 49–50; *Tr.* II, 103–104). That he appeared at the scene was not deliberate, however; he chanced upon it without knowing what he was to see; in fact, it was a long chain of events (*Tr.* IV, 4, 37–38) which led to his becoming an accidental witness of the misdeed. He was swallowed up in a whirlpool of adverse circumstances beyond his control (*Tr.* II, 101–102). Not even years after the incident was it safe for him to reveal the whole story (*Tr.* III, 6, 27–28; *Po.* II, 2, 61–62). If all the details of his case were known, one would recognize that his personal guilt was none too grave (*Tr.* IV, 4, 37–38); his behavior was shameful but not hateful (*Tr.* V, 8, 23–24). After his error, he was too frightened to do the right thing (*Tr.* IV, 4, 39; *Po.* II, 2, 17). The occurrence might have remained without evil consequences for Ovid, had he only spoken of it to his friend Celsus and taken his advice; but he omitted to inform the very man to whom he was used to confide everything (*Tr.* III, 6, 11 ff.).

The event became known in certain circles at least (cf. *Tr.* I, 1, 23). Ovid had violated no law (*Po.* II, 9, 71); yet the Emperor had a right to feel offended, although the poet had no intention (*consilium, Tr.* IV, 4, 44) of antagonizing Augustus, nor was he bent on any selfish purpose (*Tr.* III, 6, 34); his wrong could only lead to his own ruin (*Po.* II, 2, 15–16). This is Ovid's version of the unfortunate occurrence.

The *Art of Love* had been published about seven years before.[3] No doubt Augustus disliked the book in the first place, but at the time did not feel that in itself it warranted a punitive action. When he now saw fit to use it in Ovid's indictment, it is safe to assume that the first count in the bill seemed to tie up with the second charge. Thus we may infer that somehow or other Ovid became an accessory in a scandalous affair. One of the lovers, more probably the woman, must have been an important person.[4] As we have come to know the poet, we may well accept his story and believe that Ovid, from beginning to end, far from harboring sinister intentions, had no clear-cut designs whatever. He thoughtlessly stumbled deep into the tangle of a precarious situation before he knew it and, when he realized his predicament, was just stuck in a muddle and could not make up his mind this way or that. To the Emperor, on the other hand, it would not occur that one could get so thoroughly messed up by sheer indecision; he was led to assume that Ovid had behaved as he did with a purpose, and had abetted the adultery for reasons of his own. This is, of course, mere speculation, but it seems not out of place.

Ovid's allusions are too definite for the peace of our inquisitive minds; on the other hand, they are not circumstantial enough to satisfy our curiosity. The most likely conjecture is that Ovid's offense was connected with the adultery which the Emperor's granddaughter Julia is known to have committed with Junius Silanus in the same year, A.D. 8. Because of her crime, Julia was exiled by the Emperor, and Silanus likewise left the country although no formal action was taken against him (Tac. *Ann.* 3, 24, 5). What reasons there were to suspect Ovid of active assistance, we cannot tell, but it is easy to fancy, for instance, that the couple met on premises owned by the poet. In any case, Ovid learned of their love but was afraid to take the step which was expected from a loyal subject. It would indeed have been most unpleasant for him to denounce an imperial princess with whom he was socially acquainted and who had perhaps been his guest.

The aged Emperor, on his part, must have been wounded to the quick when his granddaughter's adultery became known. It was his set and well-publicized policy to use all powers at his command for restoring the sanctity of marital bonds, and his prestige was closely tied up with the success of that ambition. But for the second time by such an experience as was bound to hurt him most he learned how hopeless his moralizing endeavors actually were. Nine years before, he had been compelled to inflict stern punishment on his beloved daughter Julia because she was given to so reckless a debauchery that it could not be hushed up. Now the same offense was committed by Julia's daughter. No wonder he was incensed against the man who, in his opinion, was doubly responsible for it, first by writing a morally subversive book which became very popular, and then by complicity in the crime.[5] And yet the Emperor's own record had one hideous stain in that respect. He too had violated no statutory law but nevertheless had insulted common decency.[6]

Ovid's penalty was technically not exile but only relegation. This milder form of banishment did not entail the abrogation of civil rights and the confiscation of property. Ovid was merely obliged to reside at the place assigned to him, which was Tomis at the Black Sea shore, where now the Rumanian city of Constantsa is situated. The place was as remote as could be from any center of civilization (*Tr.* II, 194); obviously the Emperor wanted to isolate Ovid, so as to protect society from his nefarious influence. His books were withdrawn from public libraries (*Tr.* III, 1, 65 ff.) but remained unmolested in private circulation; only as far as the *Art of Love* was concerned would one not care to have it known that one harbored a copy (*Tr.* III, 14, 17–18; *Po.* I, 1, 11–12).

◇   ◇   ◇

When Ovid learned of his banishment, he was visiting with his friend Cotta Maximus on the island of Elba. Perhaps he had left the city on purpose when he heard that an investigation was impending. On the news of his punishment, he reacted with characteristic irresolution. This is what he later wrote in a letter to Cotta:

> When you asked me whether it was true
>   what an evil rumor reported about my guilt,
> I was wavering between doubtful admission and doubtful denial,
>   and you could see how fearful I was.
> (*Po.* II, 3, 85 ff.)

Immediately, most of his former acquaintances turned their backs on the one branded with the imperial disgrace, and the desertion of former friends was another bitter disappointment for the weak and kindly man.[7] Some servants behaved badly (*Tr.* IV, 10, 101). Financial difficulties also arose (*Po.* IV, 8, 32). The writer's income from his books was likely to dwindle down and his credit was shaken, while on the other hand cash was needed for immediate and later expenses. In this situation, one of Ovid's supposed friends seems to have pressed some claim he had against him, with the intention of deriving a financial gain from the poet's ruin. His ruthlessness put in jeopardy Ovid's remaining fortune on which he had to rely for his subsistence, and the sting of this meanness was to stick in Ovid's mind for the rest of his days.[8] Some real friends, however, were

generous enough to help the poet and his wife to settle the obligation; and sympathy with his dire affliction was courageously shown
Ovid from unexpected quarters (*Tr.* I, 8, 27-28; III, 5). His friend
Celsus comforted him in his despondency and talked him out of the
idea of suicide (*Tr.* I, 5, 3-6). His wife watched over his interests
(*Tr.* I, 6, 7-16) and even proposed to accompany him into exile,
but he dissuaded her (*Tr.* I, 2, 41; I, 3, 81-88); he told her she would
be more useful to him in Rome, working for a mitigation of his
punishment.[9]

Ovid made little use of the short time given him for preparing
his departure. Reeling under the smart, he had plunged into a
torpid numbness as if struck by lightning. He was unable to set
his affairs in order, to select the servants who were to go with him,
and prepare the clothing he would need (*Tr.* I, 3, 7-12). One thing,
however, he did do, and it was an absurdity. His poetry had been
the prime cause of his disaster, and thus, while he went over his
papers, he raged against his own poetry; he was as good as dead,
and thus his greatest work, imperfect as it still was, had to burn on
a funeral pyre. Here is his own description as he gave it shortly after
the senseless and useless holocaust:

> When I was leaving, I put with my own hands mournfully
>   with many other verses the *Metamorphoses* into the fire ...
> The innocent manuscripts, flesh from my flesh, were to perish
>   with me in the greedy flames of the pyre,
> either because I now hated the Muses for the charge they had
>   brought upon me,
>   or because the epic was still rough, still growing into shape.
> Nonetheless it was not utterly destroyed but yet exists
>   (I think there were more copies made of it);
> thus I now pray that it may live, and that my industrious
>   leisure may delight the reader and remind him of me.
> Yet it will not be perused with forbearance but by him who
>   understands
>   that the final hand was never laid on it.
>   (*Tr.* I, 7, 15 f.; 19 ff.)

The strange performance was a magnificent gesture[10] of raving
penance and supreme sacrifice; in sober fact, however, no more
than one copy out of many had been offered up as atonement; and

the eventual result was that the author dispensed himself from a last revision and sanctioned as final the current unfinished version, or versions (27–40; *Tr.* III, 14, 19–24).[11]

✧   ✧   ✧

The poet tarried in his house as long as he was permitted (*Tr.* I, 3). When the fatal day dawned, the acute pain finally broke through the stupor which had clouded his mind. Around him he saw his helpers bustle with thoughtful activity, but he asked them what cause there was to hurry. He set himself a certain hour for his departure and then allowed it to pass by, establishing and ignoring one time limit after another. More than once did he cross and recross the threshold of his home, and many a time he bade his last farewell and bestowed his last kisses on those he left behind forever. But there was no choice and no escape. This thing was real.

Ovid was setting out on his melancholy voyage in midwinter. He had to brave a fierce December storm while he was sailing the Ionian Sea on his way to Greece. It was during that tempest that he experienced a wonderful surprise (*Tr.* I, 11). The wind was howling and breakers were coming over; the involuntary traveler could expect the tiny craft to be wrecked at any moment; and yet he found himself composing poetry. He was happily bewildered, because he had been brought up with the Roman prejudice that poetry could never sprout in a rough climate. The delicate, fragrant flower of poetry was thought to flourish best in the sheltered seclusion of a garden or the calm countryside, amongst the tranquil charms of verdant, peaceful, innocent nature. Every Roman believed that the writing of verse required a carefree, collected mind; and comfortable, congenial surroundings; and, before all else, the boon of luxuriant leisure.[12] Ovid's present condition was perplexingly unlike that:

> I am not writing this, as I used to do, in my garden,
> nor is my body enjoying the familiar couch,
> (*Tr.* I, 11, 37 f.)

and yet he was writing verse. He took no small pride in this feat, but he was at a loss fully to explain his own behavior. Attempting to account for that which had befallen him, he assumed that some stupor was shielding his mind from outward reality, and that, on the other hand, the obsession of an inspired madness had taken hold of him.[13] Any Greek, writer or not, would have known better; the Greek nation had always implicitly understood that poetry is man's mother tongue, to be employed whenever there is a use for it. Ovid was amazed, but he welcomed the unexpected independence of his active talent:

> Be it that stupor or madness is the proper name for my fascination,
>   I care so much for it that all my care is relieved.[14]
>
>   (11 f.)

The struggle of which Ovid's soul was the perennial battlefield, a struggle between creative art and inclement reality, had entered a new stage. Playtime was over; youthful resiliency was gone; and reality was stern and vicious as never before. The war was to be one of attrition, in which reality was sure to win out, unless it were willing to relent. But at present poetry could score a tactical success which augured well for the future. Even while the poet's body was trembling in fear, his unbroken spirit remained aloof. He was still able to write, and write he did.

13. OVID IN EXILE

OVID COMPOSED book after book of elegiac verse, and through them he has left us a record of his life in banishment. We are not given all the information we should like to have, but we are permitted to relive with him the hopes and wishful dreams, the pains and shuddering fears, the fretting and lonesome musing, and the ebb and flow of his pride, during the slow-moving years of his protracted misery. The first collection he called *Tristia,* that is, *Elegies of Gloom;* and its first volume, of twelve poems, was written while he was on his way out from Rome to Tomis.

Ovid had sailed in December from an Adriatic port for the Corinthian gulf. Soon bad weather came up, as it was bound to do at that time of the year, and threatened to force the boat back to the Italian shores. The exile's heart was under a strain when the mountains of his home country once more hove into sight; much as he longed to return, it was forbidden ground for him (*Tr.* I, 4, 15–23;

I, 2, 92–94). He left the ship at the western harbor of Corinth and spent several weeks in that pleasant city. In the beginning of March he crossed the narrow Corinthian isthmus and embarked on another boat for the island of Samothrace. He took a liking to the swift craft on which he was sailing. She was called *Minerva*—or probably rather *Athena,* because it was certainly a Greek ship and she had the image of blonde Athena emblazoned on her bows. She was good for all sorts of weather:

> Equally well she batters the waves and cuts through wide silent floods, and she remains victoriously dry in fierce waters.
> (Tr. I, 10, 7 f.)

Steadfastly she carried her passenger

  along the slender line of a long journey,
(16)

and all the time she remained

  a faithful companion and guide on the anxious flight.
(10)

The *Minerva* was going on to Tomis, but Ovid left her at the island of Samothrace. From there it was only a "short hop" (*Tr.* I, 10, 21) to the Thracian mainland and the town of Tempyra, from which a highway led to the eastern shore of Thrace. Ovid preferred the overland short cut to an unbroken voyage on the narrow ship; he was to board the *Minerva* again at a Black Sea port for the last leg of his journey.[1] He grew sentimental when, arriving at Samothrace, he had to exchange the friendly Greek craft, with its competent and kindly Greek crew,[2] for the inhospitable land of savage Thrace in which he was to reside. At the parting, he dedicated an elegy to the *Minerva* and bade her God-speed. He promised to sacrifice a lamb to the goddess Minerva when the ship and the poet should have reached Tomis safely. More than a lamb he could not afford.

In Thrace, Ovid enjoyed the special protection of Sextus Pompeius, the governor of the contiguous province of Macedonia (*Po.* IV, 1, 2; IV, 5, 33–38). Ovid thought that he owed his very life to Pompey; he never felt secure among the barbarian Thracians. Furthermore, the thoughtful Pompey took care of Ovid's expenses.

---

[1] For notes to chapter 13, see pages 230–238.

Why he acted as he did, we cannot tell. Perhaps he felt it was in the interest of the Empire that Ovid should suffer no more than was ordained for him by the supreme authority; perhaps he admired the greatest living poet the nation possessed; or perhaps he had a good heart.

Ovid crossed Thrace, as planned, and embarked again. While approaching Tomis on board the *Minerva,* he completed the first volume of his *Elegies of Gloom.*

◇   ◇   ◇

Elegy tends by its nature more to a contemplative than a narrative content. The first book of the *Tristia* does not give a continuous and complete itinerary; rather, it consists of variations on the somber theme, Voyage into Exile. The restful stopover at Corinth was not in tune with this theme and went therefore unmentioned. Ovid always subordinated the particulars to the general character of his subject. In contrast to the studied realism of Hellenistic poetry, he used descriptive detail sparingly, saturating it with emotional values. But he did not therefore lapse into vague generalities; for he excelled in recasting commonplace patterns so as to give them a specific and original complexion. One of the most hackneyed topics, for instance, is the author's appeal to the good will of the benevolent reader; but Ovid, when addressing the reader of the *Tristia,* has something to say which is by no means trite. He asks for an unusual amount of benevolence (*Tr.* I, 9, 1–36); not many people can be expected to look with compassionate kindness on the laments of an outcast. The deeper is the poet's gratitude to those who still may appreciate his most recent work. Friendship, as a rule, is selfish, says Ovid:

> when clouds shadow your life, you will be alone.
>
> (*Tr.* I, 9, 6)

And he fondly wishes (1–2) that his reader be spared the anguish of disillusion such as the author has suffered by the faithlessness of former friends.

> I pray that you may always disbelieve what I just said,
> yet from my fate it must be owned to be true.
>
> (15 f.)

From now on, a new note makes itself heard in Ovid's elegies. While in his happy times he had deliberately indulged in pleasant fancies, he was compelled after his downfall time after time to insist on the truthfulness of his complaints.

How far shall we believe what he says about the pains and evils that were besetting him in his exile? Poet as he was, and writing verse as he did, he has never ceased to select, arrange, and adorn the facts, although not to the point of distorting them.[3] It is not the business of poetry to cater to the historian's legitimate curiosity and to satisfy his fastidious greed for more and ever more clean, raw, wholesome facts.[4] But if we allow the facts to remain in the background where they belong, and pay more attention to the poet's reactions to them, then, I feel, we can fairly well trust him.[5] The emotional history of Ovid in exile makes a good and true, if sad, story.

He was weak and sensitive, and therefore very human. While he was sailing in bad weather and imagining that he might be drowned here and now, he felt this:

> I do not fear death, but that kind of death is wretched.
> Take out the shipwreck and the end will be a boon.
> *(Tr.* I, 2, 51 f.)

Let those smile at such cowardly bravery who are not familiar with the typical sentiment of a man in physical danger;[6] better than they did the Greek poet Bacchylides know that "most hateful is to mortals that violent death which stares them in the face" (Bacch. 3, 51). Ovid humanly pleaded with the winds and waves, as he had pleaded with unhearing and unfeeling Dawn before. He gave sentimental reasons for his appeal to them, using his own prostration as a shield to ward off new blows:[7]

> Even if the sea should calm down and the winds were to favor my
> voyage,
> even if the elements were to spare me, no less would I be an exile.
> *(Tr,* I, 2, 73 f.)

And on the last leg of his voyage, when the waves hurled spray against the paper on which he was penning his verse, with his old boyish fancy he thought of striking a sly bargain with the tempest and getting the better of it by means of a surrender:

> The wicked gale is fighting me, indignant because I would
> write while it is brandishing bitter threats.
> Let then storm win and man be beaten; but, pray, as soon as I
> stop my song, let it stop also.[8]
> > (*Tr.* I, 11, 41 ff.)

With these lines, the volume gracefully ends.

◇   ◇   ◇

It was probably in the middle of May, A.D. 9, that Ovid reached
Tomis, where he was to spend the rest of his life. When the anxious
and strenuous business of traveling was completed (*Tr.* III, 2, 15–18),
when he had "seen the place, the ways of the people, how they
dressed and lived, and how they sounded" (*Tr.* III, 8, 37–38), when
there was nothing more to be anticipated and nothing to be done
except to stay and wait, Ovid collapsed. His courage broke down
(*Tr.* III, 2), and he fell critically ill (III, 3); he had a fever which
made him delirious (line 19); and he could not have the care which
his condition required:

> The house is not quite as it should be, there is no fitting food
> > for a sick man
> > to be found here, no one to relieve the evil with Apollo's art;
> no friend is with me to comfort me or to beguile
> > the crawling hours by telling tales.
> > (III, 3, 9 ff.)

From his first day at Tomis, the poet felt as if some chill had
clamped down on his mind and body, sapping his vitality;[9] all the
four elements were here uncongenial to him:[10]

> Neither sky nor water, neither soil nor air agrees with me.
> > Alas, my body suffers from a constant languor.
> Be it that my limbs caught the infection from my sick mind,
> > be it that my illness is caused by the place itself:
> since I reached the Pontus, I have been plagued by loss of sleep,
> > lean flesh hardly covers my bones, eating is no pleasure,
> and that color which the autumnal leaves take
> > when, with the first frost, they are stricken by the oncoming winter,
> that color envelops my frame; no strength supports me,
> > and never do I lack some pain to sigh for.

My mind is no stronger than my frame; they are both
    equally ill, and I am doubly afflicted.
And there, fixed before my eyes like a visible thing,
    stands the shape of my fortune for me to scan; . . .
    when I recall who I am and who I was,
I yearn for death.

(Tr. III, 8, 23 ff.; 38 f.)

Yet in other hours he would feel that his mind was equal to his fate
and was helping his weak body to bear an almost unbearable burden
(*Tr.* III, 2, 13–14).

The elegy from which we had been quoting begins with these
couplets:

Now I wish to mount the flying chariot of Triptolemus,
    who first sowed seed in soil untried before;
now I wish to hold the reins of Medea's dragons,
    which carried her aloft from the citadel of Corinth;
now I wish to put on thy wings,
    O Perseus, or to ply thine, O Daedalus,
so that, with the gentle air giving way to my journey,
    I might suddenly behold the sweet soil of my homeland,
and the face of the house I left, and the friends that still think of me,
    and, most of all, my wife's dear features.—
You fool, why do you vainly indulge in childish wishes
    such as never came true nor ever will?
If there is a wish to be made, adore the divinity of Augustus,
    offer ritual prayers to him whom you have learnt to know as a god.
He can lend you feathers and chariot for your flight.
    Let him grant you return, and soon you will be winged.

(Tr. III, 8, 1 ff.)

In these lines the poet once more contrasts gaudy legends with
bleak reality. But, under the cold light of personal misfortune,
things have changed their complexion. The fair sheen of glamor-
ous fables is dimmed, and sober fact stands out clearly in all its
powerful solidity. His own experience has taught Ovid a harsh
lesson. He has learned to direct his humble prayers to the Jove in
the flesh on Palatine Hill.[21] He now feels that any fantastic fable of
old would be consummated in the miracle of his return to the
modest house where he belongs.

Legend has thus sunk to a minor dignity; and it has also lost for the poet the character of a standard which cannot be surpassed by experience. He feels that the old stories are outstripped by his own sufferings. He assures us that fate subjected himself to severer trials than Odysseus ever underwent; besides, Odeysseus was a notorious liar,[12] while the poet's adventures are real (*Tr.* I, 5b; *Po.* IV, 10). His wife, he contends, has stood up under a sterner test of loyalty than Penelope did; she, and not Odysseus' wife, deserves to have her praises sung by a Homer, and yet only Ovid's feeble voice is being raised in her honor (*Tr.* I, 6).

⬦ ⬦ ⬦

What, then, was the reality which surrounded Ovid at Tomis? Tomis was a tiny coastal town in what is now called the Dobrudja. The coast there consists of an arid plateau. It does not slope gently down to the sea, but ends in a precipitous cliff. The shore line is straight and offers no indentations in which a ship may find shelter, except at one place where a promontory projects eastward. This spur is about a mile long and half as wide; its southern side is curved like a hook and provides the only harbor in the entire region.[13] On the flat surface of the promontory was the town. In Ovid's time[14] the Dobrudja was thinly populated by two races speaking two different languages. The Getae were of Thracian extraction, while the Sarmatians (or Sauromatians), who had infiltrated from the northeast, were of Scythian origin (cf. *Po.* I, 3, 59–60). These peoples had hardly tasted the rudiments of civilization; they were fierce, cruel fighters, given to a half-nomadic life and to the warlike sport of banditry. They were still in the tribal stage, and the kings of Thrace, who had recently extended to the Dobrudja the claim of their over-lordship, held only a precarious authority over the country they were supposed to rule. Tomis itself, however, had a history and position of its own. It had been founded many centuries before by Greek traders and colonists, and was organized, after the Greek fashion, as an independent city-republic. Thus Tomis was supposed to be a Greek community; but actually the complexion of the town was, if we can believe Ovid, more barbarian than Greek. Getae and Sarmatians had settled there in such numbers that they were in the majority (*Tr.* V, 7, 11–14); no separate district was set aside for the Greeks to reside in (*Tr.* V, 10, 29–30); the Greeks themselves had adopted the native garb (*Tr.* V, 10, 33–34), and such vestiges of the Greek language as survived in the speech of a few among them were atrociously mispronounced with native articulation (*Tr.* V, 7, 51–52; V, 2b, 24). As to the Latin language, no one knew any of the most common phrases (*Tr.* V, 7, 53–54). Yet even so, the town of Tomis and a few other free cities like it, scattered as they were over the drab plains, served as tenuous outposts of comparative civilization in a barbarian country on the confines of the Roman Empire. Economically, these communities lived mainly from trade and manufacture. The savages from the wilderness would ride into town to sell hides and animals for slaughter, and to buy fish, simple hardware, and goods imported by sea—for instance, grain and wine.[15] Politically, the Greek towns were not subject to Thracian rule, but were placed under the jurisdiction of the governor of Roman Macedonia.[16] Thus Ovid continued to live under Roman law (*Tr.* II, 197–200); but no Roman official or garrison was stationed in the town, and for this reason the enforcement of law was very much in doubt. The Kingdom of Thrace, on its part, was a "satellite of the Empire."[17] The political conditions, then, under which Tomis subsisted were as unsound as they were unsettled.[18] To summarize the complex situation, Tomis, a small city half Greek and half native in character, was a self-governing Roman enclave remote from the greater part of the Empire; the contiguous territory, with a barbarian population of Thracians and Scythians, belonged to Thrace more in name than in fact; Thrace, in turn, was a primitive, poorly governed kingdom semi-independent from Rome; and the nominal Thracian rule ended at the Danube, thirty-five miles from Tomis at its nearest point, with the lands beyond the river occupied by Dacians and roamed by nomadic Scythians. To ward off migratory hordes of savages which periodically invaded the country, looting, burning, and killing (*Tr.* III, 10, 53–66), Tomis had to rely, first of all, on its own walls and on the fighting strength of its citizens; secondly, on the enlightened self-interest of the Thracian king; and thirdly, on the Empire, if the Roman authorities saw fit to send out an expeditionary force. Two or three years before,

Dacian and other tribes had crossed the Danube and broken into Moesia, but had eventually been beaten back by Thracian and Roman troops.[19]

◇ ◇ ◇

The third volume of the *Elegies of Gloom* was written during Ovid's first year at Tomis. The first poem after the preface elaborates the melancholy theme, "So I have arrived, and here I am in that horrible place." Another elegy (*Tr.* III, 10) describes the first winter he went through in the incredible land. The north wind was so violent that it toppled towers and carried roofs away with it. The natives appeared more hideous than ever, now. Ovid heartily disliked their truculent looks, the beards they wore, their untrimmed hair, and the barbarian attire with pants instead of civilized garments. In the winter, Ovid says,

> they fend off the evil cold with skins and stitched breeches,
>   and of their bodies the faces only show.
> When they shake their head, the icicles in their hair will tinkle,
>   and their beard shine white with a coat of frost.
> The wine stands by itself, retaining the shape of the jar;
>   instead of draughts to drink, they help themselves to chunks.
>
> (Tr. III, 10, 19 ff.)

The Danube freezes over and ceases to be an obstacle to ravaging tribes:

> Over newly formed bridges, under which the water still glides,
>   Sarmatian oxen draw barbarian carts.
> You will hardly believe me, but, as there is no ground for me
>   to lie, you will have to grant my testimony credence:
> I have seen the immense ocean bound in ice,
>   a slippery shell held fast the waters.
> I have not only seen it, I walked on hard sea waters,
>   the top of the waves was under my dry foot.
> If you, Leander, once upon a time, had had such a sea,
>   the narrow water would never have been charged with your death.
>
> (Tr. III, 10, 33 ff.)

Thus legend lost its point in the absurd country to which the poet was banished. Leander would simply have walked over the frozen narrows; and never would Acontius have thrown the love apple

before Cydippe's feet there, because apples did not grow in the inclement northern land (73–74).

Not legend alone, but other things as well seemed to have lost
their true meaning. When on March 20 the poet's fifty-second birthday came, the first to be spent in his new abode, he greeted it as an
unnecessary event; he had better never been born, or never lived
to see that day come and visit him at such an improper place (*Tr.*
III, 13). About the same time, he wrote a fine elegy (*Tr.* III, 12)
on the advent of springtime—springtime in Italy, that is, with all
its sweet, exquisite pleasures. In delicate lines he describes the
awakening of nature, and then he says:

> and wherever the vine grows, buds push from the shoots
>   (for the vines stay far away from the Getic shores),
> and wherever a tree grows, the branches on the tree stir
>   (for the trees stay far away from the Getic lands).
>   (13 ff.)

In the barren Getic country the signs of spring are different. The
snows begin to thaw; the water for washing and cooking is no
longer dug out with a spade; and the frozen sea opens up again.
Soon ships will call at Tomis, and Ovid will meet them at the harbor
and look for sailors with whom he can talk. Most of the boats are
from Pontic ports, and with their native crews he will be unable to
converse; but there may be a few Greek, or even Italian, ships coming in from Byzantium and beyond, and the poet can hear what
the world has been doing. If anyone should tell him that the new
Roman campaign in Germany is making good progress, Ovid will
invite him to his home to celebrate. But no, he must not call it his
home; he trusts it is no more than a temporary stopping place, soon
to be exchanged, by the Emperor's leniency, for a less distasteful
habitation.   ◇   ◇   ◇

When Ovid insists that he does not consider his present abode as
a home (cf. also *Tr.* IV, 4, 86), he betrays a sensibility which prevailed throughout the first years of his stay at Tomis. During that
time, he stubbornly refused to accept the humiliating conditions
imposed upon him. He did not get used to the place of his banishment; it irritated him more with each year (*Tr.* IV, 6); and it is

obvious that he did not want to get used to it. Evidently he feared to give up his hope of release, and in fact to give up his own self, if he were to reconcile himself to Tomis and all that name stood for. He would not stoop so low as to like that atmosphere in some measure. He had always been dedicated to the finer things of life; for luxuries or pomp he did not care, but with the wonderful gift of his art he had tried to promote *cultus,* that is, a graceful civilization of the mind and heart. Crude and raw animal instincts were to be replaced by cultured pleasures, fond thoughts, attractive manners, and lovable intentions; and now he was ignominiously sentenced to live among fierce savages and dull, slovenly, ignoble colonials. In such a situation he appears to have remained deliberately glum and sullen. Lest he should contaminate and further degrade himself, he declined to come to terms and coöperate. This is probably another reason why from his poetry we learn so little about his actual life and the small things of which it was made up.[20] Doubtless, necessity forced upon him, day in and day out, a great many insidious little compromises; but these minor indignities, he may have felt, were better ignored in the elegies he sent to Rome. Forcefully, on the other hand, he set forth the generalities of his present environment, and pictured in bold strokes the sinister roughness which surrounded him on all sides. Humorous though he was by nature, he would speak of the place and its inhabitants with no redeeming touch of friendly humor, but only with a disgustful amazement.[21] Warm and kindly though his heart was, it would not go out with sympathy to the humanity whose life it was his lot to share. He was too proud to learn the languages of the natives; or rather, it took several years before he would admit that he was beginning to understand and actually to use the "beastly" tongues the very sound of which was to him "full of hostile frightfulness" (*Tr.* V, 12, 55–58; cf. V, 7, 17):

I, the Roman bard—forgive me, O Muses—
   am compelled mostly to talk after the fashion of the Sarmatians.
                                                      (*Tr.* V, 7, 55 f.)

The physical discomforts of life at Tomis were probably very bothersome for an elderly man with a delicate frame (*Po.* I, 5, 52) who previously had known nothing but ease and leisure. But worse were the mental torments of seclusion and boredom for a sensitive poet passionately devoted to the fond give-and-take of social intercourse and the fine art of the tongue and pen. Bitterly be complains of the difficulties he has in writing:

> No book is here, nor anyone to lend me his ear
>   and to comprehend what my words mean....
> Often, when I try to express my thought—I am ashamed to own it—
>   the words fail me; I have unlearnt to speak....
> Lest I should lose the vehicle of the Italian tongue
>   and my voice grow dumb for its mother speech,
> I talk to myself and practice half-forgotten words.
>   (*Tr.* V, 12, 53 f.; III, 14, 45 f.; V, 7, 61 ff.)

He felt shut out from human communion:

> While the others enjoy the bond of a common tongue,
>   I indicate by gestures what I mean.
> I am the barbarian here, because no one understands me;
>   the Getae stupidly laugh at my Latin words.
> I guess they often speak ill of me before my face with impunity,
>   jeering because I was sentenced to exile.
>   (*Tr.* V, 10, 35 ff.)

He keenly resented the disgrace that a man of his fine culture was expelled into the raw, hostile wilderness which he hated

> even as a cultivated field hates the weeds
> and as the swallow hates the frost.
>   (*Po.* IV, 14, 13 f.)

The swallow would migrate, but he was doomed to stay.

He was pent up in the narrow town as in a real prison (*Tr.* III, 14, 41), since he would hardly dare to venture beyond the gates even for a walk, for fear that brigands would ride up and kill or enslave him. For the same reason, the surrounding countryside was left almost unworked:

> Few are they who dare to till the land, and they, poor souls,
>   grasp the plow with one hand, a weapon with the other;
> the herdsman wears a helmet while he pipes on his rustic reeds,
>   and the timid sheep fear not wolves, but war.
>   (*Tr.* V, 10, 23 ff.)

Thus the landscape presented a desolate sight to an eye starved for
the tender charms of verdant nature. There was little to break the
somber monotony of the empty steppes, barren and flat like the
sea itself:

> Pontic land, you know not spring crowned with a flowery wreath,
>   you do not see the naked bodies of the reapers,
> nor does autumn bring you the grapes of the vine;
>   but a strange chill burdens every season.
> Oft you hold the sea bound in ice,
>   enclosing with a roof the wandering fish.
> You have no springs but with brackish water,
>   which quicken as well as quench the drinker's thirst.
> Scant and sorry are the trees that rise from the open
>   plains, and the land is like another sea.
> No birds chatter to me but such as, unsheltered by woods,
>   water their raucous throats from the brine.
>   (Po. III, 1, 11 ff.)

In one short line the poet thus summarizes the character of the
ghastly land:

> The forsaken earth idles, benumbed and slothful.
>   (Tr. III, 10, 70)

The place was "unlovable" (Tr. V, 7, 43); and how had Ovid loved
loveliness!

                    ◇   ◇   ◇

In addition to all that dismal unpleasantness, Ovid was haunted
by an ever-present fear: a stark physical fear of murder and violence
(Tr. V, 2b, 21–34, etc.). The nightmares of sudden death by the
sword, or slow painful destruction by the sting of a poisoned arrow
(Po. I, 2, 15–24), or of enslavement (Tr. II, 204–206; IV, 1, 77–84;
Po. I, 2, 48) and a toilsome life under a savage master—these nightmares crept even into his sleep:

> Dreams frighten me, in the likeness of real events,
>   my mind keeps awake to harm me.
>   (Po. I, 2, 45 f.)

Fright was his obsession, and only blind prejudice can deny that
much, if not all, of it was justified. In the wide plains beyond the
slender walls, danger was perpetually lurking. At any time, the sav-

ages might come, take the city, and slaughter or enslave the inhabitants. And within the town both citizens and visitors, while riding or walking in the streets, would never part with their weapons, and were not slow to draw and use their knives (*Tr.* V, 7, 13–20). There was no law but that of brute force (*Tr.* V, 7, 45–48), and at the marketplace where court was held the savages often preferred to fight it out (*Tr.* V, 10, 43–44). In addition, Ovid thought of himself, it seems, as an outcast who was game for any killer, and fancied that there was some dark plot against his life.[22]

While Ovid's lively imagination was torturing his mind with horrible pictures, the threat became more substantial than ever. In the second year of his stay at Tomis, it happened that the watch on the wall reported that horsemen were approaching. The gates were closed in time, but the enemies shot their poisoned arrows into the town, where they could be seen lying here and there (*Tr.* V, 10, 19–22) and sticking in the thatched roofs (*Po.* I, 2, 23). Meanwhile the poet, who had always hated and despised soldiering, found himself in his fifty-fourth year donning the weapons of war for the first time to mount guard and help defend the city (*Tr.* IV, 1, 69–84). The scare repeated itself a year or two later. In autumn, A.D. 12, a Getic army made a surprise attack on the city of Aegissos at the head of the Danube delta, stormed the fortified town, and massacred its garrison. The news caused alarm at Tomis. The citizens took to arms, and Ovid considered himself once more a soldier on the alert, ready for immediate action (*Po.* I, 8, 7–10).

When that crisis was over, Ovid wrote one of the most lucid elegies of his last period (*Po.* I, 8). It seems that the shock of acute peril, breaking like a flash through the murky monotony of futile brooding, aroused from their lethargy his slumbering powers. In this poem, his recollection of things irrevocably lost is more vivid, and his yearning for a purposeful life more virile, than it had been for a long time. Chafing as he was under his confinement to a narrow, dull, and dismal town, he once again fought reality with ardent dreams. "Do not imagine," he writes, "that it is the comforts of Rome I want—although, indeed, I want them, too; I keep thinking of my house and those I love, of the unique city and all its wonders; but no longer do I harbor immoderate desires.

I do not long for the fields I have lost,
   for the grounds on which Pelignian mountains look down,
nor the garden on the pine-clad hill
   rising from where the Clodian and Flaminian highways join,
the garden I planted for I know not whom, where I did not mind
   channeling fountain water to sprouting seeds;
where apple trees grow—if they still stand there—planted once
   by my hand, but never to be picked by my hand.
I have lost them, and would that I, the homeless man, could have
      instead
   at least some ground here which I might till.
I should myself, lest the familiar cares besiege my breast,
   lead the team under the gaping yoke of the plow;
I should learn the words which Getic oxen will understand,
   and threaten them with those shouts to which they are used ...
But whence, pray, shall that be, as the wall and locked gate
   stand, as a tenuous fence, between me and the enemy?
                        (*Po.* I, 8, 41 ff.; 61 f.)

◇   ◇   ◇

With his continued writing, Ovid had several objectives in mind. For one thing, the Roman public was used to expect ever new volumes from the admired author, and he was eager to supply the demand (cf. *Tr.* V, 1, 1–24). He cherished the hope that his new books, like the previous ones, would find a responsive audience both then and in times to come (*Po.* II, 5, 19–24; II, 6, 33–34; III, 2, 29–36). He trusted that his tragic laments would move the reader like the sad monologues and arias of Greek tragedies (*Tr.* V, 1, 61–62).[23] The extraordinary metamorphosis which his fortune had undergone (*Tr.* I, 1, 119–120; cf. *Tr.* III, 8, 35–36 and 38) made a pathetic subject, replete with personal human interest. Better perhaps than other ancient authors did Ovid comprehend how personal a thing poetry is; even a seemingly objective poem like the *Metamorphoses* he calls, in a sense, "my own portrait" (*Tr.* I, 7, 11–12).[24] Well, then, he was now in a position to add a new, poignant chapter to the earlier ones and with it to complete his own picture.

Directly autobiographical is the last elegy of the Fourth Book of the *Tristia* (IV, 10). There Ovid tells us where and when he was born; how devoted a brother and son he had been; and that he could boast of a heart responsive to Cupid's darts, yet had never been involved in a dishonorable affair. Next we hear about his three marriages:[25]

> I was hardly more than a boy when I was given a wife, unworthy
>   and useless;
>   the marriage lasted only for a short time.
> To her succeeded another, and she was blameless,
>   but she was not to remain in her union with me.
> The last, who has stayed with me throughout the many years,
>   had the courage to be an exile's wife.
> My daughter made me twice a grandfather
>   while she was young, but not by the same husband.
>   (*Tr.* IV, 10, 69 ff.)

That kind of information is of course of some interest for us, but nevertheless these passages sound commonplace and bourgeois. Most of the elegy, however, deals with Ovid's career as a writer and his catastrophe, and that main part is real poetry.[26] At the same time, it shows how high his pride could still rise. He feels that he has conquered adversity:

> My mind, disdaining to succumb to misfortune, made use
>   of its own powers and proved invincible.
>   (103 f.)

There is a great deal of excellent poetry in Ovid's elegies from exile, and there is to be found in them some wisdom such as only bitter experience could mature. On the other hand, the quality of his verse had always been uneven, and in the dreary years of his banishment his creative powers were inevitably sinking. He himself knew how unfavorable the conditions were under which he was writing, and unceasingly apologized for the defects of his elegies;[27] and when someone seemed to like them, he was overjoyed (*Po.* II, 5, 9–24). Every now and then, he was gripped by a fit of acute despondency. Disgusted with the stuff he was producing, he would burn up all the papers he could lay his hands on. But again some of the manuscripts would escape the flames "by accident, or perhaps by craftiness," and those would subsequently be dispatched to Rome (*Tr.* IV, 1, 101–104; V, 12, 59–66). There we find him once more at his old tricks of cheating himself: evidently he took the precaution of stowing away copies of his best elegies so that, when the next condemnatory paroxysm should come over him, they would providentially be out of his reach.

❖ ❖ ❖

Ovid's second reason for keeping up his production was of a sentimental nature. He wanted to break his isolation by a continued contact with his friends and the Roman public at large. He felt as if he had lost his identity and was no more than a shadow of his former self (*Tr.* III, 11, 25–30), but he struggled to emerge from destruction and through his verse to keep in being before the eyes of his friends and admirers at home (*Po.* III, 5, 33–34).[28] Most of his elegies are in the form of letters, either addressed to some definite person, or to the benevolent reader, or even to his detractors and enemies. He had composed a book of poetic epistles before, although those had been only fictitious. At first, he did not dare to mention openly the person to whom he was writing, except for his own wife, for fear of exposing the recipients of his letters to the imperial frown (*Tr.* III, 4b, 17–26; IV, 4, 7 ff., etc.); later, however, all but one of his correspondents gave him permission to divulge their identity (*Po.* I, 1, 17–18; III, 6, 1–6). He wrote to his wife for her birthday and told her how he planned to celebrate the anniversary; on that one day he was to put on the white toga (*Tr.* V, 5, 7–8). Talkative and social as he was, and given to "luring forth the words of the one by those of the other" (*Po.* II, 5, 46), the recluse yearned for communing in thought at least with those who were dear to him. Mentally he would travel to Rome and speak with his friend Cotta, and would listen to what Cotta was saying to him—so vivid was his imagination,—and such moments were to him blissful beyond words (*Po.* III, 5, 47–54). To another friend he writes: "You are here with me, even if you do not know it. Do the same and think ever of me" (*Po.* II, 10, 49–52). He begs for love, a thing, he says, which is not laborious for him who has the will to love (*Po.* IV, 10, 81–82). And he asks: "Do you miss me? Does it sometimes happen that your soul, forgetful of what is lacking, yet feels that some part of itself is lacking?" (*Po.* III, 5, 41–42). Nothing was more natural than that he should use the vehicle of his art for his intercourse with his friends. "Bad as my present poetry is," he writes, "I send it to Rome because I want somehow to be with you" (*Tr.* V, 1, 79–80). The correspondence, however, cannot have been very lively, because it took up to a year for a letter to go and the reply to come back (see p. 254, *d*). Ovid could not afford to have his mail carried back and forth by his own couriers; thus the letters would suffer long delays in waiting for an opportunity to be forwarded from one station of the way to the next, and some were lost (*Tr.* V, 13, 15 f.).

◇   ◇   ◇

Thirdly, Ovid intended to keep his misery in the public eye and to impress it on influential men, so that there would be a general demand for his release from Tomis. His banishment had created a sensation in Rome, and it was still much talked about many years after the event (*Tr.* II, 569–570; *Po.* III, 1, 47–60). Ovid wanted to keep alive the commotion and to channel into a useful direction the current of sympathy with his affliction. The greater was his irritation when a traveler from Rome told him that some people thought his grievances were exaggerated (*Po.* IV, 10, 35). This disconcerting intelligence led to a train of protestations and explanations on the part of the unfortunate poet (*Po.* IV, 7; IV, 9; IV, 10). He insisted (*Po.* IV, 9, 81–86) that he had not been lying when he wrote of the very sea freezing over (cf. *Tr.* III, 10, 35–50, etc.), of human victims being sacrificed at the native altars (cf. *Tr.* IV, 4, 63–85), and of the savages poisoning their arrows (cf. *Tr.* IV, 1, 77; V, 7, 16, etc.). He composed a verse epistle to a prominent man who had come out there, asking him to confirm with his authority Ovid's statements (*Po.* IV, 7, 1–12). To his old comrade Albinovanus Pedo (see p. 7), who himself had pictured in spirited verse the horrors of the northern ocean (Seneca, *Suas.* I, 15), he addressed a scientific explanation of the reasons why the Pontus was icebound in winter, although a discussion of this sort was not fitting for an elegy (*Po.* IV, 10, 35–66). He also dispatched to one of his friends an authentic quiver with arrows (*Po.* III, 8). In the letter which accompanied the curio he wrote: "There is nothing else I can send from here; the women do not know the arts of spinning and weaving, but only pound the grain and carry water; the reed does not serve for writing and conveying cultured thoughts, but for arrows, carrying a message of destruction." Small wonder, then, if on almost every page there is a hint that the reader should do his share in bringing about the poet's deliverance, or an overt request that the recipient of the letter should intercede in his favor. After several disappointments,[29] Ovid became uncertain what precisely he should suggest and rather left it to the discretion of the person addressed what particular step he should take (*Po.* III, 1, 33-34), provided he did something:

> You ask how I want you to act? Not for the life of me can I tell
>   (supposing a dead man like me has life).
> I cannot think of any one design or preference,
>   I know not enough about my own advantage.
> Believe me, foresight is the first to desert the wretched;
>   when our standing is gone, sense and counsel too abandon us.
> Please find out for yourself how you can help me
>   and what road may be open for the fulfillment of my wish.
>   (*Po.* IV, 12, 43 ff.)

We hear Ovid urging his wife to see the Empress and implore her to intervene in his favor (*Po.* III, 1, 97-160). Sometimes he praises her for her exemplary fidelity and devotion, and sometimes (cf. *Tr.* V, 2, 34-40; *Po.* III, 1, 31-94) he frets that,

> honest as she is, she is equally timid and not enterprising enough.
>   (*Po.* III, 7, 12)

Ovid also wrote to the Emperor several times. One whole volume of the *Tristia* consists of an epistle to Augustus, justifying the poet's life and writings and pleading for clemency:

> I ask not to return to Italy, unless perhaps in the distant future,
>   when my long punishment will have reconciled you;
> but I do pray for a place of exile somewhat more safe and quiet
>   so that my penalty be equal to my offense.[30]
>   (*Tr.* II, 575 ff.)

In addition, Ovid composed two laudatory poems, which have not survived, in honor of the imperial house[31] and thus gave proof that he had reformed, if there was cause for reforming. No doubt his asseverations of submissive loyalty (e.g., *Po.* IV, 9, 105-124) are not edifying, but we must not forget the habits of the times, or the very special reason he had for behaving in that fashion. And who can presume to sit in judgment over Ovid's prostration except a man who himself has stood up better under a comparable test?

It was all in vain. In vain did Ovid quote the moral of his Deucalion story (*Metam.* 1, 377–380) to the effect that timid prayers are apt to mollify the heart of the supreme power and arouse its natural mildness (*Tr.* V, 8, 25–30); in the harsh world of reality it did not work out as it had done in the fantastic world of the *Metamorphoses*. When Ovid believed he was on the verge of success, the aged Emperor died (on August 19, A.D. 14; cf. *Po.* IV, 6, 15–16), and there was little likelihood that his successor would rescind any of Augustus' decisions.

◇   ◇   ◇

A fourth reason for Ovid never to cease writing was that the activity diverted him and dulled his pains. He was seeking "relief, not renown" (*Tr.* IV, 1, 3); he kept singing just as a convict in a chain gang sings (*Tr.* IV, 1, 5). Whenever he was composing poetry, the inspired furor of production whisked his mind "beyond human suffering" (*Tr.* IV, 1, 43–44). The Muse offered him "solace, rest, and medicine" (*Tr.* IV, 10, 117–118); she carried him away from his abode in the flesh and took him where he rightfully belonged:

> O Muse, you lift me from the banks of the Danube
> and give me a place among poets on Mount Helicon.
>
> (*Tr.* IV, 10, 119 f.)

He had been robbed of everything man can take away from man, but

> My own talent goes with me everywhere and gladdens me;
> no emperor has any right over that.
>
> (*Tr.* III, 7, 47 f.)

And the last reason was that his sufferings demanded an outlet. There was so much, he felt, that he had still to tell the world, and this time it was all real:[32]

> If one of you were to ask me: Why do you sing
> of so many grievous things? I should reply: because I endured
> so many.
> I do not make this up with my art and ingenuity;
> my very fate of which I write is ingenious in inflicting injuries.
>
> (*Tr.* V, 1, 25 ff.)

Ovid is here explaining why he has resumed the composition of elegies of this sort, after publishing four books of *Tristia* and concluding them with his autobiography which was meant to be the epilogue to the collection. He felt, himself, that he ought to have left it at that:

> You will say: It is better to bear your misfortune in silence
> and mutely dissemble that which befell you,
>> (*Tr.* V, 1, 49 f.)

Nevertheless he was unable to put the lid on his anguish:

> Pain pent up inside strangles; it boils with fury
> and doubles its force because of the pressure.
>> (63 f.)

On his voyage out, he had discovered that he still could write; now he learned that he must. Thus he added a fifth volume to his *Elegies of Gloom,* and then he composed four more volumes under the title *Epistulae ex Ponto,* that is, *Letters from the Black Sea Shore.* There, then, were Ovid's reasons for continuing to write elegies.

◇ ◇ ◇

With exasperation Ovid kept the tally of the lengthening sequence of years in exile: "Twice the sun has completed its round of the ecliptic" (*Tr.* IV, 7, 1–2); "Three times the Danube and the sea have frozen over" (*Tr.* V, 10, 1–2); "While I am fighting against the cold and the arrows and against my fate, the fourth winter is wearing me down" (*Po.* I, 2, 27); "Five years in Scythia" (*Po.* IV, 6, 5); "The sixth winter" (*Po.* IV, 13, 40); and more were to come. Ovid's complaints and requests are depressing and monotonous to read through, but indeed his sufferings and yearnings were far more depressing and monotonous to live through. He himself realized how tedious his epistles were becoming:

> Asking so often for the same thing, I am running out of words,
> by now I am ashamed of my useless, unending solicitations.
> I suppose that you are tired of poems one like the other,
> that everyone has learned by heart what I want,
> and that you already know what my letter is bringing even before
> the seal is loosened from the cord I put around it.
>> (*Po.* III, 7, 1 ff.)

Therefore he half promised not to broach any more the subject of intervention on his behalf. Nevertheless, he had again to admit that "craving knows no moderation":

> I often try to write of something else and slide back into the
>   same thing.   (Po. IV, 15, 33)

His release was for him a matter of life and death, more important than the niceties of good style:

> Should I ask for help only one of my friends,
>   lest the reader might meet the same thought twice?
>   (Po. III, 9, 43 f.)

Firmly convinced that his sentence was unjust and his penalty out of proportion to his mistake, he could not but cling to his hope for a pardon, be it partial or total. To his friend Carus he wrote:

> I am sustained by a slender hope that the angered deity
>   might be placated, and you ought not take that hope from me.
> Be it that my expectation is groundless, be it that it may come true,
>   do you, pray, prove to me that it may come true,
> and bend all the power of your eloquence to that purpose,
>   to persuade me that my wish may prevail.
>   (Tr. III, 5, 25 ff.)

Again Ovid is preferring the glimmer of a pleasant deception to stark unpleasant truth.   ◇   ◇   ◇

Time went on, even though it seemed to stand still (Tr. V, 10, 5), but it brought no change. No longer did experience provide the poet with new themes for his verse; it was always the same sad tale. He felt that the fountain of his genius became more and more clogged with the accumulating silt of vexation (Po. IV, 2, 15-22). He lost the ardor of writing, but not the habit:

> What should I rather do? I am not made for dragging along my
>   leisure in idleness.
> I reckon for death time wasted in sloth.
> Nor do I enjoy dawdling in drunkenness till daybreak,
>   nor do I to no purpose occupy my hands with the dice.
> After I give to sleep the hours which the body demands,
>   how am I to dispose of the long time of wakefulness?
>   (Po. I, 5, 43 ff.)

He yet attempted to accomplish something worth his while, but his interest in ultimate perfection slackened:

> Often I wished to change a word, and let it stand;
>   my powers forsake my judgment.
> Often—why should I not tell you the truth?—
>   it annoys me to correct and carry the burden of long toil.
> In the act of writing, the pleasant exertion dulls the strain of exertion;
>   while the work is keenly on its way, the mind too is keen.
> But correcting, being a lesser task just as the critic Aristarchus
>   is less than great Homer whose works he edited,
> pains the spirit with cold, halting cares
>   and curbs the fervor of the eager horse.[33]
>   (*Po.* III, 9, 17 ff.)

Moreover, he had to go year in and year out without the benefit of a direct response:

> To write verse which you can recite to no one
>   is like dancing before people in a black darkness.[34]
>   (*Po.* IV, 2, 33 f.)

Nevertheless, rather than give in and waste his days, he "forced his unwilling hand" (*Po.* I, 5, 10; cf. IV, 2, 27–28) to put down couplet after couplet. In doing so, he discovered in himself an incredible timeproof tenacity; even Death seemed to respect it, because he was slow in coming (*Po.* I, 2, 37–38; IV, 10, 3–8). The poet envied the characters of his *Metamorphoses* for their capacity to escape from anguish by freezing into numb tree-wood or unfeeling stone:

> Such as I am, no wood will accept me,
>   such as I am, I wish in vain to be a stone....
> I live on so as never to lose the sense of bitterness,
>   and the longer I carry it, the heavier grows my burden.
>   *Po.* I, 2, 35 f., 39 f.)

The "ever-present anxiety" (*Po.* I, 10, 36) preyed on Ovid's mind. "Even as a rock is hollowed by a constant stream of water," thus adversity wore him out, and "grief became a habit" for him (*Po.* II, 7, 39–42). There was even some pride in his grief; singled out, by way of arbitrary punishment, for a senseless and purposeless misery, he felt that his misfortune invested him with a kind of distinction and tragic dignity:

> People respectfully make way for a blind man even as they do
> for a venerable consul with the insignia of puissant office.[35]
>
> (*Tr.* V, 6, 31 f.)

And he knew that his lack of fortitude was bound up with the best traits of his character; when a friend tried to comfort and exhort him, Ovid struggled bravely, but then his longing for Rome got the better of his resolve:

> My love for the place where I belong, stronger than any reasoning,
>   undoes whatever your letter had achieved.
> Whether you call it loyalty or unmanliness,
>   I confess: my heart, alas, is soft.
>
> (*Po.* I, 3, 29 ff.)

True enough, Ovid's courage did often falter. But we cannot expect a swallow (*Po.* IV, 14, 13) to fight and die like an eagle.

Meanwhile he aged. This is what he wrote to his wife about it:

> By now the worse time of life has sprinkled my hair with white,
>   by now the wrinkles of old age furrow my face,
> by now vigor and strength languish in my shaken frame;
>   whatever delighted me in youth is no longer a pleasure.
> If you were to see me unawares, you could not recognize me,
>   so severely am I wrecked by age.
> I admit that the years did it, but there is another cause also,
>   the anxiety of my mind and the constant strain.
>
> (*Po.* I, 4, 1 ff.)

⬦   ⬦   ⬦

The verse letters that fill the nine volumes of *Epistles of Gloom* and *Epistles from the Black Sea Shore* were written by the poet throughout all the years of his banishment, at the average rate of about one volume a year, or one acceptable elegy a month. This poetry was more personal than even the *Amores* had been. While the work with which he began his career had pictured typical experiences, the elegies he composed in his declining years reflect an unprecedented contingency. With no literary tradition to guide the writer,[36] it was indeed no mean task to cast into artistic shape a sensitive exile's emotional life in the strange, wild country to which an angered despot had sent him. Ovid's ingenious talent acquitted itself of the unique assignment in an admirable manner. To be sure, just as with his other verse, if we read too many poems in a row we feel keenly the heaviness of repetition as far as material content, general ideas, and patterns of thought are concerned. But a leisurely examination of individual elegies would show how firmly each of them is organized, how elegantly it is executed, and how original it is in the particular shading and handling of its theme.[37] Considering the conditions under which Ovid was compelled to subsist, the achievement does credit not only to his gifts but even so to his will. Especially during the first part of his stay at Tomis, it was a feat that he composed poetry at all; we would not be surprised if he had quitted the service of the Muses. In that first period, we may imagine the lonely and frightened man ceaselessly reliving the long train of events that had led to his ruin, and torturing himself with the thought of how he might, or ought to, have acted (cf. *Tr.* III, 6, 11–18; V, 12, 61–68, etc.); racking his brains to plot this course or that for his deliverance; sending to Rome an endless stream of letters to explore chances and possible moves; and periodically, exhausted, plunging into a spell of deep, restful apathy (*Po.* I, 2, 29–30). We know he was ill; he had to adjust himself to trying discomforts; he was, and for a long while remained, overwhelmed by the fantastic ugliness of his environment. And yet he managed to produce his verse letters. As the years progressed and his situation assumed a stationary character, the press of immediate concerns abated and quivering tension gave way to morose lassitude. Ovid carried on with his epistles, but he contented himself no longer with that production. A writer of his abiding ambition and natural industry could not forever be satisfied with a trickle of personal verse. Moreover, time was heavily hanging on his hands, and though an artist in a measure relieves himself of his sorrows when he objectivates them in his creations, the epistles, rather than diverting his attention, kept his mind on the ills that beset him. A friend in Rome who understood his affliction suggested that he use his talent for composing some work of a higher order; and he seems to have added an admonition to bear his condemnation philosophically like Socrates, who wrote verses in his prison cell (Plato, *Phædo* 60 b–61 b). Ovid replied (*Tr.* V, 12) that not even a Socrates could have composed poetry if he were in his place; the circumstances were too unpropitious; try as he did, the results were so discouraging that, each time, he had soon destroyed what he had written, only a few verse letters escaping the flames (see pp. 132 f.). Thus we learn that in the third year of his banishment Ovid struggled to compose poetry other than his personal letters.[38] From what is preserved we see that at various times he had in hand three more literary projects—two of which were to remain unfinished. This is in addition to the encomia he saw fit to prepare in honor of the dynasty.

14. THE "FASTI"

ONE OF THE poems on which Ovid worked at Tomis was the *Fasti*. The title can be translated *The Roman Calendar,* and Ovid's book is a verse almanac which lists and discusses annual events in the order in which they occur, with emphasis on the periodic Roman festivals. The author expounds the significance and supposed origin of the traditional practices; he suggests explanations for peculiar observances, and interprets the technical terms that were in use. The history of the calendar system is sketched and the names of the months are analyzed for their true meaning. Moreover, Ovid registers the constellations as they enter or leave the nocturnal skies, and indicates the weather that may be expected to prevail.

This work had already been in an advanced stage of preparation when the author was banished. On his voyage out, he carried with him a manuscript, fairly perfected, of half of the *Fasti,* and a draft, if not more, of the rest (*Tr.* II, 547–552). Then the project seems to have been shelved for some years. Ovid was in no mood to delve leisurely into Roman customs and antiquities; besides, the subject was so closely connected with the sites and the life of the capital that it was not easy to finish the *Fasti* anywhere else.[1] Not until the poet had exhausted in his epistles the theme of his present condition did he take up the *Fasti* again. He had an ulterior motive in doing so: he hoped to attract the favorable notice of Germanicus (cf. *Po.* IV, 8, 65 ff.), the heir to the throne, who happened to be keenly interested both in poetry and in the star calendar. Furthermore, in summer, A.D. 17, Germanicus was appointed High Commissioner for the eastern part of the Empire. The *Fasti* was originally dedicated to Augustus (*Tr.* II, 551–552), but in the meantime Augustus had died; so Ovid set himself to work to change the dedication, substituting Germanicus, and to insert passages in honor of the brilliant young prince who was to rule supreme over the region to which his own domicile belonged. The poet, however, did not live long enough to complete the *Fasti*. Only the first half of the work has come down to us, in an unfinished form. It is written in the elegiac meter and consists of six volumes, with the calendar of the six months from January to June. In its conception and most of its execution it dates from A.D. 7 and 8, when the author was writing the last books of the *Metamorphoses*.[2] Therefore, in order to give the work its proper place in Ovid's biography, we have to go back to the time when he was at the apex of his life and about fifty years old.

It is a common experience that the years around fifty are a critical period in the career of a successful man. By then he has to his credit some notable achievements; in certain lines, he is a man of mark. But the fixed standing he has established for himself irks him as much as it flatters him, and he becomes restless. Still full of vigor and with a good many years, so he hopes, ahead of him, he thinks it dull and wasteful to go on diligently turning out more of the same old stuff. He feels he has not yet reached the end of his rope; there are a few surprises in store for those who believe they know him well. Burning to show the world that he is by no means a closed chapter, he is anxious to throw off his accustomed routine and make a new beginning. But he has no longer the time, nor the patience, once more to build up from the bottom. Eagerly he attempts to contrive things of a different order, starting from above rather than below. He believes that he can transfer to the new activities most of the skills he had aquired in his formative and maturer years. Thus we have found Ovid casting about while he composed the final section of his *Metamorphoses* and experimenting with a number of novel themes, views, and styles.[3] Foremost among his new subjects were those derived from the native Italian history and religion. At that time, his mind was already made up to devote his next work to the tradition and religion of his homeland. But how was the theme of Roman religion to be approached and handled?

Certainly not in the manner of the *Metamorphoses*.[4] True
enough, that epic serves even today, among other things, as a delightful textbook for the study of the Greek pantheon, since the
poet has here called into active play all the numerous deities of
Greek religion. But he could do so, within the framework of his
continuous narrative, only because Greek myth abounded in divine
characters with very human features and very human experiences,
and because a coherent system existed in which each god and each
story had its proper place. Nothing comparable was to be found in
Italian mythology. And, worse still, the native religion was of an
antiquated type. Its spiritual content was in large part gone, but the
cults persisted; the Italian race was given to scrupulous observance
of traditions rather than to their gradual transformation to suit the
changing ages. What active life was left in the indigenous religion,
was mainly stirring in the many ceremonies and festivals which
were still celebrated, as in times of old, by the appointed priests and
the population at large, year in and year out in the identical venera-
ble forms.[5] The religion of Italy could therefore most fittingly be
represented in terms of recurrent functions. But the significance
of the rites and customs was fading out of memory; in fact, the
original meaning of most of them had long since been lost in obliv-
ion. Thus it was not enough for Ovid objectively to display, as in a
pictorial frieze, the sequence of various events: he was obliged to
add, by way of elucidation, a great deal of personal comment, although the explanations available to him were often unwarranted.

These were probably the reasons why, when Ovid decided to
give his *Metamorphoses* a companion and to illuminate with his
poetry the ancestral Roman religion, he chose to describe and interpret the yearly cycle of rites and festivals. Most of the ceremonies
were based on the religious history of Rome, but some on the political history, so that legends and stories of either sort had a legitimate
place in the poem. In his calendar lore Ovid included the dates for
the risings and settings of the constellations because many people,
especially countryfolk and sailors, were still keeping track of the
year's progress and the seasonal weather changes by observation of
the stars rather than by a count of days and months.[6] Ovid also inserted a number of Greek star legends.

The theme of the *Fasti* was bound to have a great popular appeal. No doubt the Romans of the Augustan age were fondly proud of their ancient cults and festive celebrations, and would love to see them reflected in poetry's beautifying looking-glass. It was one of the characteristic Roman traits to take a lively interest in the national institutions and usages; and, since so much in the observances was mysterious, the people had a right to be curious about their true meaning and probable origin. Scholars had dedicated themselves to research of this kind, and on their books, replete with both facts and conjectures, Ovid could easily draw for the material he needed. Moreover, with his *Fasti* the poet found himself for once in line with the policy of the Emperor, who was anxious to see the traditional Roman religion preserved and revitalized (cf. II, 59–60).[7] Ovid has given up the privacy of his ivory tower; for the first time, he is dealing, not with the exciting experiences of single individuals, but with regular community life. The *Fasti,* so he indicates, is his public service; his elegiacs, which previously had ministered to amatory adventures, are now put to use for a worthier cause; and boastfully he exclaims: "Who would have thought there was a road leading from there to here?" (II, 3–16).[8]

In its literary form the *Fasti* follows rather closely a Hellenistic model, the *Aetia* (i.e., causes or reasons why) of Callimachus.[9] In the Hellenistic age, antiquarian studies and interest in *aetia* had a great vogue among the savants and poets even of the Greek world, but the shading was different; there the stress was more on local peculiarities. After the manner of Callimachus, Ovid presents in a very personal fashion the explanations he has to offer. The reader of the *Fasti* is permitted to watch his author gathering relevant information and weighing different theories against one another. But Ovid does not mention books as the sources of his learning, except for the official *Fasti* and for "annals of great antiquity" which he says he has consulted (I, 7 and 657; IV, 11). Instead, he claims to have had his questions answered by the most competent authorities directly. Thus he playfully pretends to have chatted with some deity, preferably the one to whom the month was sacred or the festival dedicated; or he reports (and this may be just as fictitious) how he consulted the priest who officiated at the function; or he tells, for instance, that an old gentleman who sat next to him watching the commemoration of a victory had volunteered the explication, proud of having himself served in that campaign (IV, 377–386).[10] Just as in the *Aetia,* the typical inquiry is about the whys and wherefores.[11] Why is the rite celebrated in this particular way? Why are the persons and things named as they are? And so forth. The answer is sometimes given in a long, elaborate story. The style of Ovid's *Fasti* is mostly lucid and fluent in the true Ovidian manner;[12] but at times it is rather halting, involved, and abstruse in an imperfect imitation of Callimachus, and especially so in the First Book.[13]

Callimachus manages to display his erudition with little pedantry; he uses recondite words and cites recondite facts with a select elegance which was hard to duplicate. The literary deportment of that author combines, to the amusement of the appreciative reader, trim smartness with genial casualness. While Horace had some of both these qualities, Ovid was too tenderly emotional for either one. The *mise en scène* of the *Fasti,* with the author frequently appearing on the stage in the role of an investigator and interviewer, is meant to give an air of breezy informality to the dispensation of profound learning. In contrast, however, to Callimachus' *Aetia,* the *Fasti* does not prove its author to be a very serious student of his subject, nor do the conversational passages impress us with the personality of the writer.[14] The notion of his direct intercourse with a host of major and minor deities is too bizarre to be poetically plausible. Ovid finally realized this defect, or perhaps one of his literary friends brought it to his attention; at any rate, in the Sixth Book he inserted two remarks designed to remedy it.[15] Occasionally, he lightens the heaviness of the fiction by a welcome touch of irony and humor.[16] The preface to the Fourth Book is a most charming example. There the author pays his respects to Venus. The reason is that he needs her inspiration because she is the deity of the fourth month; but as he has ceased to serve her with his poetry, she wonders what he may want from her. While explaining the nature of his request, Ovid behaves like a man who, in the course of his business affairs, has to deal with a long-forgotten former flame of his, and is tactful enough to assure her that, in spite of their inevitable separation, he has always been in love with her and always will be.

We have no means of assessing the response accorded to the *Fasti* by its original audience. The modern scholar values it as a source-book for Roman cults and practices;[17] but he cares less for the explanations the author reproduces, and most of the etymologies make him smile.[18] The *Fasti,* however, was written neither by a scholar nor for scholars. To a present-day reader who merely looks for a fascinating book, the customs and rituals, the buildings and sites of ancient Rome no longer mean what they meant then and there, and much of the information handed down in the poem appears uninspiring. The stars, it is true, still rise and set on our own horizons; but too few among us know the names and shapes of the constellations, or care for the dates of their periodic visibility.

What matters, however, is not so much the frame of mind in which a modern public may approach the *Fasti*. If the author's genius was in tune with his theme, he could convey to any reader, howsoever remote in time and space, the mood and mode of the subject. But it was not easy for Ovid to strike the true note. That sweet nostalgia for pristine things which actuates the antiquarian did not come to him naturally. Oldness had for him no inherent merit; we have his own word for it that he left it to others to take pleasure in antiquity.[19] He delighted in whatever was neat and proper, spontaneous and humanly meaningful, no matter how plain and unadorned it might otherwise be; but he had no taste for anything primitive in a clumsy, or absurd, or inane way. The *Fasti* is excellent in such places as where, for instance, the writer puts the modest concerns of a simple shepherd into words of prayer to a rural goddess (IV, 747–776). But other passages remain lifeless because they deal with crude beliefs and senseless practices, a stuff for which this poet had no real use.

Nor was Ovid so made as to be pious in the national Roman style. He actually kept aloof from the cause he was supposed to have espoused. Once, he gives himself away by taking exception to the ritualistic notions he is obliged to represent:

Our ancestors believed that any sin, anything bound to lead to ruin,
   could be taken away by means of a lustration. . . .
Alas! Too lenient are those who fancy
   river water can wash off the grievous guilt of murder.

(II, 35 f., 45 f.)

The fine, candid lines run counter to the way of thinking the author was affecting. He did not have his heart in the task he had set for himself. In spite of his good and loyal intentions, there is less, instead of more, genuine religious feeling in the *Fasti* than in the *Metamorphoses*. To his nature the Greek religion was more congenial than the earthbound, formalistic, and superstitious ideas of indigenous origin.[20] In fact, the divergence between the author's own persuasions and the drift of his subject was too great for a compromise. Ovid was obliged time and again to cross over all the way to the other side, if only vicariously and with a mental reservation. We notice, for instance, that Ovid here, in contrast to the *Metamorphoses*, never troubles to alleviate the oddity of miracles. He will report the incredible event in all its original rawness, bluntly putting it up to the reader to accept or reject it.[21] But even while the writer plays the part of a naïve believer, he permits himself here or there a roguish wink. Thus, reporting a miracle, he remarks in parenthesis: "It must be true because even stage plays have it that way" (IV, 326); and another time (IV, 203–206), when telling an extremely improbable legend,[22] he says: "Everyone is bound to believe it because numerous generations did; it is a very ancient story," to which he adds, in lieu of a more profound explanation: "It was fated to happen just so."   ◇ ◇ ◇

The six volumes of *Fasti* we possess are obviously a good deal less perfected than the *Metamorphoses,* and were published, unlike the *Metamorphoses,* after the author's death and without his sanction. Under these circumstances, it would not be fair to criticize such details of execution as could easily be rectified.[23] But there are fundamental objections against the work; one of them is the discrepancy between the writer's professed and actual opinions. Moreover, while Vergil's *Georgics* is essentially a work of poetry, Ovid's *Fasti* could never be real poetry; to versify and adorn an almanac was not a sound proposal in the first place. Ovid was probably well aware of the technical difficulties involved,[24] but at the height of his career he confidently accepted the challenge and went ahead. His artistry shows up brilliantly at many places in the work as we have it, and if he had been permitted to carry through all the way under normal working conditions, he would no doubt have done still better. And yet, for the reasons I have indicated, I feel that the *Fasti* in its entirety—framework, star data, weather notes, and all—does not and cannot measure up to any of Ovid's other major works from any period of his life. The best attitude, I think, for appreciating the *Fasti* is to read it as if it were a book for children. The analogy holds so far as the writer is here transmitting rather disparate bits of useful information, setting forth views which his own age had long ago outgrown, and flavoring his instruction with that sort of wit and banter which adults use when they talk with youngsters.

◇ ◇ ◇

The *Fasti* contains a goodly number of engaging passages. The legends from mythology and early Roman history are told with the mature craftsmanship we expect from the author of the *Metamorphoses,* although none of them seems to possess that transcending character which in the epic of transformations often allows us dimly to behold, below the surface of the tale, some broader import. We have also reason to admire the art with which sometimes a ceremony is graphically described. As usual, Ovid is at his best when he has an opportunity to minister to the emotions as well as to the intellect.

Among the longer sections with mixed content, the first honors go, in my judgment, to the last part of the Second Book (II, 533–860). With a review of that section we shall wind up our short discussion of the *Fasti.*

The passage contains a story of gods and nymphs (II, 585–616) which is conceived and rendered in the good *Metamorphoses* manner; the narrative is concise and to the point, with a touch of friendly humor and delicate sentiment. Still more deeply imbued with feeling is the preceding description of All Souls' Day and of the annual offerings to the dead (II, 533–566). Touchingly the author depicts "the immaterial mob of shapeless souls" (554) as they once emerged from their sepulchers when they found themselves neglected on the day set aside for paying tribute to them; and he explains how on that day the tender shadows are used to haunt the upper world, craving, not for costly gifts, but merely for the customary documentation of loving memory (534–542; 565–566). Next follows, in the order of the calendar, the Festival of the Clans. In fine verses Ovid describes the passage from the day of mourning to the day of pride and hope:

> Fresh from the graves and the dear ones that passed beyond,
>   it is sweet to turn toward the living,
> and after so many losses to look upon those who are left of our blood
>   and muster the generations of our kin.
> May they gather with clean thoughts! But let stay far away the bad brother
>   and the mother harsh against her own offspring,
> and him for whom his father lives too long or who ponders the
>   years of his mother,
> and the woman who unfairly vexes her son's wife![25]
>   (II, 619 ff.)

The following theme, the festival of Terminus (639–684), gives the author an opportunity to display a rural scene, with all members of the family, old and young, taking part in the performance of the rites. The prayer which Ovid suggests for the occasion felicitously sets forth the nature of Terminus, the boundary as marked by a stump or stone solidly imbedded in the ground. Terminus is worshiped in this prayer as the one who impartially watches over the interests of both neighbors; his incorruptible service is equally important for the modest owner of a small field as for great nations; only the Roman Empire recognizes no limit for its expansion. Thus Terminus combines for Ovid the characters of an object, a norm, and a divine power. The notion, so conceived, is Grecian in type, and at the same time it is as apt as it is poetic. The volume is concluded with a fine verse rendering of one of Livy's legends from the early days of Rome.   ◇ ◇ ◇

Like a painter who first puts ground colors on the canvas and then covers them up with top colors of a different sort, so Ovid was in the habit of building up his poetry in two strata, representing two different mental attitudes. But here the parallel ends. Whereas in a painting the two layers are meant to combine into a unified whole, Ovid's art characteristically allows the two attitudes to blend in part only, but in part they are to remain distinct. In the

Amores, actuality was overlaid with illusions. In the *Art of Love,* delicate devotion was half hidden behind scientific presumption. In the *Metamorphoses,* lifelike human dramas were presented in a setting of miraculous happenings. In the *Fasti,* friendly skepticism cloaked itself, but not completely so, in credulous observance. The duplicity gave a particular charm to the *Amores,* but it proved irritating at times; in the *Art of Love* and the *Metamorphoses,* it succeeded superbly well; in the *Fasti,* the two sets of hues would not go together. And in the *Fasti,* too, the author chose more consistently than he had ever done before to borrow from the palette of another poet.

15. THE "IBIS"

THE "FASTI" was largely Callimachean in its manner, but Roman in its theme and Augustan in its purpose. Another work, composed at some time in the course of the first five years of Ovid's exile,[1] was entirely conceived in the Hellenistic spirit and still more closely patterned after a poem by Callimachus; the very title, *Ibis,* was taken over from the model. Its main part levels an immense number of weird imprecations against a man whose real name is concealed under the pseudonym Ibis.[2] We have no means of knowing who he was and for this reason must likewise call him Ibis. He is identical with that former friend or acquaintance of the poet[3] who, when the stern sentence was passed on Ovid, like a scavenger tried to enrich himself from the fallen man's fortune; if his scheme had been successful, the aging exile would have been deprived of the property on which he hoped to subsist for the rest of his miserable life (17–24). The heinous maneuver was thwarted, with the help of Ovid's friends, by his wife; but Ibis persisted in speaking ill of the poet and keeping alive the memory of his ruinous error.[4] He probably did so in order to cover up his own guilt; the better he succeeded in picturing Ovid as a criminal, the more leniently would people judge his own financial machination.

The poem *Ibis* is none too explicit with respect to the transgression of which Ibis was guilty, but it gives hints of its nature. The book is ostensibly written in order to deter the villain from further

---

[1] For notes to chapter 15, see pages 243–249.

slandering the unfortunate poet.[5] In the year 10 or 11, Ovid had addressed to Ibis a terse and vigorous elegy with the same purpose (*Tr.* IV, 9).[6] The fine elegy admonished its unnamed addressee to mend his ways;[7] it threatened that, unless Ibis heeded this warning, another poem would reveal his identity and the deed he had perpetrated, so that the whole world in all time to come would hold him in the contempt he deserved; and it pitted the prestige of an illustrious writer against the ignominy of the other man's vile performance.

This elegy, Ovid followed up with the *Ibis.*[8] The *Ibis* gives the same warning and backs it up with the same threat, but it is far more elaborate and ponderous than the elegy; for these very reasons, however, it is less forceful than the short poem. Ovid now spends more than three hundred couplets on the theme. In the opening lines he remarks bitterly that never before in his life has he used his pen as a weapon; but under the circumstances he cannot help writing an invective; it is the aggressor's fault if the poet is soiling his own clean record.[9]

Ovid's *Ibis* is a highly artificial and history-bound product and does not make pleasant reading. But it is interesting, among other things, because it illustrates the writer's propensity for moving on more than one plane of reality. The poem contains elements from three distinct modes of reacting to the same outrage; of these, the first may be called realistic, the second romantic, and the third grotesque. The three modes correspond to three divisions of the text.

The two framing pieces, preface and epilogue (1–66, 639–644) are realistic. They introduce and send on its way the actual volume which the reader will be holding in his hands. Explaining the character and purpose of his poem, the author states his case in general terms and alludes to the wrong Ibis had done him; he declares a lifelong war on the wretch and announces that he is going to open the hostilities with a book of imprecations. As yet, however, he is not aiming at the person (*caput,* 50) of his enemy, but only going through the motions of a fight and warming up for the real battle, in case such a battle should prove necessary. The knave will still be allowed to hide under pseudonymity, and the details of his crime, by which he could be recognized, will not yet be disclosed. But only for a short time (52) will the writer restrain himself. If the malefactor fails to reform, Ovid will revile him by name in the fashion and verse of Archilochus; that is, he will circumstantially expose his behavior and ruin his reputation beyond repair.[10] Ovid further sets forth, with great candor, that for the present book he plans to forego his own manner and taste and do the main part of it in imitation of Callimachus' *Ibis*.

The second section (67–250) is on a romantic level. The scene has undergone a transformation. No longer do we watch the author writing a book; we behold him posed before an imaginary altar in the midst of an imaginary crowd and executing, under the tacit assistance of the bystanders, a sinister ritual of dire maledictions. More than that, the intentions of the preface are directly contradicted. While it had been said there that the use of a pseudonym was meant to protect Ibis from being hit in person, the speaker is by now no longer assailing a mere dummy, and he makes a point of it. Ovid prays that the use of a fictitious name may not prevent his curses from striking home and destroying the person he has in mind. He hopes that they will take effect even so because both the curser and the accursed, if no one else, understand who is to be punished and for what crime (93–96).[11] The mental communion between the culprit in Rome, with his bad conscience, and the avenger at Tomis, with his righteous fury, is then pictured in the shape of Ibis standing at the altar with a victim's paraphernalia and offering his throat, while Ovid is brandishing a knife to slaughter him (103–106). At the same time, the poet's grievances have changed their nature. Ovid now charges his enemy with frequent attempts against the writer's life (131) and contends that Ibis' existence is a detriment to the whole community (220). On this level, anything may assume weird proportions,[12] but the facts and persons involved are not entirely obliterated. To his exile Ovid refers in a fairly natural manner (67–68; 132; 145–153). Of Ibis we are told that he was fittingly born on the black continent (222, cf. 501) at a spot where hell communicates with the upper world (226), and that his mother was delivered of him on one of Rome's black days, the anniversary of the *Clades Alliana* (219).[13] The birth story is further embellished on the line that from his first breath the monster was destined[14] to base actions, foul-mouthed slander,[15] and abject misery (209–244). In concluding this part, the author skillfully develops from his fantastic tale a kind of second preface (245–250) which serves as transition to the main section.

In addition to the dismal predictions about the fate of Ibis, the romantic part contains a number of curses against him. These maledictions are slightly but not overly extravagant in tenor and form; substantially they are such as any outraged man might pronounce in the heat of his anger. The main part of the *Ibis* (251–638), however, consists of nothing but foppish curses which follow one upon the other by the hundreds, after the example of Ovid's Hellenistic models. And after that same example, they are uniformly molded in the same pattern, each of them calling down upon Ibis the same fate which had befallen this or that character from legend or history. Many recondite examples are cited, and the writer could thus display his learning or, more precisely, the use he had made of books. Every story is skillfully condensed into a few lines, and the presentation is designed to be enigmatic (57–63).[16]

This third section is grotesque, for one thing, because the bookish character of its content is inconsistent with its supposed emotional mainspring. The particular nature of the quarrel and the personalities of the opponents are entirely lost sight of, buried as they are under the mass of farfetched material. The section is also grotesque by reason of the temerity with which the curses contradict one another. The accumulation of so many deaths to be inflicted upon one and the same victim turns the whole into a cranky play of morbid lucubration.[17]

If Ovid had been a different person, he could have wished upon the abominable man all the slow tortures of the body and mind which were besetting himself—such tortures as he knew well how to describe. In that case, the venom of actuality would have given a real sting to his curses. But he did nothing of the sort,[18] or next to nothing.[19] Not before he reached the end of his examples from legend and history did he use his own example. It is his last and climactic imprecation that he wants Ibis to live and die at the shores of the Black Sea among the arrows of the savages (637–638). Realistic like the prooemium (cf. 22), this malediction leads deftly over to the short, realistic epilogue.

Violent agitation caused Ovid to compose the *Ibis*,[20] and yet it is the most affected of his works. Not even when he was justly infuriated was he able to sustain for long the original vigor of his invective; the genre was incompatible with his gentle nature. He was soon compelled to break away from a direct discussion of the issue and to play on the theme, in a romantic and theatrical vein at first, but eventually lapsing into a stilted grotesque. At the same time, he gave up more and more his own natural manner, and ended with slavish imitation of a foreign model. Indeed, little that is genuinely Ovidian is left in the main section of the *Ibis*.[21] Besides, the poet had never stomached the interest in magic as it was rampant among the Hellenistic writers and their Roman followers.[22]

Here, then, is an eccentric book by Ovid which can only be appreciated, if at all, against the background of its literary precedents.[23] Why did the poet try his hand at such a work in the first place? It is unlikely that he hoped in earnest to intimidate Ibis by the learned damnations; and, in fact, he gives himself to understand that, while the curses are not serious, a devastating pasquil as he may write it later will prove a far more formidable weapon with which to subdue his opponent.[24] The threat had already been pronounced by him before *(Tr.* IV, 9), and no practical purpose was served by a repetition. Ovid's real object in composing the *Ibis* was probably to give fuller vent to his anger, and this is indicated when he says that Wrath and Grief acquit themselves of their part throughout the poem (86).[25] Moreover, he was anxious to duplicate a work by the greatest of the Hellenistic poets, and he could kill much of his useless time in elaborating the involved riddles of his *Ibis*.

16. OVID'S LAST YEARS

THE LATEST volumes of Ovid's letters from exile show the author becoming acclimatized, both in body and in spirit, to the conditions under which he was compelled to live. His health had settled down to a stationary condition. Already in his third year at Tomis he had written this to his wife:

> Do not worry. My body, formerly weak
>   and unable to stand up to toil,
> is equal to its task; the strain has hardened it,
>   or perhaps it is because I cannot afford to be ill.
> <div align="right">(<i>Tr.</i> V, 2, 3 ff.)</div>

The idea of the last line is elaborated in the *Epistles from the Black Sea Shore:*

>   The will conquers all things,
>   it lends strength even to my body.
> To sustain a burden, you must hold it up with a stiff neck.
>   If you allow your muscles to bend, you will collapse.
> <div align="right">(<i>Po.</i> II, 7, 75 ff.)</div>

He has no longer to complain of any acute illness; but perhaps he was suffering from some chronic disease:

> I have no pains, nor do I burn with a panting fever,
>   the pulse pursues its accustomed course,
> but my palate is listless and the set table arouses disdain;
>   I lament whenever the hated hour of a meal arrives.[1]
> <div align="right">(<i>Po.</i> I, 10, 5 ff.)</div>

And mentally he is evidently beginning to be broken to the yoke, to use a favorite image of his, even though he would not openly admit it. The indications are there of at least an incipient change of heart. We have already read how he dreamed of owning and tilling some piece of ground in the neighborhood of Tomis (p. 131). Tentatively he reconciles himself to his lot and revises his former aspirations:

> It is enough if on this ground, where I have to live,
>   I succeed in being a poet among the uncivilized Getae.
> What is the use if I strive for fame in a distant world?
>   Let that place which my bad luck assigned me be my Rome.
> <div align="right">(<i>Po.</i> I, 5, 65 ff.)</div>

And he goes on to argue that, even if the people in Rome should admire his present mediocre verse, it could affect the segregated writer no more than if the stars in heaven were to resound his praise. Resignation, he asserts, has the additional advantage that he can take it easy with his poetry, since he has no competitor in

---

[1] For notes to chapter 16, see page 250.

the land of his residence (59–64). Of course this is sarcastic and Ovid does not half mean it; but even so, such ideas would not have entered his mind before. In another elegy, one of his saddest and most forceful, he goes a step farther. It is the letter which begins: "Asking so often for the same thing, I am running out of words" (see p. 137). Ovid feels that he has too often implored his friends in Rome to bring about his deliverance, and too often his hopes have been dashed. Those who might help him are probably tired of his endless solicitations. "Therefore," he continues, "I shall change the drift of my letters and no longer try to swim against the tide. Forgive me if I expected too much of you." And somewhat further on he writes this:

It helps to embrace a hope, provided it does not dissolve every time;[2]
   If you want a thing to happen, you must believe it will happen.
But the second best is fully to despair of salvation
   and to recognize, once and for all, the reality of ruin.
Many wounds worsen when they are being treated
   and are better not touched at all.
The end is more gentle if one is swallowed by a sudden wave
   than if he struggles to float on raging waters.
Why did I suppose I could leave the Scythian
   land and enjoy a happier country?
Why did I ever hope for a milder lot for me,
   ignoring the obstinacy of my misfortune?
It only aggravates my torment; whenever I conjure up the shape of
     familiar places,
   my grievous banishment is renewed and made fresh once more....[3]
Unless the Emperor's wrath denies me even that,
   I shall bravely die at the Black Sea shore.
         (Po. III, 7, 21 ff.; 39 f.)

True enough, Ovid is writing in bitter indignation; he does not really give up his hope, but covertly threatens to do so if his friends continue to be remiss in helping him. Nevertheless, we note that for the first time he envisages a reversal of his attitude and speaks of fortifying himself with the courage of despair.

It is apparent that Ovid now sees his situation more realistically and allows the actual facts to sink into his mind. He has ceased to marvel that he is living in the land of the Getae and Sarmatians, and his lifelong habit of talking in vain to things that have no ears is subsiding. Now and then, he doffs the cumbersome armor of uncompromising anguish and lays aside the weapons of remonstrance and vituperation. He consents to make a truce, if not a permanent peace, with Tomis.

When he now speaks of his house in the town, he omits to add a protest against the term "home" (*Po.* IV, 9, 105 ff.)⁴ He confesses to have acquired a command of both the Getic and Sarmatian languages (*Po.* III, 2, 40). In fact, he ventures to write poetry in one of the native tongues:

> I blush to say it: I have composed a booklet in the Getic language,
>   assembling barbarian words so as to fit our measures.
> And I have found favor; you ought to congratulate me. I begin to have
>   the title of poet among the uncivilized Getae.
>   (*Po.* IV, 13, 19 ff.)

We may well wonder how the daring experiment succeeded.⁵ No doubt it was little more than play, but Ovid's irrepressible talent was playing with the native medium of communication for the benefit of a local audience.

His mellowed mood opened the poet's eyes to the fact that the people of Tomis were none too well pleased with the lurid colors in which he constantly pictured to the world at large his life amongst them. Thus, for the first time in his verse epistles apostrophizing the local public (*Po.* IV, 14), he took pains to explain that his complaints were not meant to reflect on them. Much as he detested the place, which was indeed as bad as the Stygian underworld, he loved the inhabitants of Tomis, who as a matter of fact used to decry, themselves, the location of their town. He goes on to express his sincere gratitude for what they had done for him. By receiving him in his affliction with mild friendliness, they had proved true to their Greek extraction. His own home country in central Italy could not have been more hospitable and indulgent. Although he had come to them as a marked man, he was the only one with no official status who was honored with the Freedom of the City, a distinction which was bestowed upon the poet even by other towns in the region (*Po.* IV, 9, 101–104). Moreover, the community of Tomis had voted, over his own protest, to crown him with a laurel wreath. Thus ancient Tomis appreciated the presence within its modest walls of the most illustrious man who has ever resided there, just as the modern Rumanian city of Constantsa proudly remembers the famous Roman. At last Ovid could feel himself once more well liked (*Po.* IV, 9, 89) and his human dignity restored in some measure. On his own part, he now made friends even with the natives and took them into his confidence. Ovid contends that, when he described to them all the sufferings he had undergone, the truculent warriors groaned with compassion (*Po.* II, 7, 31–32), and when he told them of the loyalty of some of his friends, the barbarians expressed their comprehending approval (*Po.* III, 2, 37–38). However much or little truth there may be in poetic assertions of this sort,[6] they certainly betray a change in Ovid's attitude. The expatriated man no longer dissociated himself from those in whose midst he was compelled to live. His coolness thawed, and he probably also felt that he could not afford to keep aloof. For obvious practical reasons, he tried to win the favor of the Thracian kings. He praised Rhoematalces (?) for his valiant fight against the invaders from beyond the Danube (*Po.* I, 8, 17–22), and when young Cotys had become king of northern[7] Thrace, Ovid, with his chronic fear of murder or enslavement, implored the ruler of the surrounding country to give him his powerful protection (*Po.* II, 9). Unlike his race, Cotys was a kindly man with pleasant manners;[8] he had received a Greek education and took pleasure in writing verse; thus the Roman poet addressed him as a brother bard.[9] In this fashion, Ovid tried to make himself popular rather than be morose and refractory. In his private behavior, he wanted to be as inoffensive as possible, and especially to live down the notoriety he had acquired with his unfortunate *Art of Love*. He asserts that he has forgotten his old love games (*Tr.* V, 7, 21) and in all his years at Tomis has never given cause for complaint in that respect (*Po.* IV, 9, 95–96). It was therefore hardly in line with the poet's own intentions when in the eighteenth century a ballet was produced in Paris in which the natives of the Pontian coast celebrated funeral games in Ovid's honor because he had introduced the tender arts of love to their savage country.[10]

17. THE "HALIEUTICS"

OVID WAS NOW in his middle and later fifties, and found other things
with which to distract his mind. He was eventually taking a positive
interest in his surroundings, and the life of the very sea at whose
shores he was forced to dwell caught his sympathetic fancy.[1] He
spent long hours in watching anglers, in talking with Greek[2] fishermen, and in examining the catch they brought home in the holds
of their craft. He informed himself on the species of fish, their
names, their diverse habits, and the methods by which each kind
was caught. To supplement what he could learn by observation and
conversation,[3] he studied Greek books on the natural history of fish;
and then he began to write a poem in hexameters on *The Fisherman's Art,* to which he gave the Greek[4] title *Halieutica.* He died
when he had hardly begun; 130-odd lines, probably from the first
part, have survived.

The fragment we possess is in a very poor shape.[5] Not only has the
text suffered badly in the process of transmission from Antiquity
to modern times; it seems that the author's original manuscript was
no more than a rough draft,[6] partly messy and hard to decipher,[7] to
begin with. At places the text consists of fragmentary clauses, jotted
down on the spur of the moment;[8] there are a number of gaps which
were to be filled out later;[9] the same thought appears twice in different phrasing;[10] and several sentences are faulty in their structure.
Some lines, on the other hand, are only slightly disfigured, and the
majority are unobjectionable.

The sketchy fragment is none too coherent, but the trend of the
argument is fairly clear.[11] What Ovid had in mind to set forth was
about as follows. Animals are possessed of an amazing resourceful-
ness; diverse as they are in their shape and constitution, nature has
seen to it that each species knows how to make the best both of its
strong and its weak points. (This is illustrated by striking examples,
and so is the next topic.) Land animals, however, are less well fitted
for survival than those of the sea. They often contribute to their
own destruction; the foolhardy ferocity of some, and the senseless
timidity of others, play into the hands of the hunter. They are easier

---

[1] For notes to chapter 17, see pages 251–253.

to chase, moreover, because the hunter is assisted by the spirited horse and the intelligent dog. Besides, his game live on terra firma, while the denizens of the sea enjoy the protection of an element alien and inhospitable to man. The fisherman has thus no hope of success unless he can outwit his prey by a superior cunning (82), and so he will welcome the advice which *The Fisherman's Art* is dispensing. Offshore fishing, however, will not be discussed:

> I shall not exhort you to proceed to the habitat of fish
> on the high seas and to venture out into deep water;
> you will cast line or net better on the confines of both elements.
> (83 ff.)

The discerning fisherman will consider the nature of the shore:

> whether the place is rough and rocky and requires the use
> of patient hooks, while a smooth beach allows net catching;
> whether a lofty cliff casts a frigid shadow
> on the water (for certain fish avoid that, and others flock to it);
> whether the sea bottom is green with weeds that grow in the depth ...
> (87 ff.)

We can easily imagine the poet himself sitting among anglers on the "lofty cliff" at the edge of the promontory on which Tomis was situated,[12] and perhaps trying his own luck with the hook and line. And we also understand why he thoughtfully keeps his disciple at the "confines"; he has probably never gone out very far on a fishing craft, because he hardly took pleasure in boating (cf., e.g., *Ibis,* 147–148). But he does give in the *Halieutics* a long list, neatly descriptive, of high-seas fish as he had inspected them on land or read of them in books. The fragment breaks off in the middle of a similar catalogue of inshore fish.

The *Halieutics* arouses the biographer's special curiosity because it was the poet's last project. In assaying its literary quality, we have to disregard whatever flaws are likely to be due to the fact that we are dealing with a very sketchy draft. If we thus give our text a fair hearing, we find that the style is surprisingly fresh and brilliant and the presentation pleasantly animated in the best Ovidian manner. For example, that inexplicable endowment of animals which we term the instinct of self-preservation is well described in these concise lines:

They all fear death, of which they know nothing; it is given to all
to sense their enemy and their means of protection, and to understand
the power and limitations of their own weapons.

                              (7 ff.)

The poet shows a fine sense for the natural behavior of the sundry
animals, wild or tame, and he interprets their actions with a lively
comprehension of their concerns, but with no undue sentimentality.[18] In a digression on those beasts that serve man he gives a very
good description of the proud bearing of horses (66–74)—too good,
in fact, for spoiling by a translation. Then he praises the dog thus:

> Which is the chief glory of the dog? Is it his headlong daring,
> his admirable intelligence in hunting, or his strength in pursuit?
> Now he will sniff the breeze with uplifted nostrils,
> then search for traces with his snout on the ground;
> he announces his find, giving voice and calling
> his master; and when the game flees from the hunter's attack,
> the dog follows after over high ground and low.
>
>   (75 ff.)

The subject of the work does not appear promising; but what
Ovid has made of it seems to prove that his resilient art was again
on the upsurge when death overtook him.[14]

18. THE END

OVID PROBABLY died in the year 17 of the Christian era.[1] At that time
he was fifty-nine years old and had lived at Tomis for eight years.
How the end arrived, whether in a natural way or through some
such violence as Ovid had always dreaded, we have no means of
knowing. Death came as a liberator to the man who knew that he
had outlived himself. In the very last lines of his collected works
we hear him plead thus with the detractor who begrudges him his
greatness:

> I have lost everything; life alone has been left me,
>   to provide the perception and stuff of adversity.
> What is to be gained by driving the steel into a corpse?
> I am no longer fit for a new blow.
>
>   (Po. IV, 16, 49 ff.)

---

[1] For notes to chapter 18, see pages 253–255.

But in spite of all his misery he felt that it was only his private exist-ence which had been crushed, while his glory as a poet had risen even higher. His social and civil death enhanced, rather than destroyed, his fame. The opening lines of the same elegy celebrate his spiritual triumph:

> O jealous man, why do you rend the poems of castaway Ovid?
> 　Genius is not harmed by the day that ends life.
> Renown grows after the pyre, and I had a name
> 　already while I was among the living.
> 　　　　(*Po.* IV, 16, 1 ff.)

It was the poet's destiny to spend his last years "at the banks of Styx," as he puts it (*Tr.* IV, 5, 22; *Po.* I, 8, 27), in between the realms of the quick and of the dead. His bodily sojourn at the shores of the Black Sea was certainly not of his own choosing, but his mind was ever used to haunt the difficult regions of some Inbetween.

His graceful poetry had been weaving back and forth between the brute facts as known to the intellect and the finer realities as sensed by the heart; between the art of love and the passion of love; between a stable nature of the self and its capacity for transforma-tion; between proud isolation and tender communion of souls; between obsolescent views and those that were coming up. He still had a secure grasp of things ancient and all they stood for, but he reached out for them from a point slightly beyond.

His place in the history of mankind was between two worlds, between the wonderful self-contained world of Antiquity and that newer one which was to bring Christianity and a different civiliza-tion, but began with empty disillusion and dumb, hopeless con-fusion. While the bleak new day was inexorably rising, the light of all the familiar lodestars went out, and man was about to become, to quote once more[2] Ovid's elegy on *The Dawn,*

> a sailor lost and erring among the wastes of the ocean.

It was Ovid's mission to sing the song of Dawn and to perpetuate the fugitive beauty of that uniquely precious moment of transition:

> This is the hour when I delight to rest in the tender arms of my lady;
> 　now, if ever, is she close to my side.
> This is the hour when slumber is rich, and cool the air,
> 　and clear the chant from the soft throats of birds.

j) Too many attempts have been made in the past, under neglect of the considerations set forth under (*a–i*), to demonstrate that Ovid was a "rhetorical" poet; instead of explaining the text of his works, students have often been content to point out its alleged "rhetorical" character. Some scholars have justly protested against this practice (see the preceding note and moreover, among others, R. Heinze, *Ovids elegische Erzählung,* Ber. d. Sächs. Akad. d. Wiss. 71, 1919, Heft 7, *passim;* H. Magnus, *Philol. Wochenschr.* 42, 1922, pp. 940–943; F. Lenz, *passim,* see note 1). It may indeed be wise to let the question of Ovid's rhetoric rest until more urgent tasks are completed.

Let us, then, try to explain Ovid's poetry in terms of poetry rather than dump upon it our grievances against the school rhetoric of his time. After this is done, there will still be ample scope for scolding as well as commending the poet. First of all, however, let us try to understand Ovid as he wanted to be understood.

4 (p. 2). Cf. Edward K. Rand, *Ovid and His Influence,* Boston, 1925. Ovid's popularity in Antiquity, even among less educated people, is attested by the numerous quotations from his works in inscriptions (cf. R. Ehwald, *Bursians Jahresbericht* Nr. 109, 1901, pp. 202–203). In the early centuries of Christianity, the hostility to pagan literature in general militated against the study of Ovid (cf. Rudolph Schevill, *Ovid and the Renascence in Spain,* Univ. Calif. Publ. Mod. Philol. 4, 1, 1913, pp. 6 ff.). From the eighth to the eleventh century, Ovid's influence, as indicated by the number of known manuscripts written at the time, was surpassed not only by Horace and Vergil, but even by Lucan (cf. Hilda Buttenwieser, *Manuscripts of Ovid's "Fasti,"* Trans. Amer. Philol. Assoc. 71, 1940, p. 49).

5 (p. 2). Quoted from Schevill (see preceding note), pp. 12 f. In this paragraph I quote amply from authorities because I have not studied in detail Ovid's influence on posterity. Recently, E. K. Rand published, in *Studies in the History of Culture,* Menasha, Wis., 1942, pp. 103–121, an article on "The Metamorphosis of Ovid in *Le Roman de la Rose.*"

6 (p. 2). Cf. Hilda Buttenwieser (see note 4), p. 50.

7 (p. 2). Quoted from Schevill (see note 4), p. 199.

8 (p. 2). Quoted from Rand (see note 4), p. 150. For representations in art of the Daphne metamorphosis from the Middle Ages to about 1800, cf. W. Stechow, *Apollo und Daphne,* Leipzig, 1932.

9 (p. 2). Cf. Emile Ripert, *Ovide,* Paris, 1921, p. 244.

10 (p. 3). "No classical poet was more popular in the Middle Ages than Ovid. It would hardly be an exaggeration to say that distinctively modern

literature has its springs in the French poets of the 12th century, and that these poets were inspired and (paradox as it may seem) 'modernized' by the inspiration they drew from Ovid." This remarkable assertion (quoted by Rand [see note 4], p. 168) is to be found in Philip H. Wick-steed and Edmund G. Gardner, *Dante and Giovanni del Virgilio,* West-minster, 1902.

11 (p. 3). When Ovid did try to provide his *Metamorphoses* with a philosophical foundation, he did not succeed very well (see p. 110).

12 (p. 3). His indelicacy, however, is naïvely blunt rather than of the tense and sultry sort. See p. 71.

13 (p. 3). Cf. *Ars Amat.* II, 683 f. (see p. 185, note 46). Likewise uncon-ventional was his aversion to the idea of using philters and witchcraft for amatory purposes (see p. 62, with note 27, p. 203).

14 (p. 4). For the Pygmalion story, *Metam.* 10, 238–297, see pp. 93–96.

NOTES TO CHAPTER 2, OVID GROWS UP, PP. 4–10

1 (p. 4). Cf. *Am.* III, 15, 5–6; III, 8, 9 ff.; *Tr.* IV, 10, 7 f.; *Po.* IV, 8, 17 f.

2 (p. 4). For details see A. L. Wheeler, "Topics from the Life of Ovid," *Amer. Jour. Philol.* 46 (1925), pp. 1–28.

3 (p. 5). *Poterat videri* can only mean, I believe, "it could have been, but was not, taken for ..." I have omitted the rest of § 8, which, I think, is a footnote on both *Latronis admirator erat* and *solutum carmen:* "Just as Ovid's rhetorical prose was poetic, so his poetry was replete with loans from Latro's rhetoric" (cf. p. 186, note 55). As soon as we cut out the footnote, the relation of *iam tum* and *tunc autem cum studeret* becomes obvious, and the *tunc autem* clause, which has puzzled scholars, makes good sense.

4 (p. 6). W. Hoffa, however (*De Seneca patre quaest. select.,* Diss. Göttingen, 1909, p. 19), takes Seneca's words to mean that Ovid, while studying mainly with Arellius, was at the same time an admirer of Latro.

5 (p. 6). Ovid repaid his debt to rhetoric by "filling the age not only with amorous arts but also with *sententiae";* cf. Seneca, *Exc. Controv.* III, 7.

6 (p. 6). Seneca's words, *molesta ei erat omnis argumentatio,* are often quoted but rarely discussed. *Argumentatio* is the tricky syllogistic by means of which the orator tries to convince the audience that the facts of the case are such as he alleges them to be (cf., e.g., *Ad Herennium* II, 2: *argumentationes quas Graeci ἐπιχειρήματα appellant;* Cicero, *De Inventione* I, 34–96; Cicero, *Pro Sex. Roscio* 98: *Etiamne in tam perspi-cuis rebus argumentatio quaerenda aut coniectura capienda est? Nonne*

vobis haec quae audistis cernere oculis videmini, iudices?). An examination of witnesses played no part in *argumentatio;* the allegations were to be made plausible merely on their intrinsic probability, and yet the actual themes for school *controversiae* as we know them were utterly improbable, and devoid of circumstance at that. Shall we blame, then, a budding poet if he felt that *argumentatio* was "annoying"? Contrary to the general assumption, moreover, Seneca himself, far from censuring Ovid for his aversion to *argumentatio,* professes the same view, using the identical term "annoying": *argumentationes . . . molestae sunt et minimum habent floris* (*Controv.* IX, pr. 1; it makes little difference that in one case *molesta declamanti* is meant, in the other *molestae audientibus*). Since he did not care for it, Seneca's book disregards *argumentatio* and deals only with *sententiae, divisiones, colores.*—Ovid's distaste for *argumentatio* was to the advantage of his poetry. There is very little *argumentatio* in his verse; one instance is *Am.* II, 7, 19–22, with the delightful recantation in 8, 9–14.

7 (p. 6). It seems strange that those modern critics who loathe Ovid's "rhetoric" should reproach the poet for not swallowing school rhetoric hook, line, and sinker.

8 (p. 6). In preferring the *suasoria,* Ovid followed his master Arellius Fuscus (cf. Seneca, *Suas.* 4, 5), and the soundness of his judgment is confirmed by the concurrence of as competent a rhetor and writer as the historian Tacitus. Tacitus, in his *Dialogus* (35), lashed out against the absurdity of *controversiae* as practiced in the schools, and against the general view that *suasoriae* were easier and should be taught to immature beginners.

9 (p. 6). For the term *ethica controversia* cf. Fortunatianus, *Ars Rhetor.* I, 10 p. 88, 28–31 Halm; Mart. Capella V, 473. An *ethica controversia* turned not so much on questions of fact or law as on the interpretation, in terms of individual character, of human actions. We are told that, for this reason, both the *forma elocutionis* and the *modus actionis* were different from ordinary *controversiae.*

10 (p. 6). A. D. Wheeler (see p. 170, note 2), p. 9, ingeniously suggests that the wife misunderstood the message: the husband wrote of his going abroad, but she thought he had departed for Hades. This, however, is refuted by the way the case is discussed throughout the chapter; the debaters assume that the husband wanted his wife to believe he was dead (see §§ 1, 4, and 7). The treatment of the case further shows that no motive was given for the husband's strange behavior; the debaters had free play in explaining it (see §§ 5 and 7). The case, then,

was put up for discussion just as Seneca sets it forth, with a crucial point of the issue left blank. No wonder the school speeches were airy.

11 (p. 7). Like many others in the rhetorical schools, this case is taken from Greek, not Roman, law. A rescript by Diocletian (*Codex Justin.* 8, 46, 6) says: *abdicatio, quae Graeco more ad alienandos liberos usurpabatur et apoceryxis dicebatur, Romanis legibus non comprobatur* (G. Thalheim, *R.-E.* 1, 2836; Ludwig Mitteis, *Reichsrecht und Volksrecht,* Leipzig, 1891, pp. 212 ff.). From a papyrus we learn that the apoceryxis must be approved by a court of law (Paul Meyer, *Jurist. Papyri,* Berlin, 1920, 24 foll.). Hence a question of *abdicatio* could be argued in a Greek court (lines 87 ff. of the papyrus).—I am indebted to Wolfgang Kunkel for the information contained in this note.

12 (p. 7). *Facilius in amore finem impetres quam modum.* The subject of *impetres* is not the lover, but someone who tries to impose his own will on the lover; in this case, the father.

13 (p. 7). For Ovid's point *senes sic amant,* cf. *Metam.* 9, 551–553: *Iura senes norint, et quid liceatque nefasque fasque sit inquirant legumque examina servent; conveniens Venus est annis temeraria nostris.*

14 (p. 7) I leave out the lines as Seneca quotes them. The first is *Ars Amat.* II, 24 (*semibovemque virum semivirumque bovem*), which will be discussed below (p. 183, note 38). The second is similar to the first in its sound pattern only: *et gelidum Borean egelidumque Notum* (*Am.* II, 11, 10). Here the point is that the apprehensive lover stands in dread for his voyaging lady of any weather; he is frightened by the wind blowing from the west or the east, the north or the south, cold or otherwise. In both lines, the pattern is too loud and gaudy for the taste of many people, but it is distinctly expressive of a definite idea, and Ovid had a case when he stuck to these two lines—supposing there is so much to the story. The third line is unfortunately lost in Seneca's quotation.

15 (p. 7). The prevalent feeling was that a *naevos* would slightly disfigure an *egregium corpus* (*Tr.* V, 13, 14; Horace, *Sat.* I, 6, 67), but Ovid's poetry contains examples of an ingratiating *vitium,* cf. *Ars Amat.* I, 290–292: a fine white bull with one black spot between the horns; *Am.* III, 1, 10: *et pedibus vitium causa decoris erat; Ars Amat.* III, 295: *in vitio decor est, quaedam male reddere verba; Fasti* 3, 495: *vitio tibi gratior ipso est.*

16 (p. 7). Albinovanus Pedo is given this epithet by Seneca the Philosopher, *Epist.* 122, 15.

17 (p. 7). While Seneca the Father says: *Non ignoravit vitia sua sed amavit,* Quintilian calls Ovid *nimium amator ingenii sui* and wishes that

he *ingenio suo imperare quam indulgere maluisset* (*Instit. Orat.* 10, 1, 88 and 98). Seneca the Philosopher likewise judges that Ovid made improper use of his wonderful *ingenium* (*Natur. Qu.* 3, 27, 13–15). He is referring to the description in the *Metamorphoses* of the deluge, a passage he thinks to be partly admirable and partly ridiculous. The details of his criticism are more revealing for Seneca than for Ovid. For one thing, by an ingenious lapse of memory Seneca transfers to the story of the deluge, where the rising flood turns mountain peaks into new islands, a line from Ovid's Phaëthon story (2, 264), where the falling waters cause new islands to emerge from the bottom of the sea. Secondly, Seneca is incensed against Ovid's line (1, 304): *Nat lupus inter oves, fulvos vehit unda leones,* and in the blindness of his anger he makes a pedantic objection: *Natari in diluvio et in illa rapina potest? Aut non eodem impetu pecus omne quo raptum erat mersum est?* Seneca fails to see that with *nat* and *vehit unda* Ovid had meant precisely that, viz., "they were swept by the waters," and the critic himself presently uses *natat* in exactly that sense (*orbem terrarum natare*). What, then, caused Seneca to be so intolerant? The context makes it clear that he could not endure Ovid's talking of sheep and wolves while all mankind was perishing and the whole world was in uproar and confusion. Ovid, on his part, had a warm feeling for all living creatures; but Seneca, as a true Stoic, found it anticlimactic that the suffering of mere animals should intrude on the sublime spectacle of a cosmic catastrophe, and thus he exclaimed: *poetarum ingeniosissimus ... tantum impetum ingenii et materiae ad pueriles ineptias reduxit* (for Seneca's terms, *ingenium, materia,* and *puerilis,* we have a parallel in Ovid's own *Amores,* III, 1, 25, where *Tragoedia* says to the poet: *Materia premis ingenium,* scil., by choosing juvenile subjects). Seneca's tragedies show his propensity for picturing colossal events, with the very elemental powers out of gear; thus he would resent it if, in his opinion, so exalted a motif was spoiled. (In *Philologus* 83, 1928, pp. 459–466, Fr. Levy compares Ovid's and Seneca's descriptions of the deluge.)

18 (p. 7). There is also, however, behind the bravado in these words a good deal of weary resignation; the Ovid of the exile was no longer sure of himself. Outright despondence is voiced by Ovid in another passage from *Ex Ponto,* a confession which otherwise closely parallels Seneca's statement that Ovid very well knew his own defects, and that his judgment (*iudicium*) was sound but he had not the inclination—or heart (*animus*)—to eliminate them. In *Po.* III, 9, 7–26 (see p. 139), Ovid says this: "I see the faults in my own works, my judgment (*iudicium*) is not corrupted by fatherly love to my products, but I lack the strength to

follow up my judgment, and I shirk the prolonged exertion. The halting pedantry of correcting pains the genius (*animus*) and like reins holds back the impetus of the eager horse." Seneca had spoken of the inclination or impetus (*animus*) going astray and taking delight in things of poor taste; Ovid the exile, on the other hand, complains of his impetus (*animus*) faltering.

19 (p. 8). Seneca is quoting Mamercus Aemilius Scaurus (cf. von Rhoden, *R.-E.* 1, 583, no. 139), a quick-minded, witty critic (*Controv.* 10, praef. 2), who would never allow a foolishness to go unpunished (*Controv.* 1, 2, 22), and was complacent only with his own productions (*Controv.* 10, praef. 2–3). Scaurus censured both the rhetor Votienus Montanus and Ovid for the same fault, calling Montanus "the Ovid among the orators" and scoring certain passages in Ovid's poetry as being "in the Montanus manner" (*Controv.* 9, 5, 15–17). To illustrate that each of them *"nescit quod bene cessit relinquere,"* he analyzed on the same lines a passage from Montanus (§§ 15–16) and a sequence of three exclamations by Hecuba in Ovid's *Metam.* 13, 504–505 (§ 17).

20 (p. 8). He also visited, together with his friend the poet Macer, the cities of Asia Minor and Sicily. Whether or not these travels were connected with the journey to Athens is unknown.

21 (p. 8). His brother had died in 24 B.C., so that Ovid became sole heir to his father's possessions. Ovid was a late child; when he was born, his father was over forty (cf. *Tr.* IV, 10, 77–84 combined with lines 95–97).

22 (p. 9). Hesiod ranked the poet next to the king (*Theog.* 79–103); Pindar (although he was not an Aegeid) talked to kings on an equal, or better than equal, footing.

23 (p. 9). Cicero tried to combine in his own person spiritual and political greatness, but he strictly subordinated the one to the other. The role he assigned to poetry is patent from his oration *Pro Archia Poeta*. He wrote the speech with the intention of vindicating the dignity of poetry in the face of narrow-minded prejudice, but how tame is his defense! His main claim is that poetry stimulates political ambition by perpetuating the deeds of a great man. Besides, he guardedly contends that it provides a liberal recreation, increases the power of oratory, and has a moralizing influence. Poetry is for him, in a word, a dainty handmaid of political excellence.

24 (p. 9). Cf. R. Heinze's introduction to Horace, *Carm.* I, 6.

25 (p. 9). In *Ars Amat.* III, 411–412, Ovid complains that poetry enjoys no standing, and that a writer's intensive labors, carried on for long hours deep into the night, are styled as laziness (*inertia*).

26 (p. 9). For the reason why that particular setting was selected see below, p. 229, note 12, and the text to which the note belongs, p. 116.—The view that free poetry has its place outside of normal life was native in Rome, but it also seems to have been gradually evolved in the Greek world from the time of the imperialistic kingdoms of Hellenism. Concurrently with its progress, the pastoral idyls grew more and more unrealistic and delicate, from Theocritus, through the spurious poems in the Theocritus collection, down to Vergil.

27 (p. 10). For the role which love was bound to play in the poetry of the age see also pp. 26–28 and p. 189, note 67.

Notes to Chapter 3, The "Amores," pp. 10–35

1 (p. 11). That is, when he was about 18 years old. Cf. Wheeler (see p. 170, note 2), pp. 14–16.

2 (p. 11). For the chronology of Ovid's earlier writings see Max Pohlenz, *De Ovidi carminibus amatoriis,* Progr. Göttingen, 1913; and p. 193, note 1.

3 (p. 11). All this, I think, is just as true for Propertius as it is for Ovid.

4 (p. 11). In this sense Ovid says *artes teneri profitemur amoris* (*Am.* II, 18, 19). For the fact that he is here referring not to the *Ars Amatoria* but to the *Amores,* see E. K. Rand, *Amer. Jour. Philol.* 28 (1907), p. 295, and M. Pohlenz (see note 2), pp. 9–12. See also, below, p. 199, note 8.

5 (p. 12). There is, however, another Ovidian passage which does contain the motif. In the Leander epistle, XVII (XVIII), 111–118, he describes the reluctant departure at daybreak of the lover who must not be discovered in his lady's bower; the nurse plays here the part of the warner. Perhaps the medieval minstrels were inspired by that passage, also.

6 (p. 12). A similar structure, with the body of the poem consisting of an address, recurs several times in the *Amores:* I, 3 (first two couplets narrative); III, 2 (last hexameter narrative); III, 10 (first couplet narrative).

7 (p. 12). Cf. the refrain *dô tagete ez* in Heinrich von Morungen's *Tageliet, Minnesangs Frühling* 143, 29 ff.

8 (p. 12). The ancient Romans actually used to rise at daybreak.

9 (p. 13). The striking phrase *sua sidera servat* (11) establishes a personal bond between the sailor and "his" stars. I do not know whether anywhere else the actual stars "of" a particular person are mentioned; but parallels are close at hand, significantly, for metaphorical "stars," symbolizing the sheen of love. In Ovid's *Amores* II, 16, 44, we read *oculos, sidera nostra, tuos* (cf. Prop. II, 3, 14, and ἀστὴρ ἐμός in the epigram,

ascribed to Plato, *Anthol. Palat.* 7, 699). The same elegy also contrasts the enjoyment of the lady's presence with journeys on sea and land and with country life; furthermore, it refers to Hero's beacon which guided her lover through the waves of the sea (31–32).

The latter idea is fully elaborated in Ovid's Leander epistle (*Epist.* XVII, alias XVIII, 85–86 and 147–168). The light in Hero's bower is here identified with the flame of Leander's love (*meus ignis in illo est,* 85) and that flame is said to set the course for the swimmer. Leander, likening himself to a sailor (148), declares that he does not consult everybody's stars (*publica sidera,* 150), but his own personal lodestar: *ipse meos igitur servo quibus uror amores,* 168. This line is indeed a close parallel to *sua sidera servat nauta* in *Am.* I, 13, 11–12; cf. also *non errat,* 156, with *nec errat* in line 12 of *The Dawn*). (For the notion of love's self-sufficiency see p. 50, with note 7 on p. 196.)

The notion of dawn dispersing, and the star that brings on night uniting, families and lovers, already occurs in Sappho's fragment 120 Diehl.

Parallels abound in modern literature. The concept of starry night providing man with the orientation which the tumult of day withholds from him is set forth by Conrad Ferdinand Meyer in a fine poem, *Unter den Sternen* (*Gedichte,* Leipzig, 1912, p. 86). While Meyer does not specifically refer to love, Richard Wagner has built the entire second act of *Tristan und Isolde* on the contrast between night which permits the lovers to find their true selves and the blinding glare of delusive, desolate day (*der öde Tag*).

10 (p. 13). Hesiod in the *Works and Days* (580–581) had spoken of dawn "which by its appearance sends many travelers upon their way and lays the yoke on many oxen" (cf. also Ovid, *Metam.* 4, 664–665). Apollonius of Rhodes (*Argon.* 3, 743–746) described the advent of night which makes the sailors look up to the stars and causes travelers to wish for sleep.

11 (p. 13). Line 18 echoes line 14; the rhyme contrasts the tender victims with the rough dispensers of cruelty.

12 (p. 14). Except that, for reasons not known to us, the ambitious politicians remain unmentioned.

13 (p. 14). There is method also in the wishful fancies. Ovid thinks of a windstorm or thick cloud to prevent Dawn's progress because some people believed that the movements of the heavenly bodies were controlled by winds (cf. Lucretius V, 509–516, 637–649) and others assumed that winter nights are long because the rise of the sun is retarded by "thicker air" (cf. Lucr. V, 696–700). Thus Ovid playfully applies to the

mythological symbol of the chariot the mechanistic theories which had been invented to replace and refute mythology.

14 (p. 14). E.g., a heart which will not respond to the appeal of Love; cf. Pindar frag. 123.

15 (p. 14). The couplet *Quid si Cephalio,* printed in our editions as lines 31–32, poses a complex problem which also involves the four lines 11–14.

Lines 11–14 as well as 31–32 are missing from the text of the two best manuscripts, the P(uteanus) and S(angallensis) but are carried by the rest of the manuscripts, the so-called recentiores. Lines 11–14 and 31–32 also appear on the margin of P, added by a later hand, probably in the 14th century. However, while the recentiores carry 11–14 between lines 10 and 15, the later hand in P marked the four lines for insertion between lines 18 and 19; and likewise, while the couplet 31–32 is written in the recentiores after line 34, the later hand in P marked it for insertion between 30 and 33. (The data for this paragraph were taken from Friedrich Lenz, *Parerga Ovidiana,* Rendic. Accad. Lincei, Classe Scienze Morali, Ser. 6, Vol. 13, Rome, 1938, pp. 386 ff., and from a letter in which Mr. Lenz was kind enough to supply additional information. It is to be noted that the term "the recentiores" stands for all manuscripts known to Mr. Lenz, except P and S.)

This, then, seems to be the situation. In the 14th century, a reader of P noticed that another manuscript had four more lines in one place and two more in another, and he added the missing lines on the margin of P, but made both times a mistake in the marking of the place. The modern editors go in one case with the recentiores and place 11–14 where they belong, between 10 and 15. In the other case, however, they follow the casual corrector who has perpetuated himself on the pages of our best manuscript and print the couplet, in brackets denoting interpolation, between 30 and 33. This seems incomprehensible. If the couplet is to be considered as spurious because it is missing from the best manuscripts, then it originated in the inferior tradition and that tradition is the prime authority for its position. But even if the distich is genuine, the conclusion remains the same. All the manuscripts which have the distich as part of their continuous text assign it the one and same position, between lines 34 and 35; in the one case alone where the distich had been lost and was recovered from a more complete manuscript, its position was accidentally changed in the process.

Fr. Lenz (in the Rendic. Accad. Lincei) contends that lines 11–14 are spurious, for these reasons. (1) The lines can be dispensed with.

(2) Unlike the persons mentioned in 15–26, the sailor does not begin his work at dawn. (3) While *Aurora* is the grammatical subject in 9–10 (*properas, supprime*) and in 15–24 (*vides, vocas,* etc.), this is not so in 11–14 (*ante tuos ortus, te veniente*). (4) Although Ovid does use alliteration in other poems, he abstains from it in this elegy except for the suspicious lines 11–14, which contain four instances of alliteration.— These arguments have not convinced me. The reasons why I think the lines are genuine are implied in my discussion of the passage (above, pp. 12–14, with notes). The four lines were probably omitted from the common source of P and S because of the homoeoteleuton *manu* 10 and *manus* 14.

With respect to the distich 31–32, we have first to establish our text. In the pentameter, we have the choice between the readings *flagrasset* and *flagraret* (see Lenz, p. 390); the former seems preferable. In the hexameter, *Cephalio* does not scan; obviously the word was miswritten under the influence of line 39, where Cephalus is mentioned. The emendation is inevitable; there are no other words which both satisfy the meter and resemble *Cephalio* but either *Cepheo* (*Met.* 4, 669; Prop. IV, 6, 78) or *Cepheno* (*Met.* 4, 764; Pliny, *Nat. Hist.* 6, 28). The difference in meaning between the two, if any, is very slight, and we therefore need not worry which of them we may prefer, or which of them may be the true reading in some of the passages we have cited. And it so happens that the emendation, which was forced upon us mechanically, refers to the Aethiopians of whom Memnon was the king, that is, to Negroes. It can hardly be an accident that the word fits so well into the context. This is the context:

> 33 Invida, quo properas? Quod erat tibi filius ater,
> 34   materni fuerat pectoris ille color.
> 31 Quid si Cepheno nunquam flagrasset amore?
> 32   An putat ignotam nequitiam esse suam?
> 35 Tithono vellem de te narrare liceret;
> 36   femina non caelo turpior ulla foret.

"Aurora, you have borne a black child; this shows how black your heart is. In fact, Memnon was evidently sired by a Negro lover of hers; hardly can she suppose that her immodesty has remained a secret. Would that your husband could afford to tell all he knows; your reputation would be worse than any other in heaven." *Quid si,* with impf. or plup. subj., "It were a different matter if ... ," recurs four times in Ovid with the same meaning: "You were less to blame if ..." (*Am.* III, 6, 89; *Her.* 7, 53;

Tr. I, 8, 29–34; II, 497; cf. Vergil, *Aen.* IV, 311–313; also Petronius 42, 6: *Quid si non illam optime accepisset*). The couplet contributes a very amusing point; and without it, the connection between lines 34 and 35 is less smooth and easy. So far, so good.

On the other hand, three objections can be raised against the assumption that the distich is genuine. Why was it missing from the archetype of the better tradition? The answer is that omissions do occur even without any apparent reason, so that the fact itself is not a sufficient reason for condemnation of the couplet. Secondly, hexameters with no more than one dactyl are infrequent, and the poem already contains two such lines (22 and 35). And lastly, I can see no plausible reason why Ovid should have broken for this one distich the direct address to Aurora (for a justified aside cf. *Am.* I, 14, 51–54; a rather willful switch from the second to the third person takes place in I, 12, 21–26 and in II, 5, 35–56, as against 1–17 and 57–62; see p. 187, note 60). It is to be wished that the remaining difficulties could be resolved. It is hardly credible that a mere interpolator should have composed the witty couplet and foisted it into a position which it fills so admirably, apart from some minor defects. And why, if he was as clever as that, did he not make it perfect?

16 (p. 14). In line 39, S reads *manibus,* while P writes *magis.* The recentiores have *malis,* which is probably a conjectural emendation for *magis.* Modern scholars try further to improve on *malis* by changing it to *mavis.*

Quem malis (or *mavis*) cannot be justified by the apparent parallel, *quod malles,* in *Tr.* V, 5, 59. In the *Tristia* the clause contributes a new idea, but in the *Amores* it does the opposite: it duplicates in a weak form that which the distich expresses with felicitous force. The *quem mavis* is pitifully lame in itself, and its insertion hamstrings the brisk rush of the couplet. *Manibus complexa,* on the other hand, is unobjectionable (cf. *manibus complexa est,* Lucan 5, 809), and *si quem Cephalum* (cf. *si quis Aeacus,* Prop. IV, 11, 19) with its innuendo is excellent: "With any young man of the Cephalus type in your own arms, you would wish like myself that the night should never come to an end."

17 (p. 14). In line 27, Dawn was supposed to drive Night from the skies; here it is rather Night who, by leaving the skies, compels Dawn to succeed her. Assumptions of this unsubstantial sort are shifted around at will to suit the argument.

18 (p. 15). If *forma* is the correct reading in line 44, then *illius* refers to *Luna,* and the argument is of the same type as in *Am.* II, 17, 11–20: "If Luna, who is no less beautiful than you are, fell in love with a mortal and

lingered around the skies, why should you be too proud to do the same thing?" The idea of proposing a more satisfactory match for Aurora was suggested by *me conciliante* in line 42.

19 (p. 15). The type of joke recurs, although in much feebler form, in *Tr.* III, 1, 55: *Aspicis exsangui chartam pallere colore?*

20 (p. 15). For the use of a term like *adsuetum* to describe the regularity of nature's timetable cf. *solitos* in *Tr.* V, 10, 11.

21 (p. 15). I am not able to mention any close parallel from extant literature, but this may be due to an oversight. Moreover, a contest between Night and Day (or Winter and Summer, etc.) is a widespread folkloristic motif which may have been exploited in Hellenistic poetry (cf. the quarrel between Laurel and Olive in Callimachus' *Aetia*).

22 (p. 16). Ovid himself says, *Am.* I, 6, 66, after mentioning the rise of Lucifer, *inque suum miseros excitat ales opus.*

23 (p. 16). The meaning of this line becomes clearer when we compare *Anthol. Palat.* 5, 296 Stadtmueller = 5, 297 Dübner.

24 (p. 17). If direct evidence is needed for Ovid's disbelief in the legendary tradition, we can point to the following facts. (1) In *Tr.* II, 64, Ovid declares that the transformations as he tells them in his *Metamorphoses* are not to be believed. (2) In *Tr.* IV, 7, 11–20, he mentions fictitious monsters like Medusa, the Minotaur, and Scylla in order to express the notion of patent impossibility, while in his mythological vein he often speaks of them as if they were real and in the *Metamorphoses* tells Scylla's story and adds: *si non omnia vates ficta reliquerunt* (14, 60 ff.; 13, 732–737). (3) In *Am.* III, 6, 13–18 and *Tr.* III, 8, 1–12, Ovid brands Perseus', Medea's, and Triptolemus' flight through the air as figments of poetic imagination. (4) In *Am.* III, 12, 21–42, he does the same with a great many legendary characters and stories. (5) In *Ars Amat.* I, 637 ff., Ovid declares that he only hesitantly and with reserve believes in the reality of gods; the passage will be discussed later (see pp. 90–91).

25 (p. 18). *Dialogi Meretr.* 8, 1; cf. also Prop. III, 8; Ovid, *Ars Amat.* II, 447–454, etc. The device of putting a person to shame by cutting off his hair (or beard) or ripping open the dress down to the girdle enjoys a considerable antiquity; it is mentioned in the Bible (II Sam. 10:4). As appurtenances of an amorous quarrel the two modes of punishing the mistress, or one of them, are mentioned, in addition to Ovid *Am.* I, 7, 47–48, by Xenopho of Ephesus 5, 5, §§ 2 and 4; Propertius II, 5, 21 and 23; III, 8, 8; Tibullus I, 10, 61–62 (cf. below, note 30); Horace, *Carm.* I, 17, 27–29. The subject of Menander's *Perikeiromene* is illustrated by Goffredo Coppola (*Menandro,* Torino, 1927, p. 87) with an interesting parallel:

"Lo sfregio del taglio dei cappelli si può paragonare a quello che l'amante nella camorra napoletana si crede in diritto di fare alla donna che lo tradisce, deturpandole il viso con un colpo di rasoio. I due sfregi, s'intende, sono identici pel valore che essi hanno per l'amore, che i più delle volte le donne aman volentieri chi con un atto di violenza mostra di comprenderne la debolezza."

26 (p. 19). Ovid frequently illustrates the appearance of a person by comparing him to a character from legend. The reference seems pointless to us, but it would evoke a definite image in the mind of Ovid's original reader, who had seen many wall paintings on which the familiar stories were rendered in set traditional types and patterns.

27 (p. 19). According to Vergil, *Aen.* II, 402–403, Cassandra was dragged from the temple *passis crinibus* (cf. also *Am.* I, 9, 38). While Ovid had the *Aeneid* in mind when referring to Cassandra (17–18), he probably thought of Catullus' *carm.* 64 for Ariadne (15–16).

28 (p. 19). All the three examples from legend (13–18) extol the charming looks of the poet's mistress, but only the first does no more than that. The other two, far from being repetitious and gratuitous, add delicate sentimental touches to the picture, on an ascending emotional scale. While the second example sympathizes with the lady's cruel disappointment, the third worships her as a hallowed being, desecrated by profane hands. Like the examples of Ajax (7), Orestes (9), and Diomede (31), those of Ariadne and Cassandra exaggerate the poet's misdeed.

29 (p. 19). Or: his own Venus (line 32).

30 (p. 19). The two couplets 45–48 seem to me out of place; this speculation is foreign to the mood in which the rest is conceived. Ovid is here succumbing to the influence of his predecessor Tibullus. In I, 10, 53–68, Tibullus is praising peace in contrast to war, and the amorous fight in contrast to bloody battle. He wonders how far the chastising may properly go. Beating the girl would, so he argues, be sacrilegious; one ought to do no more than rip her blouse to pieces or tear her hair, and it is an ideal relationship when the man is able to draw tears from his lady by his anger alone. Tibullus preceded Ovid also in sketching the aftermath of the excess, with the girl crying and the man cursing his own hands (55 f.). The invention of the pattern, however, was not Tibullus' either. Menander's *Perikeiromene* opens with both the man (lines 52–54) and the girl (68–70) weeping, after he had cut off her hair in a fit of jealousy.

Roman erotic elegy was greatly indebted to Greek New Comedy, as Friedrich Leo has pointed out (*Plautinische Forschungen,* 2d ed., pp. 143–148; cf. also A. L. Wheeler, "Erotic Teaching in Roman Elegy and the Greek Sources," *Class. Philol.* [Chicago] 5, 1910, pp. 440–450, and 6, 1911, pp. 66–77). It was, however, not merely through the medium of books that Roman youth became familiar with Greek ways of love. Either in Athens, where many Romans spent a happy time, or at Rome itself, where many Greek women lived with their Greek relatives and friends, Greek mistresses would initiate awkward young Romans in the Greek code of love, the Greek gamut of sentiments, and the Greek diversity of passionate incidents. Among Greek surroundings, the young man learned through personal experience how to act and to speak, how to suffer and to enjoy, in the Greek style. (In *Ars Amat.* II, 122, Ovid advises the lover to perfect himself in Greek as well as Latin eloquence in order to keep alive the affection of his mistress; this shows that even in Rome love had often to be made in Greek.)

31 (p. 20). The tears had been pent up (*suspensae diu* 57), as it were, as long as the lady was frozen with terror (cf. *Metam.* 13, 539–541). The simile of melting snow, for cold numbness giving way to grief with tears flowing freely, stems from the *Odyssey*, 19, 205–209. Ovid used the simile again, but with a different slant, in *Po.* I, 1, 67–68.

32 (p. 20). Several times Ovid concludes an elegy with lines more sober or lenient than the rest of the poem: the tension is relieved (I, 7); the illusion vanishes (*The Dawn,* I, 13); or the indignation relents (II, 14; I, 10, see p. 29).

33 (p. 21). For the notion that the hands are slaves of the person, cf. the Hypermestra epistle, *Her.* XIV, 59–60: *Manus haec ... morte foret dominae sanguinolenta suae.* In that epistle, Ovid uses the motif of the hands in a manner very similar to that of *Am.* I, 7. The epistle begins and ends with Hypermestra's hands in shackles (lines 3 and 131); the writer mentions her own hand again and again and describes it as almost a murderer (lines 5, 8, 19, 50, 56, 76); and at the peripety of the narrative, precisely as in *Am.* I, 7, 57–66, tears begin to flow and the intended victim's arms are mentioned for the first time (66–70). The pattern could not have been so closely duplicated by the author unless it had a certain significance in the first place, which justifies our calling attention to it.

34 (p. 21). In a preceding distich, Ovid's concept was still conventional (*Ante meos umeris vellem cecidisse lacertos; utiliter potui parte carere mei* 23–24) and the poet was abreast with Tibullus (*optarim non habuisse manus* I, 6, 74); but with *Quid mihi vobiscum* (27) he has advanced beyond his predecessor's point of view.

35 (p. 21). For the climax *tears: blood* cf., e.g., *Her.* VII, 188: *ensem, qui iam pro lacrimis sanguine tinctus erit.*

36 (p. 21). Unlike the Ovid of *Am.* I, 7, 27, the Sophoclean Ajax did not think of disavowing his former self and detaching himself from the action he had committed in his insanity; nor did the Hercules of the *Trachiniae* (1091 ff.) repudiate his own arms when they had become powerless, but on the contrary addressed them with the words: "You are the very same that overcame the Nemean lion."

37 (p. 21). It is one thing, however, that the self of a person is in a flux, and another that it is merged in another self. While examples of the former occurrence, which may arise from a great variety of causes, are frequent in Ovid's poetry, those of the latter are rare because that experience comes to pass with full force only when a lover is in an ecstatic frame of mind such as Ovid has not often occasion to describe. (For the exceptional character of the elegy I, 7 see below, p. 188, note 63.) The parallels to *Am.* I, 7, 60 which I have at hand are these. Laodamia, who stands in dread that her husband may be killed in the war, fears *ne meus ex illo corpore sanguis eat, Her.* XIII, 80. (Expressions like *Metam.* 13, 495, *video tuum, mea vulnera, pectus,* are more remotely parallel.) Alcyone, mourning for her husband who was drowned at sea, says: *Nunc absens perii, iactor quoque fluctibus absens, et sine me me pontus habet, Metam.* 11, 700. (For an example of a playful merging of identities, in *Am.* III, 2, see p. 24). In the fable of Hermaphroditus and Salmacis (*Metam.* 4, 285–388, see pp. 88–89), the woman coalesces into one being with the man she loves. It may well be that it was Ovid who invented the miraculous merging of the lovers; all the other authors who refer to it have the story from him (cf. Jessen in *R.-E.* 8, 717).

38 (p. 21). Or, for that matter, whether we like or dislike the wording of the notorious line *semibovemque virum semivirumque bovem* (*Ars Amat.* II, 24). The phrasing pointedly indicates that the fruit of an unnatural union between bull and woman (cf. *conceptum crimine matris* 23) was a monstrous combination of two natures, both of which had an equal claim on his identity. Similarly, the phrasing in *Her.* II, 70: *tauri mixtaque forma viri* describes the two components of the Minotaur as combining, not into one being, but only into a "compound shape," while in *Her.* X Ovid describes the Minotaur with the circumlocutions *parte virum parte bovem* (102) and *taurique virique* (127). Thus the obnoxious line is only one of four instances in which Ovid, by means of different verbal figures, points out the divided identity of the monster, and it follows that it was not the playful ring of the words alone that caused him to give his verse the shape to which his critics objected (see above, p. 172, note 14).

39 (p. 21). See pp. 79–85; 88–89; 99.

40 (p. 22). Ovid is so persuasive partly because he knows how to predicate his arguments not on his own frame of mind but on that of the other person. One instance is *Am.* II, 8. Ovid is having a flirtation with his lady's chambermaid Cypassis and has succeeded in talking Corinna out of her suspicion against the two (II, 7). In the elegy II, 8 he makes it appear to Cypassis that it was she who by her awkward behavior had almost given away their secret when he saved the situation by his presence of mind and a clever denial; and presently he demands that she reward her benefactor (*pro quibus officiis,* 21) by giving him the coming night, or else he will go tell Corinna everything. Thus, viewing the situation with the eyes of Cypassis, he brazenly ignores that he had only been serving his own ends and would hurt himself if he carried out his threat.

41 (p. 22). Take for example *Am.* I, 6, where Ovid tries to insinuate himself into the favor of the concierge by a comprehending sympathy with that man's concerns (cf. line 1 *indignum;* 19–20; 23; 41–42; 45–46). The leading characters of Sophoclean tragedy, on the other hand, never take an interest in the petty problems of those in lowly stations, such as the messengers.

42 (p. 23). It would take more than one man's lifetime to work out the history in antiquity of the human self and its relations to things and other selves. In an early phase, a community between persons was possible only so far as their concerns were bound up with one another. It was out of the question that their souls would meet (much less that they would merge); all that could be hoped for was that their designs headed for the same objectives (cf. Bruno Snell, *Gnomon* 7, 1931, pp. 84–85).

43 (p. 25). A strange sense of propriety forbade the Romans to publicize even the most innocent details of their family life (hence the colorless praise of the virtuous wife in Propertius' Cornelia elegy, IV, 11), while extramarital love could be depicted with no restraint whatever. The taboo (for once daringly broken by Propertius in his elegy IV, 3) was not in force in Greece; Xenophon, for instance, depicts in his *Oeconomicus* (VII, 35–42) the activities of a good housewife in a charming passage which culminates in the remark that the master of the house will become the lady's servant. Tibullus imitated the passage (the young Cicero found it worth his while to translate the *Oeconomicus,* cf. *De Off.* II, 87); he speaks, however, not of his wife but of his mistress (I, 5, 21–30). In Ovid's *Amores* there is just the barest hint that even in regular marriage the lovers can expect experiences similar to those of which the book

is full. In the opening poem of the Second Book (II, 1, 5) the author writes: *Me legat in sponsi facie non frigida virgo.* Considering the conventions, this remark was rather risqué.

44 (p. 25). It is well known that the term *vir* is indefinite; either the husband is meant, or the man who at the time is the lady's recognized lover (cf. *Ars Amat.* III, 483–484). The parents or other relatives of either lover are hardly ever mentioned (I, 8, 91); the lovers are too much engrossed with themselves to waste any thought on them.

45 (p. 25). The *Amores* concerns itself very little with anything that has no direct bearing on the sentimental issues with which it deals. The modern reader feels sometimes annoyed by the author's exclusive concentration on his main theme, and heaves a sigh of relief when once, by exception, he is permitted to visualize a concrete setting of rural scenery and to sympathize with the lover's deep attachment to his paternal soil (II, 16). This concentration in the *Amores* on the lover's narrow purview contrasts with the attitude of Attic New Comedy to which Roman love poetry was deeply indebted (see above, p. 181, note 30). Comedy always showed up the monomaniac lovers against a background of sober reality.

46 (p. 25). It is therefore a mistake to call the women prostitutes. Ovid took no pleasure in favors accorded for foreign reasons. For the slave prostitutes, who were not masters of their own bodies, he had nothing but pity (*Am.* I, 10, 21–24). In addition to resenting any admixture of the mercenary (see p. 29), he disliked to have his mistress submit to him in mere dutiful compliance (*Ars Amat.* II, 687–688), and he detested the use of drugs because they interfere with the free will (see p. 62). He scorned homosexual love, in which the one partner is no more than a victim to the other's desire (*Ars Amat.* II, 684).

47 (p. 26). *Am.* II, 12 reflects the poet's first conquest of Corinna; but it is preceded immediately by an elegy which assumes that he has been united to her for a long time (II, 11). In plot chronology, II, 12 should likewise have precedence over I, 5 and over II, 7 and 8.

48 (p. 26). The only instances in the *Amores* are the groups I, 1–3; II, 2 and 3; II, 7 and 8, with an equal number of couplets; II, 9 and 9 b; II, 13 and 14.

49 (p. 27). The Romans, ruling as they did the whole Mediterranean world, and year in year out sending their leading men to its four corners to enlarge, protect, and govern their empire, ought to have been interested, at least, in geography. And yet Strabo attests that even in that factual and practical field they had little initiative and curiosity (cf. Strabo 3, 166; *Neue Jahrb. f. Wissenschaft und Jugendbildung* 9, 1933, p. 37).

50 (p. 27). Cf. Horace, *Epist.* II, 1, 117. However, not long ago Cicero, one of the finest connoisseurs in some fields of literature, had remarked that if the span of his life were doubled he would still refuse to waste his time in reading the Greek lyric poets (Seneca, *Epist.* 49, 5).

51 (p. 28). Some aspects of the history of the motif are clarified by Alfons Spies, in *Militat omnis amans,* Diss. Tübingen, 1930. Among the things the author has overlooked is the change the motif underwent on passing from New Comedy to Roman elegy. Athens was conducting no wars of its own, and a young Athenian who joined a foreign army was something of a prodigal son. For this reason, the character of a soldier in New Comedy served often as an object of ridicule, and scenes like IV, 7 in Terence's *Eunuchus,* or 217 ff. in Menander's *Perikeiromene,* poked fun at a soldierly way of conducting a love affair. In Rome, by contrast, an army officer of good family enjoyed a high social standing, and when the Roman elegists elaborate the analogies between lovemaking and soldiering they do so in order playfully to justify and glorify their own avocation.

52 (p. 28). The idea that love is self-sufficient and requires no assistance from outside recurs in the Leander Epistle; see p. 50.

53 (p. 28). In *Am.* II, 10, 31–38, the death in battle of a soldier and the death in the waves of a greedy merchant are contrasted with a lover's life and death in the pursuit of his occupation (the lover's death is added for the sake of symmetry only). The passage is interesting because of its close parallelism to Semonides of Amorgus frag. 1, where lines 13–16 speak in the same way of the soldier and the merchant, while lines 22–24, in all probability, lead to the praise, by way of contrast, of the pleasures of love. Thus this pattern of Ovid's can be traced as far back as the seventh century B.C.

54 (p. 28). For the comparison between mercenary soldiering and prostitution, cf. also *Am.* I, 10, 17–20.

55 (p. 28). For the phrasing of *Am.* III, 8, 55–56, Nicolaus Deratani (*Artis rhetor. in Ovidi carm....perspicuae capita quaedam,* Moscow, 1916, p. 83, according to H. Magnus, *Philol. Wochenschr.* 42, 1922, p. 943) compares Latro (Seneca, *Controv.* II, 1, 17): *Census senatorium gradum ascendit, census equitem Romanum a plebe discernit, census in castris ordinem promovet, census iudices in foro legit.* (Cf. p. 170, note 3.)

56 (p. 28). In his passionate protest Ovid forgets to explain of whom he is speaking, but the reader sees immediately that he means the people at large who believe in money and power.

57 (p. 29). The first four couplets are solemn and lofty in the grand

Propertian manner (cf. Prop. I, 3, 1–8); then suddenly the tone changes with dramatic abruptness.

58 (p. 29). For the artistic effect of the concluding couplet see above, p. 182, note 32.

59 (p. 30). Cf. *Her.* X, 79–80 and XIII, 150.

60 (p. 30). When a man says that he has remained quite sober at a banquet (II, 5, 13–14), we know what we have to think. We are to understand that Ovid had a cup or two too much and believes he has seen things which were only figments of his imagination. The condition of the author also explains the confused nature of his morose musings. In an unaccountable manner, the elegy alternates between direct address to the lady and narrative in the third person, and in lines 29–52 the poet builds up a charming scene (a milder duplicate of I, 7) which seems to form, but cannot possibly be, an immediate sequel to the banquet scene (12–28).—In line 29, *Quo nunc mea gaudia differs* is hardly correct. *Mea gaudia differs* means "you delay my delights," cf. III, 6, 87; *Epist.* XVIII, 3, etc.; *quo differs* means "for what purpose do you delay?" cf. *Metam.* 13, 518; and *quo nunc mea gaudia differs* means (if anything at all) "why do you not now accord me your favors?" In the sense required here, "you transfer" or "bestow," *defers* is the correct word, while *differo* with a similar meaning is extremely rare (Hyginus, *Fab.* 63: *disco quem ventus distulit in caput Acrisii*).

61 (p. 30). Cf. *Epist.* XV (XVI), 286.

62 (p. 30). Line 5 says: "She does not sin, whoever can deny having sinned." Another time, Ovid sets up a very different tenet because the situation is different. I am referring to III, 4, 3–5 (for 1–2 cf. Prop. II, 6, 39 f.), where he tries to persuade the present keeper of his mistress to give her more freedom and unscrupulously uses for his ulterior purposes a remarkably fine moral argument (III, 4, 3–5): "Only that woman is modest [so he now contends] who is so even if she has nothing to fear from a transgression; she who commits no sin because it is not feasible, does commit the sin. However well you protect her body, her mind remains immodest." The passage seems strangely to anticipate a verse from the Sermon on the Mount (Matt. 5:28): "But I say unto you, that whosoever looketh on a woman to lust after her, hath committed adultery with her already in his heart." Ovid was here evidently influenced by Stoic doctrines, and it is well known that Stoicism had some things in common with Christianity.—Ovid's reasoning has a close parallel in a fragment preserved by Jerome, *Adv. Jovinianum* I, 47 (= Migne, *Patrol. Lat.*, Vol. 23, p. 277 B–C): *Verum quid prodest etiam diligens custodia, cum uxor servari*

impudica non possit, pudica non debeat? Infida enim custos est castitatis necessitas; et illa vere pudica dicenda est, cui licuit peccare si voluit. Jerome says that he is quoting from the "aureolus Theophrasti liber de Nuptiis," but the authorship of the fragment is disputed (cf. Otto Regenbogen, *R.-E.* Suppl. 7, 1487).—In the 13th century, Pseudo-Heinrich von Morungen recast the ideas of *Am.* III, 14, 1–18 thus (*Minnesangs Frühling* 137, 4–9):

> Wê der huote die man reinen wîben tuot;
> huote guote frouwen machet wankelmuot.
> Man sol frouwen schouwen unde lâzen âne twanc.
> Ich sach daz ein sieche verboten wazzer tranc.

63 (p. 31). The whole elegy III, 14 ranks with I, 7 as the most emotional of the collection; they betray a rare abandonment to passionate sentiment. The poet was perhaps still in his teens when he wrote them. The first edition of the *Amores* may have contained more poems in the same vein, but Ovid purged them out in his maturer years because he then considered them as too eccentric, letting stand only the two best.—For a number of very good observations on the elegy III, 14 see Fr. Lenz, *Studi Ital. Filol. Class.* 12 (1935), pp. 227–235.

64 (p. 31). These lines are the most exceptional in the exceptional elegy, but otherwise there is no reason for condemning them. Jealousy is able to flood a lover's heart with a sweeping wave of desire, cf. *Her.* VI, 76 (Hypsipyle): *Cor dolet, atque ira mixtus abundat amor,* and *Ars Amat.* III, 597–598. True enough, the reaction is not sensible; yet it is an established fact that love is not reasonable, and Ovid, for one, informs us that Madness walks in the train of Love. But his philological critics will not believe their poet; they try to rationalize or athetize the *furor.* Palmer was inclined to throw out the admirable pentameter we quoted from the *Heroides,* and many scholars declared the powerful couplets *Am.* III, 14, 37–40, or the second of them, as interpolated. The authority for condemning the second distich is Lucian Müller (*Philologus* 11, 1856, p. 88), and it seems worth while to quote verbatim the puny reasons he has to offer: "Cur tunc potissimum amaret, cum Corinnae perfidiam nosceret? Dein *odi frustra* nihil potest significare nisi *debeo amare,* at ineptissime tum adicitur *quod amare necesse 'st.* Deinde quomodo potest optare ut sit mortuus, cum iam v. 37 dixerit se mori? Nimis celeriter a mortuis resurgit. Quare versus 39–40 haud dubie pro glossemate habendi, orti e periphrasi distichi prioris." We may well wonder who might have been capable of such a "periphrasis." Not even external evidence is lack-

ing to confirm the authenticity of the four lines. For the *tunc* pattern in 39–40, and the *morior* in 37, cf. Tib. II, 6, 51–53; for line 37, Ovid, *Fasti* 2, 753; for the form and sentiment of line 40, *Her.* XII (Medea), 116 and 121–122.

65 (p. 31). Cf. also II, 1, 19–20.

66 (p. 32). Cf. J. F. D'Alton, *Roman Literary Theory and Criticism,* London, 1931, p. 413.

67 (p. 32). It has been remarked above (pp. 9–10) that poetry enjoyed no adequate standing in Rome; most people rated it as an idle amusement, good enough for dallying away leisure hours but unworthy of earnest engrossment. The same can be said with respect to love. Roman erotic poetry cannot be properly understood unless we realize its very iniquitous position. A triple handicap was imposed on it: the disparagement of poetry; the disparagement of love; and third, the prohibition against concerning itself with the affection between a man and a woman who hoped to be married, or were married, to each other (see p. 184, note 43). Nevertheless, Roman love-poetry survived and throve, though not unscarred, for two reasons. First, erotic poetry was the one form for the expression of sensibility (see above, pp. 27–28); and second, amor vincit omnia.

68 (p. 32). II, 1, 11 ff. It is quite possible that Ovid actually tried his hand at the ambitious project, but gave it up when he found that it transcended his poetic powers (cf. *Tr.* II, 333–334); he may have experimented with a number of themes and styles to make sure which were best suited to his talent and inclinations (cf. I, 1). But I can see no basis for any further conjectures about Ovid's attempted *Gigantomachia* (cf. S. G. Owen, *P. Ovidi Nasonis Tristium Liber Secundus,* Oxford, 1924, pp. 63–81); in fact, it seems to me improbable that, as Owen suggests, Ovid publicly recited his fragmentary *Gigantomachia,* and that the cautious Emperor, informed of it, was offended with the manner in which the poet symbolically glorified Augustus' victory over the revolutionary forces; or again, that two short fragments of 4 and 2 words respectively (nos. 12 and 13 Lenz) belong to the *Gigantomachia.*

69 (p. 33). Ovid's phrase *verbosae leges* receives substance from a passage in Cicero's oration *Pro Murena* in which the orator pokes fun at the pompous and abstruse verbosity (*satis verbose* § 25) of legal formulae.

70 (p. 34). The incident reminds one of the Candaules story (Herodotus I, 8–12); also cf. Ovid's *Ars Amat.* I, 739–754. Even closer is the resemblance to an epigram ascribed to Plato (*Anthol. Palat.* 7, 100). For a parallel from the *Amores* see III, 11, 19–20.

71 (p. 35). The degradation of love progressed from Propertius to Ovid, but not in all respects. Ovid scorned homosexual relationships, but Propertius indulged in them. The story Propertius tells in I, 10, 1-12 is more shameless than anything to be found in Ovid's works, and one would wish that Propertius had rather complied with the directions Ovid gives in *Ars Amat.* II, 601-640.

NOTES TO CHAPTER 4, THE "HEROIDES," PP. 36-46

1 (p. 36). The standing reference to the *suasoria* would have more point if the *suasoria* shared with the *Heroides* some of their major characteristics; that is, for instance, if the speaker of a *suasoria* were supposed to be deeply in love with the person whom he is trying to influence; if he were supposed to be in a dire predicament himself; if, instead of giving disinterested advice for the benefit of the other, he were unburdening his own cares, pleading his own cause, and making his own claims on the person he addresses; and if it were required that the *suasoria* be ineffectual. More pertinent is the comparison of the *Heroides* with the monologues and arias of tragedy; Ovid himself recommends that these elegies be "sung with mimic voice" (*Ars Amat.* III, 345: *composita cantetur Epistula voce:* for *componere* in the sense of "adjust one's voice, etc., to the part one is to play," cf. Tibullus [Sulpicia] III, 13, 9, and Suetonius, *Calig.* 50, 1 *componere voltum;* Quintilian, *Institut.* I, 11, 19 *componere gestum,* etc.).

2 (p. 37). The epistle of Hypermestra (XIV) seems to be an exception because tradition has it that she was afterward united with Lynceus; but the details of the story which Ovid had in mind are obscure, and there is room for the possibility of a complication the shadow of which darkened the picture in a similar fashion as in the Briseis epistle (III; see p. 37).— With respect to the 8th epistle (Hermione), tradition is likewise unanimous in giving the story a happy ending; eventually, after the death of Pyrrhus, Orestes remarried Hermione. But the precise background of Ovid's epistle is again unknown. According to "practically all poets," Pyrrhus was killed in a brawl with the Delphians (cf. *schol.* Pindar, *Nem.* 7, 62 a and b); in which case Hermione's deliverance from her marriage to Pyrrhus was not brought about by Orestes and her letter was useless. (It is true that in Euripides' *Andromache* [996-1006; 1114-1116] Orestes has his hand in the assassination of Pyrrhus, but we can disregard that version because Ovid's epistle cannot possibly be based on it; certain crucial points disagree.)

3 (p. 38). Self-deception and inconsistency is what we must expect from

these pathetic Ovidian epistles. Even Dido and Phyllis implore the addressee as if they had not given up hope entirely, although they say that they have. Only Canace's letter (XI) is conceived, for good reasons, in a spirit of unmitigated despondency.

4 (p. 38). In V, 1–4 (si sinis), the writer wonders likewise whether the addressee will care to read a letter coming from her.

5 (p. 38). It follows that Ovid probably invented the idea that Phaedra wrote such a letter. This disposes of any conclusions with reference to the plot of Euripides' first *Hippolytus*.

6 (p. 38). The resemblance was even more striking when the poetic epistles were not yet collected in a book, but circulated, as was the custom, one at a time, among Ovid's friends.

7 (p. 38). For the notion of the addressee watching the writer with the eye of his mind cf. VII, 183.

8 (p. 40). In XIII, 104, I suggest the emendation *celer* for *dolor*, together with *veni* for *venis* which was conjectured by Bentley:

101   Cum venies, remoque move veloque carinam,
                inque tuo celerem litore siste gradum;
             sive latet Phoebus seu terris altior exstat,
104   tu mihi luce *celer,* tu mihi nocte *veni*—
             nocte tamen quam luce magis; nox grata puellis
                quarum suppositus colla lacertus habet.

The notion of *dolor* is incompatible with the context, since the pentameter leads up to the description of a blissful night of love. For *nox grata puellis* cf. *Am.* I, 13, 9, *ingrata puellis,* scil. *Aurora* (likewise, in line 117, *bene iunctus* echoes the *bene iuncta* of *Am.* I, 13, 6); for *lacertus suppositus* under the lady's neck, which can only be her lover's arm, cf. [XV] Sappho, 127–128. The repetition of the word *celer,* along with that of the verb *venire,* does not seem objectionable, because the writer is elaborating the idea of the preceding distich: "Come as fast as you can—come fast, be it day or night—come even faster at night than by daytime!" For a still more pointed repetition of *celer venias* cf. V, 57–58.

9 (p. 41). Hypermestra, a virgin bride (XIV, 55; cf. *schol.* Pindar, *Nem.* 10, 10 b), is too bashful to betray her love and addresses Lynceus not as husband but as cousin (*frater*).—Unlike the Byblis of *Metam.* IX, Canace (XI) is represented as childishly naïve, ignorant, and docile; she never understands what is happening to her, and finally kills herself because her father told her so.—Phaedra, on the other hand, makes a shameless offer and knows it (IV, 155), but nevertheless she uses no

immodest language.—The most risqué couplet (XIII, 115–116) is set down by a young bride picturing to her husband the bliss that awaits them on his return.

10 (p. 42). For *tango* (89) in the sense of 'make an impression, arouse interest, *moveo*,' cf. *Her.* 5, 81 (in an identical phrase, *nec me tua regia tangit*); 7, 11; *Metam.* 2, 293; 527, etc.). The immigrant's bath (90) symbolizes his permanent establishment in his new residence; it is equivalent to "shaking off the dust" of the old country. See Univ. Calif. Publ. Class. Philol. 12 (1943), pp. 293–294.

11 (p. 43). A. Palmer declares the distich 89–90 to be very frigid in expression and is inclined to consider it spurious. The couplet seems frigid because Ovid's Phyllis, too proud to beg for love, charges Demophon with spurning, not her hand, but the crown and country she offered him. Throughout the epistle, she appeals to her lover's sense of honor rather than his affection. She is also too discreet to describe to him the loneliness of her nights, beyond mentioning that when the stars shed their cold light she is used to explore the weather in the hope that it may be favorable for his return (123 ff.).

12 (p. 43). Thus with Heinsius, who wrote *si* for *nisi;* the next couplet explains the idea further. Soon Phyllis adds, in restrained and dignified words claiming for their relationship the status of wedlock:

> Promissus socios ubi nunc Hymenaeus in annos,
> qui mihi coniugii sponsor et obses erat?
> (33 f.)

What is the precise meaning of *sponsor et obses?* The hexameter says that their association was meant to be a permanent one; the marriage, however, had been contracted informally (so the pentameter goes on to indicate), and there was no one present to guarantee its validity (*sponsor*) except Hymenaeus, that is, the consummation, celebrated with the intent of permanence, of their love. Hymenaeus served at the same time also as "hostage" because her desertion by Demophon would kill the legality of their intimacy.

13 (p. 44). In one respect Ovid actually improves on Homer. The exemplum of Meleager who was eventually persuaded by his wife to give up his wrath, makes a closer parallel when laid in Briseis' mouth (91–98) than in that of the old gentleman Phoenix.

14 (p. 45). The *Amores* contains a number of elegies conceived in a similar spirit, the poem on *The Dawn* (I, 13), for instance, which consists, as we have seen, of entreaties directed to one who cannot be assumed

to listen to them. Other examples are *Am.* I, 6; I, 12, 7–30; II, 3; II, 9; III, 6. There is, however, no παρακλαυσίθυρον in the collection.

15 (p. 46). For Ovid's claim to have invented the genre, see *Ars Amat.* III, 346. It would detract little from his originality if, as seems to be the case, Propertius wrote his one poetic epistle (IV, 3) before Ovid had begun to compose his fifteen verse letters. True enough, the Propertius elegy resembles in many respects some of the epistles from the *Heroides,* and it is a very fine piece of poetry at that. But Arethusa is not a woman of legend; the reader does not know what is in store for her, and that shadow of ironic or tragic futility which is essential for Ovid's *Heroides* is absent.

NOTES TO CHAPTER 5, THE "MEDEA," PP. 46–47

1 (p. 46). The chronology I have adopted is based on the following facts and considerations.

a) Ovid was born in March, 43 B.C.

b) Ovid began to recite his own verse about 25 B.C. (see p. 175, note 1); about 20 B.C. he gave up his political career and began to live for poetry alone (above, p. 8). The first poems he composed for publication were erotic elegies (cf. *Tr.* IV, 10, 57–60, etc.). It follows that he began seriously to work in the line of the *Amores* no later than about 20 B.C., but possibly as early as about 25 B.C.

c) *Am.* III, 9 was written in 19 B.C. and immediately put into private circulation.

d) *Am.* I, 15 was written after the death of Vergil and Tibullus, and before the death of Horace, that is, between 19 and 8 B.C.

e) *Am.* I, 14, 45–49 was written either in (or shortly after) 16 B.C., or at the time of Drusus' campaigns against the Sugambri (13–10 B.C.).

f) The first edition of the *Amores,* in five books, was nearing completion when Ovid wrote the *Heroides* and made the first tentative studies for his *Medea* (*Am.* II, 18; III, 1). For details, see text and notes of this chapter.

g) When Ovid gave out the first edition of the *Amores,* he took leave of elegy (*Am.* III, 1; III, 15) in order to devote himself to tragedy; it follows that the *Heroides* (I–XV) was published before the first edition of the *Amores.*

h) The interval was probably not long, since Ovid had already decided to switch over to tragedy while he was still preparing for publication both *Amores* and *Heroides;* thus he must have been anxious to be done with both of them as soon as possible. He lingered for a while (*Am.* II, 18;

III, 1), but certainly not for many years; in the meantime, the *Medea* was already taking shape.

i) The earliest possible date for the first edition of the *Amores* is about 15 B.C. (see point *e*).

j) The latest possible date for the first edition of the *Amores* can only be arrived at by a bold and rough guess. The three books we possess contain 50–51 elegies; the five-book edition may therefore have had about 85 elegies. Ovid began to work on it no later than about 20 B.C (point *b*); if from then on he produced at the slow rate of 12 acceptable elegies a year on an average, the five books were completed within 7 years, in about 13 B.C.; that is, 6 years after *Am*. III, 9 had been written (point *c*).

k) If Ovid, after publication of the *Amores* in five books, worked on the *Medea* for 2 to 5 more years, the tragedy was published between about 13 B.C. and 8 B.C. (cf. points *i* and *j*).

l) The second edition of the *Amores,* in three books, was published before the year A.D. 2, because it is mentioned in *Ars* III, 343 (provided that *tribus libris* is the correct reading).

m) Some of the foregoing conclusions would have to be modified if the elegies *Am*. I, 14; II, 18; III, 1; and III, 15 had not at all, or in part not, or not in the present form, been contained in the first edition. Even then, however, point (*j*) would remain as it stands. In points (*f*)–(*i*) and (*k*) the second edition would possibly have to be substituted for the first. The only important consequence would be that the completion of the *Medea* (point *k*) may have followed upon the second, rather than the first, edition of the *Amores,* so that the tragedy could have been published as late as 2 B.C. It cannot be dated after the *Ars Amat.,* because it was from his personal love poetry rather than from the didactic books on love that Ovid turned to tragedy (cf. *Am*. II, 18 and III, 1, 15–22).

n) The possibilities mentioned in point (*m*) are remote, because the preface to the second edition does not give the impression that Ovid had added new elegies or tampered with the old ones. He only says that he reduced the bulk by two-fifths, which seems to mean that he omitted two elegies out of every five.

o) I have therefore based my discussion of Ovid's development on points (*a*)–(*k*). The points (*j*) and (*k*) are, of course, open to argument; but I think that my maximum figures are generous. If they are still too low, the interval between the completion of the *Medea* and work on the *Ars* was shorter or nonexistent.

2 (p. 46). The sequence seems logical: the young author had begun with personal verse, telling of his own experiences; then, without inter-

rupting his work on the *Amores*, he also composed the *Heroides*, which were more exalted in style and more dramatic in subject; and finally he relinquished elegy entirely and turned to real drama.

3 (p. 46). For the precise meaning of the phrase *tragoedia crevit*, in *Am*. II, 18, 13-14, compare *Metam*. 1, 403. There the word *creverunt* is used to express that the rocks had begun to assume, but had not yet quite attained, human shape; at this stage they resembled, so the author explains, unfinished marble statues. Thus *cura nostra tragoedia crevit* means that a tragedy had begun to take shape under the hands of the poet. Furthermore, the future participle in line 4, *ausurus grandia*, indicates that the drama was no more than a project when Amor interfered with Ovid's work on it.

4 (p. 47). Cf. *Tr*. II, 519-520 and V, 7, 25-26. The latter passage shows that even after Ovid's relegation his poetry was acted and danced by mimes. For dance recitals of love scenes in the theater cf. *Rem*. 751-756 and Ludw. Friedländer, *Darstellungen aus der Sittengeschichte Roms*, 9th ed., Vol. 2, Leipzig, 1920, pp. 127 ff. Ovid's *Heroides* were especially suited to being sung and danced (see p. 190, note 1).

NOTES TO CHAPTER 6, MORE EPISTLES OF FAMOUS LOVERS,
PP. 48-53

1 (p. 48). Only for reasons of convenience has the discussion of the later epistles been assigned this place in the book. We have no means of determining the exact date at which Ovid composed the double letters, but it can hardly be doubted that he did it at some time between the publication of the *Amores* and A.D. 8. On the one hand, *Am*. II, 18 mentions none of the double epistles; on the other, Ovid could not have composed the epistles of Paris and Helen after he had been punished for having written poetry for the instruction of prospective adulterers. Max Pohlenz, *Hermes* 48 (1913), pp. 3-7, suggests that epistles XV and XVI (XVI and XVII) were composed while Ovid worked out *Metam*. 12, but his arguments do not seem conclusive; nor can we use as chronological criteria the similarity between *Ars Amat*. II, 359-372 and *Epist*. XV (XVI), 299-316; XVI (XVII), 159-162, or the fact that in *Ars Amat*. I, 457 the inscription on the apple thrown by Acontius is styled a "letter" and mentioned as an example of a love letter in a similar fashion as in the Cydippe epistle XX, 145-150. In their metrical form, the six epistles seem closer to Ovid's later works, but the divergence is very slight; the three instances of the petameter ending on a four-syllable word may be due to a mere whim (cf. S. B. Clark, Harvard Studies in Class. Philol. 19, 1908, p. 127).

2 (p. 48). The title *Heroides* was therefore no longer fitting; perhaps Ovid renamed the enlarged collection *Epistulae*. The authentic titles of Ovid's *Heroic Epistles, Face Cosmetics,* and *Art of Love* cannot be made out for certain. This is embarrassing for the conscientious scholar, but otherwise a matter of slight import.

3 (p. 48). Only one of the six replies, the letter of Odysseus, was not bound to ruin the artistic effect of its counterpart, and only that one was later mentioned again by Ovid (*Po.* IV, 16, 13-14).

4 (p. 49). Cf. also *Ars* I, 669-672 with *Epist.* XVI, 29, and 673 ff. with *Epist.* XVI, 185-188; *Ars* I, 611-614 with *Epist.* XVI, 36-40, etc.

5 (p. 49). See notes 7 and 9, below.

6 (p. 49). With respect to individual notions and phrases, we can compare, for instance, XVII, 174-179 with certain lines from the Narcissus story in the *Metamorphoses:* XVII, 174 resembles *Metam.* 3, 450 and 453; XVII, 177, *Metam.* 3, 372; XVII, 179, *Metam.* 3, 453 (*posse putes tangi*).

7 (p. 50). *Idem navigium, navita, vector ero.* Ovid had extolled once before in a similar manner the self-sufficiency of love, *Am.* II, 12, 14: *Ipse eques, ipse pedes, signifer ipse fui.* That line, however, was written in a more sportive mood (see above, p. 28), and for this reason we do not mind there the playful phrasing. In the Leander epistle, the taste of the conceit is debatable; certainly it does not happen to coincide with our own taste. But one should not mock at Ovid's "rhetoric" without giving a thought to the idea he expresses in so striking a fashion (cf. p. 183, note 38). Here, moreover, the poet has taken the precaution of leading up methodically to his conceit (145-147), and the notion of self-sufficiency underlies large parts of the elegy (see my paraphrase in the text above), although it is never, characteristically, enunciated in bald general terms.

In Musaeus' *Hero and Leander,* on the other hand, the idea that love is able to see itself through is once made explicit (196-201); in addition, there are traces of it, part of them faint, in other passages which have their parallels in Ovid's Leander epistle. Ovid's line *Idem navigium, navita, vector ero* (148) is duplicated by the Greek text in the form αὐτὸς ἐὼν ἐρέτης, αὐτόστολος, αὐτομάτη νηῦς (255). That verse, however, comes here rather abruptly, except for the remote preparation in 212, where the swimmer is styled a vessel freighted with love. In this connection Musaeus likens Hero's beacon to a lodestar (212-215; cf. also 6-10 and 306), just as Ovid does in lines 149-156 (for which see p. 176, note 9); but there is more force and feeling in Ovid's verses than in those of Musaeus. In Musaeus 149-156, Leander fortifies himself for his hazardous expedition by arguing that the fire of love within him ought to be more than a match to the water without; his abstract reasoning sounds "rhetorical" when compared to Ovid's lines 87–90 and 161–166. The idea of love's self-sufficiency is obliterated in Musaeus 239–241 ("Leander's love was rekindled together with Hero's beacon"), but it is patent in the context of Ovid's powerful words *Meus ignis in illo est* (85). Also interesting is a comparison between Musaeus 8–10 ("Hero's beacon deserves a place among the stars in the heavens") and Ovid's lines 168–169: Ovid takes a further step from his star simile (149–167) and makes Leander write that his lady deserves a place among the stars in the heavens (preluded by 153–154). There are more parallels between Ovid and Musaeus; evidently, both poets used the same model (cf. Georg Knaak, *Hero und Leander,* in *Festgabe für Franz Susemihl,* Leipzig, 1898, pp. 46–82). Compare, for instance, Ovid 39–44 with Musaeus 322.

8 (p. 50). This reminds us of the *Amores* (see p. 31), and so does the fact that Leander speaks of his arms as if they had a life of their own (20–22; 161–166), cf. pp. 20–21.

9 (p. 50). The fear is also paralleled in Musaeus, 243.

10 (p. 50). This is expressed with a fine zeugma, *deposito pariter cum veste timore.* With another zeugma, Leander complains that, while his and Hero's souls are united (125), the whims of the weather should be permitted to meddle with their happiness: *Cur ego confundar quotiens confunditur aequor?* (129; cf. also 172 *cumque mea fiunt turbida mente freta*), and Hero replies: *isdem corpus Leandri, spes mea pendet aquis* (XVIII, 149; for the simile cf. Pindar, *Oly.* 12, 5–6). Ovid is fond of that quick-witted figure of speech, the zeugma (for a list of a number of instances, see R. Ehwald on *Metam.* 9, 135), but, needless to say, he does not use it without proper discrimination. Rather than juggling words, he yokes together different aspects of the same fact, so as to impart a stereoscopic depth to the picture. Excellent examples are: *Herculis illam imperiis thalamoque animoque receperat Hyllus, Metam.* 9, 278; *et frustra coniunx oculis animoque Canentis exspectatus erat, Metam.* 14, 417; *attonitusque malis, exsul mentisque domusque, Metam.* 9, 409; *Laurea delapsa est audito crimine amantis et pariter voltusque deo plectrumque colorque excidit, Metam.* 2, 600 (cf. 3, 99–100; 4, 175; *Ars Amat.* 1, 551); *fulmen misit in aurigam pariterque animaque rotisque expulit, Metam.* 2, 312; *ille ferox ipsamque precesque reliquit, Metam.* 14, 377; *illato lumine, vidit et scelus et natam, Metam.* 10, 473; *Arcuit omnipotens, pariterque ipsosque nefasque sustulit, et pariter ...imposuit caelo, Metam.* 2, 505; *actaque magni Herculis implerant terras odiumque novercae, Metam.* 9, 134.

11 (p. 51). *Erimus plures* (154) can mean "we shall be dead," and in this sense all the three lines (154–156) will come true. This is in the manner of "tragic irony." The parallel Hero draws in 127–128 is likewise ominous, cf. Antipater of Thessalonica, *Anthol. Palat.* 9, 215.—For the omen of the lamp (151–152) cf. Agathias, *Anthol. Palat.* 5, 262 Stadtmüller (263 Dübner).

12 (p. 51). For the significance of the dream, 199–202, Knaak (see above, note 7) compares Artemidorus, *Onirocr.* II, 16 (p. 110, 18 Hercher) : Δελφὶς δὲ ἔξω θαλάσσης ὁρώμενος οὐκ ἀγαθός, τῶν γὰρ φιλτάτων τινὰ ἀποθανόντα σημαίνει.

13 (p. 51). In antiquity, the apple served as a symbol of love; cf. B. O. Foster, Harvard Stud. Class. Philol. 10 (1899), 39–55.

14 (p. 51). Or, rather, Cydippe read it aloud because her nurse, who had picked up the apple, was illiterate and asked her mistress to read the inscription to her. One shudders to think of the consequences if chance had willed it otherwise and the nurse had taken the oath.

15 (p. 51). For the popularity which the passage enjoyed cf. *Rem.* 381–382.

16 (p. 52). Ovid suppresses Acontius' withdrawal to the country and his love-lost address to the trees, and substitutes for them the lover's voyage to Naxus, his loafing around the door of Cydippe's house (XX, 31–36), and his entreaties to be admitted. Ovid's Acontius is more practical.

17 (p. 52). Acontius takes pains, however, to make it plain (XIX, 21–32) that he is not artful by nature or habit; it was his love which made him so; Love, ingenious as he is to further his own ends, gave him expert legal advice.—The syntactic difficulty we encounter in line 30, *consultoque fui iuris amore vafer,* results from the fact that we are compelled by our spelling to distinguish the affection *amor* from the god *Amor,* while Ovid was free to consider them as identic. Thus he uses here, as I take it, the instrumental ablative, *amore vafer fui* (no other construction was possible), and nevertheless adds the apposition *consulto iuris,* not to *amore* but to *Amore.*

18 (p. 52). Ovid's Cydippe discusses intelligently the juridical problem of her case (XX, 133–143) and denies that an oath is valid when there was no deliberate intent (*consilium prudensque animi sententia, iudicium* 137–138) to swear it. Acontius, on his part, holds the contrary theory (XIX, 27–30), according to which the words in themselves are binding (*verbis adstrinxit* 28). The argument reflects the dispute between the older, formalistic, school of jurists and those who took the intent (*animus*) into account (cf. Paulus, *Dig.* 44, 7, 3). It is well known that Ovid

had some juridical training (M. Pokrowskij, *Philologus* Suppl. 11, 1907–1910, pp. 353–404, however, overdoes the juridical explanation of passages from Ovid's works).

NOTES TO CHAPTER 7, THE "ARS AMATORIA," BOOKS I AND II, PP. 53–63

1 (p. 53). Scholars have so far paid little attention to the change in Ovid's attitude toward love because they unanimously lump together into one "juvenile" period the whole body of his erotic poetry, from the *Amores,* at which he began to work at the age of eighteen, down to the *Remedia,* written when he was forty-three. In this fashion, the first quarter century of his literary career is telescoped into a moment of negligible duration; the devoted and exuberant youth is blended with the ripe master lover; and the emotional background of individual poems cannot be correctly appreciated.

2 (p. 53). The last couplet is a reminiscence of Tibullus I, 10, the same elegy from which Ovid borrowed some ideas for *Am.* I, 7 (see above, p. 181, note 30).

3 (p. 54). *Am.* I, 7; see above, pp. 18–21.

4 (p. 54). In the elegy, the rending of the dress was mentioned only hypothetically, as a thing he might have done but did not do (*Am.* I, 7, 47–48). In the *Ars,* the girl pretends that he had ruined the dress, but the poet feels fairly certain that he had not touched it.

5 (p. 54). Ovid means to say that what he is going to explain is not based on mere speculation or hearsay. Nevertheless, the experiences with which he will deal were typical and had been described in literature many a time before. Literary tradition and actual life were of the same texture.

6 (p. 55). Cf. *Remedia* 9–10 (the lines seem genuine): *docui qua posses* (scil. *Amor) arte parari, et quod nunc ratio est, impetus ante fuit.*

7 (p. 55). In fact all poetry is, in a fashion, didactic, in that it interprets life, proposes ideas, and conveys emotions. The ancients were very conscious of the power poetry wields over our plastic souls. We are likely to think, feel, and act after the example set before us in forceful verse.

8 (p. 55). The didactic element becomes explicit, for example, in Propertius I, 10, 15–30 and Tibullus I, 4. When Ovid later tried to justify his *Art of Love* with the plea that others had written in the same vein with impunity, he spoke of both Tibullus and Propertius as giving "precepts" (*Tr.* II, 561 and 456; cf. A. L. Wheeler, "Propertius as Praeceptor Amoris," *Class. Philol.* 5, 1910, pp. 28–40). The exemplary and didactic character of erotic poetry is manifest already in Anacreon; his frag. 39

Diehl seems to give instruction on the approach to a young boy, some-what similar to what Ovid teaches in *Ars Amat.* I, 767–768 (cf. also *cerva* in line 766 with Anacreon's νεβρός and μήτηρ κερόεσσα). See also note 17, below.

9 (p. 55). Ovid was the first to write comprehensively on the art of love in poetic form and with high literary aspirations (cf. F. Leo, *Plautinische Forschungen,* 2d ed., Berlin, 1912, p. 146), but the same subject may have been treated before him in books of a disreputable character (*ibid.,* note 1).

10 (p. 55). Throughout the *Ars Amatoria* the material is arranged in a fairly orderly fashion, but there is no pedantry in the organization. The exposition is animated by side glances, brilliant aphorisms, legendary examples, digressions of moderate dimension, lively ejaculations, and personal confessions. The different topics are not rigidly kept apart, but are allowed to intermingle or overlap. Sometimes the reader will lose his bearings.

An example of a rather confusing change of subject is the last part of the First Book. In I, 525, the author announces that he is devoting his next chapter to Bacchus. He opens the chapter, after the fashion of a Homeric singer, with a myth in honor of Bacchus the lover (527–564) and then goes on to explain the opportunities a banquet offers. These opportunities come to a climax when the banquet is over and the guests are leaving (603); the lover has now at last a chance to talk directly with the girl he admires. He is advised to mingle with the crowd and to manage to get near the lady. "This is the time," says Ovid, "for you to declare your intentions openly; do not hold back out of timidity" (607). At this point the author, without warning the reader of the switch and without re-solving the concrete situation he has pictured, begins to lapse to a new topic which is itself composed of two elements: rules for the decisive attack on the lady's heart (cf. 619–620, etc.), and admonitions to discard timidity and other inhibitions (cf. *pudor* 608; 705; *timide* 631; *turpis* 723–733), because the normal code of propriety does not apply to love.

11 (p. 55). On the other hand, he mentions both kinds in I, 92: *quodque semel tangas quodque tenere velis.*

12 (p. 56). Ovid had already twice narrated a legend in the *Amores* (III, 6, 45–82 and III, 10), and the *Heroides* contained likewise narrative elements (esp. XIV, Hypermestra, 21–84).

13 (p. 57). Such phenomena as shaken identity, or the merging into oneness of the souls of the lovers, are foreign to the spirit of the *Art of Love.*

14 (p. 57). As a consequence of the unsentimental attitude the author professes, the class of women Ovid has now in mind is not quite the same as that with which the *Amores* was primarily concerned (see above, p. 25). The women of *Ars Amatoria* I and II are more likely to "desecrate love by mercenary tricks" (I, 435) and their standing is somewhat nearer to that of prostitutes, while those of the Third Book approach that level still closer (see below, p. 205, note 8). In *Tr.* II, 303–304, where it is in Ovid's interest that the line between respectable ladies and the women with whom his *Art* is concerned be sharp and clear, he interprets the remark in *Ars Amat.* I, 31–34 to refer to prostitutes only.

15 (p. 57). With 587 f. cf. Martial V, 61. In II, 595–600 it is made plain that the lover is expected to abide by the rules of the game and give his rival a chance, in contrast to a legal husband, who may, if he so chooses, enforce his rights recklessly. (In II, 153–158 married life is compared to its disadvantage with the free association of lovers.)

16 (p. 58). With 673 ff. cf. *Epist.* XVI (XVII), 185–188.

17 (p. 58). The clue to the correct explanation of I, 767–770 is *diffidet sibi*. The lover who is approaching an inexperienced and shy girl is advised not to show how expert in love and how wanton he is, because then the poor thing would believe that she is no match for him, and would suffer the degradation of throwing herself into the arms of an inferior man. The reasoning is somewhat more involved than in Anacreon, frag. 88 Diehl, but Ovid too shows concern for the happiness and education of the girl as well as the man. (Cf. also note 8, above.)

18 (p. 58). I, 466 reads *Saepe valens odii litera causa fuit*. In spite of the phrase *causa valentior* which occurs in *Po.* I, 10, 35, I take *valens* here to go with the subject *litera,* not with the predicate *causa* (for the pattern compare *Saepe tacens odii semina voltus habet,* III, 512). The *valens* receives its color from *vires,* scil. *oratoriae,* in 463.

19 (p. 59). Cf. also II, 507.

20 (p. 59). Ovid does not say that he has a beginner in mind, but a practitioner of long standing would not be self-conscious on such an occasion. (The figure of the timid lover serves the author as link between two chapters in his exposition, see above, note 10.)

21 (p. 59). Ovid felt differently about that point when he had won Corinna; see *Am.* II, 12, 15.

22 (p. 59). While the last part of the First Book (from I, 607 on) dealt in large part with scruples to be overcome, the latter part of the Second (from II, 493 on) is chiefly concerned with self-knowledge, self-control, and humility.

23 (p. 59). In a sense, Ovid's *Art,* and especially so the Second Book, marks the culmination point in the development of the idea that affection is an intellectual achievement. The earliest evidence for that idea are Homeric phrases like ἤπια οἶδεν.

24 (p. 59). All three examples follow upon one another in Ovid's text (II, 288–336), but for the purposes of my exposition I have changed the order.

25 (p. 60). Ovid often speaks of favors given and returned in terms of business transactions. There was a traditional theory of friendship and love according to which affection was viewed as an investment which should be placed wisely so as to yield adequate returns; or the friend or lover was compared to a farmer who expends labor and seed grain in order to harvest a good crop (cf., e.g., Theognis 105–112; Alcaeus, frag. 109/110, 24–27 Diehl; Petronius 42, 7). In a similar spirit, Ovid twice compares the benefits which the attentive lover hopes to reap to those for which the legacy hunter is pining (*Ars Amat.* II, 271–272 and 332), with the implication that, if sordid greed can produce such acts of considerate courtesy, tender love should certainly be able to inspire them.

26 (p. 61). Another example is this. It was a common observation in antiquity that the typical lover does not mind if his idol is no perfect beauty; a feature which appears as a blemish to others is a special charm in his eyes, and he gives the particular quality a laudatory term, calling, for instance, a hooked nose "majestic" (cf. Plato, *Rep.* V, 474 D–E; Lucretius IV, 1157 ff.; Horace, *Sat.* I, 3, 38 ff.). Ovid, however, in II, 641–662 proceeds on the assumption that the lover does mind the deformity of his chosen lady, but is intelligent enough, in his own interest (642), to dissemble his disgust and speak to her of that feature in commendatory terms; and he adds, characteristically, the comforting remark that such tolerant patience will carry its own reward: with time and habit, the lover will cease to notice whatever had at first offended him. Thus Ovid turns into calculating flattery that which was traditionally taken as an error in judgment, due to infatuation.—It has been suggested that the passage from Lucretius was the source of Ovid's precepts (cf. K. Prinz, *Wiener Studien* 36, 1914, pp. 49–50 and 81). But Lucretius himself drew only on the stock-in-trade of love psychology. The many Greek words he uses show that he had a Greek model before him, and one of his lines, *parvula pumilio: chariton mia, tota merum sal* (1162), is paralleled in Theocritus 30, 4–5: καλῶ μὲν (lege μεγάλω) μετρίως, ἀλλ' ὁπόσον τῷ ποδὶ (?) περρέχει τᾶς γᾶς, τοῦτο χάρις (cf. the opposite in Catullus 86, 4: *nulla in tam magno est corpore mica salis*).

27 (p. 62). We cannot doubt that the notion of coercive and unnatural methods was genuinely repulsive to Ovid. He mentions the subject four more times, *Medic.* 35–42, with the same two arguments: a drug is harmful (*nocens,* 38) and magic is ineffective; *Rem.* 249–290; *Her.* VI, 83–94 (note the fine last couplet); and in this book of the *Ars Amatoria,* II, 415–426. In that passage, he rejects powerful drugs but admits innocent stimulants; at the end, however, he recants the use of "magic" devices generally as alien to his purpose (425–426).

28 (p. 62). Next follows (121–122) another (cf. I, 459 ff.) admonition to the student of love to cultivate his eloquence and his proficiency in both the Latin and Greek languages (see p. 182, note 30). The topic of skill in conversation leads to a charming digression in which Odysseus, not a very young or handsome man, is pictured as fascinating Calypso by his talk (II, 123–142). The end of the legendary scene is connected with the main topic by a most elegant transition. From Calypso's humorous warning (preluded in 126) against a trust in the unreliable waves which have just swept away sand *figures* of greatness, the author turns once more to his own warning against a trust in the unreliable *figure* (143) which the years will soon sweep away.

29 (p. 62). In *agri* 'wilderness' the earliest connotation of the word is still alive. Obviously *ager* originally meant the wilderness separating one settlement from the other, and this connotation survived in words like *peragro, peregre,* ἄγριος (in contrast to ἥμερος), Ἄρτεμις ἀγροτέρα (for the formation cf. ὀρέστερος), etc.

30 (p. 62). Lucretius had mentioned love as one of the civilizing factors in V, 1011 ff. Ovid's *constiterant uno loco* (478) and *cognitus* (476) may be reminiscences from Lucretius' *coniuncta in unum* (1011) and *cognita sunt* (1012). Cf. also Cicero, *De officiis* I, § 54.

31 (p. 63). The theory that all refinements are promoted by love also throws light on Ovid's opinion, frequently voiced by him, that the prim chastity of olden times was nothing but a crude backwardness (*rusticitas*), from which his own age had fortunately progressed to more enlightened habits.

NOTES TO CHAPTER 8, THE "MEDICAMINA FACIEI," PP. 63–64

1 (p. 63). Cf. *Tr.* II, 487–490. With Rubenbauer in the *Thes. Ling. Lat.,* I take *fucandi cura coloris* to refer to the preparation of dyes for clothing material rather than, with S. G. Owen in his commentary to *Tristia* II, to "painting the complexion."

2 (p. 63). Or whatever else the original form of the title was.

3 (p. 63). The date of the *Medicamina* is uncertain, except that it was written before *Ars* III; cf. *Ars* III, 205.

4 (p. 63). Cf. *vestri mariti* (25), *nupta* (26), and *probitas* (49). Hence also the difference in the rules for adornment. For the ladies of the *Medicamina* it is proper (*nec indignum* 23) to have dresses heavy with gold and to wear expensive jewelry (18–22), while the women of *Ars* III are cautioned against the use of either (129–133; 169–172).

5 (p. 63). *Cui* (*pro* libri) *se quaeque parent et quos venentur* (*venerentur* libri) *amores;* cf. M. Pohlenz (see p. 175, note 2), p. 21.

6 (p. 63). Line 32, which is all but identical with *Ars Amat.* I, 624. Compare also line 33 with *Ars* I, 627.

NOTES TO CHAPTER 9, THE "ARS AMATORIA," BOOK III, PP. 64–67

1 (p. 64). The classicistic trend had a lasting success as far as the literary language was concerned; in that respect it was to remain predominant for about thirteen hundred years. The Latin of the Ciceronian and Augustan age became the standard language for all writers with literary pretensions, and the forward development of the language was thus driven underground. This is why the latest stage of the Latin language is commonly styled, not Late Latin, but Vulgar Latin. Not before the verge of the modern era did writers in Latin lands dare to publish works written in the living tongue, the *lingua volgare,* using as vehicles of literary expression no longer ancient Latin but what we call the Romance languages. The Greeks, too, had their Atticism, with the consequence that up to the present day the gulf between the spoken and the written language has been intolerably wide.

2 (p. 65). Since the *Remedia* was written A.D. 1 or 2, *Ars* III must have been composed A.D. 1.

3 (p. 65). III, 673–682. The lines sound more than usually caustic and seem to be meant that way. For one thing, the amorous scene is sketched in a dry and succinct manner; it takes the author no more than two couplets to run through the crescendo sequence of tender complaints (675–676) and tempestuous fury (677–678) on the part of the lady. Secondly, two more couplets promise a sure and prompt success for the maneuver (679–680) because the admirer is supposed to be blinded by his vanity, thinking himself irresistible (681–682). The attitude of the writer is as sober as can be, and the lucidity of his concise exposition is exemplary.

4 (p. 66). One of Ovid's infrequent personal remarks makes it manifest that he no longer warms fully to his subject. In the context he has pointed out that when the affair threatens to become dull and monoto-

nous the girl will do well to provide a bogey rival for her favors; and in this connection he says: "Lo, I confess it: I do not love unless I feel slighted" (III, 598; see p. 188, note 64). The contrast in content and tone with II, 447–454 (see above, p. 61) is obvious; Ovid now needs the sharpest stimulus for being stirred at all.

5 (p. 66). The passage III, 501–524 deals not so much with the character of the girl as with her demeanor, and when the author cautions the woman against losing her temper, his only argument is that rage disfigures the face.

6 (p. 66). In III, 369–380, Ovid warns the women not to squabble while playing a game, and goes on to explain: If we begin to quarrel, we forget our manners and our real disposition shows up.

7 (p. 66). Actually, it is probable that the women, although socially far below their male partners, were often their intellectual superiors, and especially so the Greeks among them. Even in Menander's New Comedy, where all characters were of Greek nationality, the women, as a rule, are represented as more sensible, refined, and tactful than the men. The more significant is their disparagement in the Third Book of the *Ars Amatoria*.

8 (p. 67). The Third Book of the *Ars* alone (cf. above, p. 201, note 14) represents the mistress as a former slave. The context makes the hint sound sardonic, but that may be a mistaken impression. Ovid is once more declaring that he does not intend to instruct married wives in the deception of their husbands; they are, so he says, bound by their modesty and by the law of the land. "But it would be outrageous," he continues, "to tie down like a slave (cf. 488) you who but recently were set free from slavery" (III, 611–616). This goes far beyond remarks like those in III, 25–28 and 483, or the admonition in line 58 that the girl is not expected to be modest and has a right to do what she likes. Not only is it, no doubt, a false generalization when "she" is supposed to be a freedwoman; it is, moreover, grossly indelicate to remind her in public of the condition which is alleged to have been hers only a short time ago. Did Ovid put it on so thick as a safeguard against the suspicion that, in spite of his protestations to the contrary, he had society ladies in mind and was promoting adultery? (When in *Tr.* II, 303–304, Ovid insists that this allegation is absolutely untrue, the wording implies that the terms *meretrix* and *liberta* are equivalent, just as "respectable" and *ingenua*.)

9 (p. 67). The general plan of the book is this.

I) Introduction, about 50 couplets.
  A) Personal Preface (–56)
  B) Protreptical exhortation (–98).

II) Elementary Instruction, 200 couplets.

    A) *Cultus:* (1) *Cultus* is indispensable (–132); (2) hair, dress, daintiness, and make-up (–250); how to hide deformities (–280); how to laugh, weep, and walk (–310); (3) accomplishments: singing, playing instruments, familiarity with poetry, knowledge of games, with appendix on good manners while playing (–380).

    B) How to make acquaintances: (1) Frequent appropriate places (–432); beware of professional woman-killers and dishonest admirers (–466); how to react on the lover's first tentative letters, with appendix on precautions in love correspondence (–498).

III) Advanced Instruction, about 150 couplets.

    A) Control your temper and moods so as to look pretty and be pleasant at all times (–524). (B) Marshal your lovers so as to use each to your best advantage (–576). (C) Keep your lover in wholesome suspense (–610). (D) How to elude the *vir* and the guardians (–658). (E) Mistrust those who share your secrets (–666). (F) Pretend to be tenderly devoted to your lover (–682). (G) Beware of rash jealousy, with appendix on the legend of Procris (–746). (H) How to behave at a banquet (–768).

IV) Intimacies (–808).

The main division (overlooked by F. Wichers, *Quaestiones Ovidianae,* Diss. Göttingen, 1907) into elementary and advanced instruction (*parva* and *maiora*) is clearly marked out at the beginning of the sections, in 99–100 and 499–500. The "small" things are matters easy to understand and to master, while the "greater" achievements require some measure of self-control (cf. the passage II, 535–538, where *maiora* equals *ardua,* referring to self-control, and the use of the term *maius opus* in the appendix to section II, A, line 370), comprehension, and discrimination (analogous to II, 493–end, see p. 201, note 22). A secondary, and rather dim, line progresses from part II, A, *How to be attractive,* through part II, B, *How to get your man,* to section III, *How to deal with him when you have him*—which is the most difficult task of all (cf. II, 14).

    10 (p. 67). Freely paraphrased, lines 747–750 say: "But let us now return to our subject; there will be no more digressions, since I am tired and want to be done with the one or two subjects which remain to be dealt with." In contrast to the *Remedia,* which mentions the *fessa carina* at the very end (811), here the phrase is used earlier.

Notes to Chapter 10, The "Remedia Amoris," pp. 67–72

1 (p. 67). In the passage 699–706, one difficulty has been removed by Bürger, Housman, and Prinz, who replaced *furiali* (699) by *furari* ("I shall not rob Amor of his bow, as Odysseus stole that of Philoctetes"). But it still remains obscure why Apollo should be asked to appear at this moment, and what it means that he heeds the call. K. Prinz (*Wiener Studien* 39, 1917, pp. 95–96 and 288) remarks that the invocation is pointless and that the words *ut facis* (704) are especially inappropriate. I think he has laid his finger on another corruption, and suggest changing *facis* to *faves: utque faves coeptis*, "as truly as you favor my project." The whole context, from 687 on, will then run very smoothly: "In order to avoid a relapse, resist her stirring appeals for a reconciliation and keep mum rather than try to make her understand your point of view, or else she will convert you to hers. This sounds as if I had the sacrilegious intention of despoiling Amor of his powers; but I only wish to give healthful advice. O healer Apollo, confirm the propriety of my directions and show that you favor them by appearing to me in person. Lo, Apollo does appear; I am vindicated."

2 (p. 68). In line 312, Ovid for once indicates, if very vaguely, why he wished to cut himself loose from a certain girl: *Conveniens animo non erat illa meo;* that is, probably, their temperaments did not match very well. But then he makes a point of trying to persuade himself, contrary to the truth of the matter, that her beauty had a great number of flaws (315–322). In the preceding passage, by contrast, there is an inkling of the maxim that the actual stumbling blocks should be used to lay the affection low (299–308).—A strange twist is involved in the couplet 563–564: "He who has a strict father, if everything else leaves nothing to be desired, let him keep his strict father before his mind's eye." The leading idea of the passage, however, is not: Think day and night of the obstacles to your love in order to fortify yourself in your resolution, but rather: Keep your mind busy with other worries in order to crowd out any thought of love. Moreover, to make confusion worse confounded, the remark "if everything else leaves nothing to be desired" flatly contradicts the programmatic invitation of lines 41–42: "Take you recourse to my directions, O disappointed youths whose love is *frustrated in every respect.*"—A slip in another direction is the couplet 511–512; here the author is mending rather than rending the attachment.

It was a cardinal mistake of Ovid to leave the background for his advice completely blank. It would have been quite another matter if he had chosen to develop his precepts from topical case histories taken from life or legend, such as, for instance, Odysseus' escape from Circe and Calypso.

3 (p. 68). In *Am.* I, 7, 31–32, Ovid had said that an offense against the spirit of love was comparable to Diomede's attack on Venus; now, in *Rem.* 5–6, he denies that he is attacking Venus as Diomede had done. He was right then and is wrong now.

4 (p. 68). Sixteen out of forty-two precepts, according to K. Prinz, *Wiener Studien* 36 (1914), pp. 47 ff.

5 (p. 69). *Odium* is here obviously 'rancor,' 'animosity,' while in 308 it meant rather 'disgust.'

6 (p. 70). Not even in this context is business life mentioned; but it appears later among the sources of worries from which the lover can derive some distraction from his preoccupation (569–570).

7 (p. 71). *Am.* II, 16 (see p. 185, note 45) and III, 13. It is not true that Ovid, as a confirmed city dweller, had no feeling for country life; for additional evidence cf., for instance, the story in the *Metamorphoses* of Vertumnus and Pomona (pp. 106–107); *Tr.* III, 12, 5–16 (cf. p. 126); *Po.* III, 1, 11–24 (p. 129); *Po.* I, 8, 41–60 (p. 131); *Fasti* 1, 663–704 (see p. 241, note 13); 2, 639–678 (p. 150).

8 (p. 71). For one exception, and the reason for it, see p. 216, note 49.

NOTES TO CHAPTER II, THE "METAMORPHOSES," PP. 72–111

1 (p. 74). The *Metamorphoses* has benefited from the epic dignity in that Ovid's propensity for going into details of sexual life was curbed through it.

2 (p. 74). Richard Heinze has sagaciously traced the differences between Ovid's elegiac and epic narratives; see *Ovids elegische Erzählung,* Ber. d. Sächs. Akad. d. Wiss. 71, Heft 7, Leipzig, 1919.

3 (p. 74). I do not mean to imply, of course, that Ovid consciously reasoned that way. I rationalize an achievement which actually was accomplished, in all probability, by instinct and intuition rather than by a deliberate effort to conquer a known obstacle.

4 (p. 75). The theory is based on a mere historical accident. The books of Homeric epics omitted the prefaces because the rhapsodist was expected to improvise them according to the circumstances of his recital.

5 (p. 75). The conventional motif for an incipient epic was the wrath of a god; thus Ovid has Juppiter "conceive a wrath worthy of him" (1, 166), and because of his "fierce wrath" Cupid engineers the "first" of a long series of love stories (1, 452–453).

6 (p. 75). Ovid's use of the word *chaos* in *Metam*. 1, 7 seems to supply the reason for its modern connotation. The term is taken from Hesiod, *Theog*. 116, while the concept it serves to express stems from Anaxagoras. In other passages Ovid applies the word more correctly, cf. e.g., *Ars Amat*. II, 470 *inane chaos;* originally *chaos* means "the void." Hesiod believed that the emergence of the Universe was preceded by *chaos,* the void; later, *chaos* was identified with the primordial condition—no matter what that condition was—of nature. This misuse of the term dates back at least to Zeno the Stoic (cf. *schol*. Apollon. Rhod. 1, 496–498 b Wendel). In *Fasti* 1, 103–114, Ovid playfully adds a new identification. From the premises *Chaos = beginning* and *Janus = beginning* he draws the conclusion *Janus = Chaos;* hence the somewhat chaotic appearance of the god.

7 (p. 76). It takes the author no more than three words to cloak the earth with vegetation (44) and one less to bring all the gods into the picture (73).

8 (p. 76). The modern reader would probably be less impressed by Ovid's account of the creation if he could compare it with the Greek originals from which it was derived. The story of Lycaon is the first example in the epic of the most common type of metamorphosis, as far as the plot is concerned, but in its execution it leaves us cold because it is merely grim and unflavored by feeling or humor. The first real Ovidian touches occur in the picture of the South Wind who with his "hand" squeezes water out of the clouds (264–269); here, and later in the magnificent description of Triton sounding the retreat for the waves (333–342), the felicitous blending of physical and quasi-human elements is characteristic.

9 (p. 77). The story of Aglauros (2, 708–834), for instance, ends with the girl transformed into a stone statue by reason of her *invidia. Invidia* had been described before (760 ff.) as cold, pallid, sluggish, stiff, and hardly able to rise; with almost the same words, Aglauros in the moment of petrification is pictured as cold, pallid, sluggish, stiff, and unable to rise (820 ff.); the punishment fits the crime (see p. 213, note 33).—The Aglauros legend is manifestly aetiological; it was probably inspired by one of those archaic sitting statues which are so monumental that the person seems to be seated for eternity.

10 (p. 77). The matter of meaningful repetitions and echoes in the *Metamorphoses* deserves to be studied with a responsive mind, but at the same time with tact and restraint. In our passage, there is a rhyme pattern which repeats itself. It occurs first in lines 325–326: "And God saw that one man survived out of so many millions, and that one woman survived

out of so many millions," and again in lines 361–362, where Deucalion declares that he would have followed Pyrrha unto death: "If you too were swallowed by the sea, I too were swallowed by the sea." This is a masterful way of indicating, first, how closely their destinies were bound together by their common survival, and second, how closely their souls were bound together by their mutual attachment.

11 (p. 77). *Remollescunt* and *flectitur* from line 378 are taken up by *molliri, mollita* in line 402, and by the *flectitur* which is projected back into line 408 by virtue of the contrast to *flecti nequit* in 409.

12 (p. 77). If Ovid were not the sensitive poet he is, but the clamorous rhetorician he is commonly represented to be, he would have thrown his fine point in every reader's face. Actually, he is often so discreet that many of his best ideas go unnoticed; and as long as his readers have their ears pricked for the thunder and crackle of "rhetorical" fireworks, will they miss the better part of what the poet is trying to tell them with the easy grace of his soft-spoken presentation.

13 (p. 78). Ovid did believe in spontaneous generation (cf. 1, 422–423; 15, 361–371), but not in a miracle such as was performed, according to the legend, by Deucalion and Pyrrha. Nevertheless, he makes the revival of the human race appear less absurd by following it soon up with a description and explanation of the spontaneous generation of animals (1, 416–421).

14 (p. 78). Cf., e.g., Empedocles frag. 127 Diels-Kranz, and Callimachus, *Iambi,* frag. 9, 211 ff. Pfeiffer.

15 (p. 78). For the idea that the deity of love can also induce lack of love, cf. *Iliad* 3, 415–417; Sappho, frag. 26, 10–12 Diehl; and Ovid's *Amor Lethaeus, Rem.* 551 ff.

16 (p. 79). Simonides of Ceos, a poet strangely modern for the time in which he lived, was the first writer to elaborate the sentiments which are bound to arise in normal human beings when they are subjected to the abnormal experience of a miracle performed on them. The theme became popular in Hellenistic poetry.

17 (p. 79). The Io passage, *Her.* XIV, 85–109, is patently out of place where it stands, and yet there can be little doubt about its authorship because it has a truly Ovidian ring. It seems that, at the time, Ovid's mind had already begun to be so obsessed by the theme of a metamorphosis alienating the person from his own self that he could not help elaborating such a scene. He may have justified the digression by the example of Attic tragedy, in which it frequently happens that songs recalling events from the family past interrupt the development of the main story. (For the

rapport between the *Heroides* and the lyric parts of tragedy see p. 190, note 1.)

18 (p. 79). The idea that Io was madly trying to escape from her transformed self was a remarkable progress over the ancient tradition according to which Io the cow was chased relentlessly either by a gadfly or by a horrible vision that pursued her. In the *Metamorphoses* (1, 725–727), Ovid returned to the earlier version, but line 641 can be taken as a faint echo of the more modern interpretation he had given Io's flight in the *Heroides*.

19 (p. 79). For another apostrophe of the same character, *Metam.* 3, 432–436, see p. 83.

20 (p. 80). For the trait that Io, Juppiter's mistress, became the property of Juppiter's wife, cf. *Her.* III, 71–80 (see p. 45).

21 (p. 80). Of the bear that threatens the sheep, Horace says: *Vespertinus circumgemit ursus ovile* (*Epodi* 16, 51; quoted by R. Ehwald as a parallel to Ovid's *gemitu testata dolores* 2, 486).

22 (p. 81). There is a line in the Homeric epic saying that of all the constellations the Bear alone may not "bathe" in the ocean (*Iliad* 18, 489; *Od.* 5, 275). Ovid repeats the prohibition in his Callisto story, and motivates it by Juno's wish that the pure water should not be soiled by a concubine (*ne puro tingatur in aequore paelex,* 2, 530). To this ruling he supplies a prelude, by a scene in which Callisto is prevented by Diana from bathing in a stream for the same reason (*nec sacros pollue fontes,* 2, 464, and similarly in *Fasti* 2, 174 and 192). The use of preludes of this sort (cognate to the device of echoes as described above on p. 77 and in note 9, p. 209) has a certain cushioning effect. The Indian theory of drama prescribes that any event occurring in the play should be preceded by some subtle reference to such an event, in a simile for instance, so as to prepare the spectator's mind and lessen the shock of surprise. With respect to the Callisto story, these observations receive added significance from the fact that the preluding scene (2, 453–465) was probably of Ovid's own invention. This forceful scene is in turn prepared by a fine and characteristic passage (441–452) with a touch of humor at its end. Ovid seems also to have created the meeting between mother and son; see R. Heinze (note 2, p. 208), pp. 106–110.

23 (p. 82). The notion that Hercules emerged from the fire purged of mortality has parallels in Greek legend. The infant Achilles, son of a mortal father and a divine mother, was put on the fire at night in order to burn his mortal flesh away, while by day he was anointed with "immortality" (*ambrosia*), according to Apollon. Rh. 4, 865–879; and Apollo-

dorus (III, 171 = III, 13, 6) adds specifically that the fire was to destroy the paternal inheritance of mortality. Similar is the fable of Triptolemus (*Hymn. in Cer.* 233–264; Ovid, *Fasti* 4, 549–560; Apollodorus I, 31 = I, 5, 4, etc.) except that he had no divine parent. (For further parallels see J. G. Frazer's edition of Apollodorus, Vol. 2, pp. 313–317, and his commentary on *Fasti* 4, 553.) But the deification of Hercules as Ovid describes it diverges in several crucial points. He was a mature man, while the others were infants; he actually became a god, while they did not; he passed through death, while they were to be preserved from it; and he arose from death by virtue of his own double nature alone, while they had to be imbued with immortality by means of magic.

24 (p. 82). Doubtless Ovid had in mind not Hercules alone, but also the Emperor Augustus (cf. the use of the adjective *augustus* in line 270), who was often thought of as another Hercules.

25 (p. 82). *Duplex status, non confusus sed coniunctus in una persona: deus et homo* (Tertullian, *Adv. Praxeam* 27, cf. Adolf Harnack, *Lehrb. d. Dogmengesch.*, 4th ed., Tübingen, 1909, Vol. 1, p. 601; Joseph Turmel, *Histoire des dogmes,* Paris, 1932, Vol. 2, p. 286). Harnack insists (pp. 215–216) that in the official church before Tertullian, or perhaps Melito, no one thought of assuming for Jesus a duplex entity with two natures. Of Melito we now possess a homily in which he speaks not only of Christ's having become, in succession, first man and then god (§ 7), but also of his being "man and god by nature" (§ 8, cf. Campbell Bonner, *The Homily on the Passion by Melito,* London and Philadelphia, 1940, pp. 89–91 and 28–29).

26 (p. 82). The wording shows that the two natures are by no means meant to coincide with soul and body; the cleft goes through both.

27 (p. 82). I have not investigated the history of the theory and can only quote two more authorities for it. Seneca says in *Hercules Oetaeus,* 1966–1968: *Quidquid in nobis* [i.e., *in Hercule*] *tui* [*i.e., Alcmenae*] *mortale fuerat, ignis evictus* (cf. Ovid 250) *tulit. Paterna caelo, pars data est flammis tua.* This may or may not have been taken from the *Metamorphoses.* Lucian, however, hardly borrowed from Ovid when he wrote (*Hermotimus* 7):…ὥσπερ φασὶ τὸν Ἡρακλέα ἐν τῇ Οἴτῃ κατακαυθέντα θεὸν γενέσθαι· καὶ γὰρ ἐκεῖνος ἀποβαλὼν ὁπόσον ἀνθρώπειον εἶχε παρὰ τῆς μητρός, καὶ καθαρόν τε καὶ ἀκήρατον φέρων τὸ θεῖον, ἀνέπτατο ἐς τοὺς θεούς, διευκρινηθὲν ὑπὸ τοῦ πυρός.

28 (p. 82). The simile of the snake may be influenced by Vergil's *Aeneid,* 2, 471 ff. There it is applied to Neoptolemus; Vergil evidently implied that Neoptolemus was a rejuvenated Achilles (cf. *nitidus iuventa*

473), and combined with this idea the notion that a snake was more than ordinarily vicious when it had shed its skin (cf. Vergil, *Georg.* 3, 437).

29 (p. 82). It is true that the term διφνής (for beings like the Centaurs) goes back to the 5th century at least, but it did not then carry any such implications as emerged in Ovid's time. Herodotus, while musing over the Hercules problem and the chronological difficulties it involved (2, 44), came to the conclusion that Hercules the son of Amphitruo and Hercules the god were not the same person.

30 (p. 82). The Delphian commandment, "Know thyself," is thus enigmatically reversed.—As the story unfolds, Narcissus dies because he beheld a person he should never have seen. This motif connects the Narcissus legend both with the two preceding tales, those of Actaeon and Semele, and with the following story, in which Pentheus will be destroyed because of what he has seen (3, 517–518; cf. also 3, 98). Obviously, the Narcissus story has been assigned its place not merely "for the sake of variety" (R. Ehwald). The economy of the *Metamorphoses* is not exclusively determined by such factors as genealogy, chronology, geography, the influence of source books, etc.; ideas, too, play some part in the grouping of the stories (cf. p. 93; pp. 96–97, and note 77, p. 221), and ideas, with their recurrence within the same neighborhood, make not only for coherence but also for a measure of profundity.

31 (p. 83). Lines 353 and 355 are borrowed, with slight modifications, from Catullus 62, 42 and 44, and thus they already suggest, in preparation of the metamorphosis, the comparison with a fine flower as Catullus has it there. The word *tetigere* (355), however, is better taken in the sense of "impressed, moved" (cf. p. 192, note 10) than in that of *intacta* in Catullus 62, 45.

32 (p. 83). It would appear at first sight that Echo was the obvious person to pronounce the curse. For one thing, however, a vindictive action would not fit her responsive nature; and for another, passion of a youth for a boy was to be foreshadowed. Hence the masculine gender in line 404.

33 (p. 83). For the concept that a sinner is most fittingly punished by suffering the extremities of his own sin, cf., e.g., Ovid's stories of Aglauros (see p. 209, note 9) and of the Propoetides (see p. 93). This is probably one reason why Dante rated Ovid so highly.

34 (p. 83). Such a place, sheltered from the sun (412), is the natural habitat of the narcissus flower (Sophocles, *Oed. Col.* 676 and 683).—The scenery as pictured here is the same as the favorite landscape of pastoral poetry, except that Ovid advisedly excludes any stirring of life (408–410): Narcissus the self-lover is by and with himself alone.

35 (p. 83). Similarly, the writer tries to enlighten the bewildered Io in *Her.* XIV, 93 ff. (above, p. 79).—Ovid applies the apostrophe for several reasons. Frequently he breaks the illusion of his own narrative in order to argue in person with his characters about the moral issue involved. In this class belong the following apostrophes: 2, 435, where Juno is reproached for her cruelty (cf. *Fasti* 2, 178); 2, 676 ff.: "You did not listen, Apollo, because you were unable to help for two reasons"; 3, 131 ff.: "You seemed perfectly happy, but human happiness is always precarious" (the Cadmus legend was a standard example of the instability of human conditions, cf. Pindar, *Py.* 3, 86–106; *Oly.* 2, 19 ff.); 5, 111–113: "The fate which overtook you was out of character for you"; 5, 242–247: "You deserve the fate which is to overtake you"; 10, 162 ff.: "Apollo did for you all he could"; 10, 311 ff.: "Cupid is not to blame for your passion"; 10, 542 ff.: "She told you so, but you would not listen." The apostrophe is unusually elaborate in 4, 192–206, where Ovid, the poet of love, gloats over the fitting revenge (190–192) which Venus took on Sol.

36 (p. 84). To the color scheme, white and pink (509–510), Ovid preludes three times: in lines 423, 481–484, and 491. *Croceus* in line 509 stands for 'reddish' in general, not distinguishing a particular shade, as can be seen from Ovid's describing the *crocus* flower as *ruber* (*Fasti* 1, 342; *Am.* II, 6, 22, next to *Punica; Ars Amat.* I, 104) or *puniceus* (*Fasti* 5, 318).

37 (p. 84). In my judgment, there are two minor flaws in Ovid's wonderful story. The boy's laments are too long drawn out, and lines 504–505 are in poor taste. On the other hand, there are more fine points in it than one would care to discuss. The story "had a great vogue" in the Middle Ages, according to E. K. Rand (see p. 169, note 5), p. 117.

38 (p. 84). It is possible that the combination was Ovid's original idea. Luigi Castiglioni (*Studi intorno alle fonti e alla composiz. delle Metam. di Ovidio,* Pisa, 1906, pp. 215–219) does not feel that Ovid can be credited with so much ingenuity, but we do not have the material to decide the question one way or the other.

39 (p. 85). This rapport between the two characters seems obvious enough, and it must have been noticed by a great many readers; nevertheless, I have as yet found it mentioned nowhere. A thorough bibliographical search would probably unearth a number of references to it.

40 (p. 85). The phrase I am using, 'to share the self,' is modeled on the remarkable use Ovid twice makes in this story of the word *copia.* Both times, the word holds a key position. In 391 and 392, Narcissus and Echo exchange between them the clause *Sit tibi copia nostri,* negatively from his side and positively from hers; and in 466 Narcissus, epigrammatizing

the futility of his self-love, exclaims: *Inopem me copia fecit*. Only in these two places does Ovid apply the word *copia* to the possession by one lover of the other; he seems to have coined this forceful use specifically to express the pivotal idea of this story. (It is true that also in *Rem.* 541 the word *copia* is applied to love embraces, but there the use is unspecific, and the meaning is rather "overabundance," cf. *cumules*. On the other hand, the phrase *inter se corpus sociare, Am.* I, 8, 5, already involves the notion that each lover yields to the other a share of himself, although there it is only his "body" that he makes available to the other.)

41 (p. 85). A poet more rhetorical than Ovid was would have made a neat point of the paradoxical combination in Echo of an irresistible urge to talk (cf. ἀθυρόστομος Ἠχώ Sophocles, *Philoct.* 188) with a strictly limited capacity for talking, in the manner of Archias (or Parmenio, *Anthol. Palat.* 9, 27), who calls her λάλος κοὐ λάλος.

42 (p. 85). There is no leering indelicacy or sarcastic brutality in Ovid's humor; it evokes not roaring laughter, but the friendly smile of appreciative comprehension. Take for instance 2, 450–452, where Diana in her innocent chastity fails to notice Callisto's condition, while her nymphs (they are, as we know, constantly molested by Satyrs) are at once aware of it. The humor in the *Metamorphoses* is so rich and finely shaded that it happily defies classification. Several times, the double identity resulting from a metamorphosis is exploited for the amusement not only of the reader, but even of the character himself, for instance in 2, 430: "He laughed when he heard how she preferred himself to himself," and similarly in 8, 862–868; or in 2, 704 f., where Mercury reveals to Battus the trap into which he had fallen: "It is I whom you are betraying to me" (the question marks are wrong). Ovid's wit verges on the mordant (as in the last example) only when wicked people receive their deserved punishment; in that case, it gives no bitter sting but rather a sweet satisfaction. Ironic double entendre is frequent, and some of it seems still to be unrecognized. In the story of the Lycian peasants, the thirsty Latona asks them to let her drink from the pond, and adds: "You will have given me life in the water" (*vitam dederitis in unda*, 6, 357). The phrasing strikes us as strange (although Ovid took the precaution of leading up to it with a careful preparation): when the peasants refused, Latona gave them life in the water (369, cf. βίον ἔδωκεν αὐτοῖς καθ' ὕδατος Anton. Lib. 35).—In 7, 813–820 the elaborate double entendre is part of the plot; the last line, however, rises to a triple entendre. There Cephalus exclaims, addressing the Breeze: "My mouth is forever yearning for your breath" (*Meo spiritus iste tuus semper captatur* [cf. 4, 72; 7, 557] *ab ore*); and when he had

killed the woman he loved, "she exhaled her spirit into his mouth" (861). This is tragic irony of the pathetic type. (The grim type seems extremely rare; one example is 6, 655, where Tereus takes *intus* to mean 'in the house.') We can still follow the steps by which Ovid reached the sophistication of triple entendre. The first was that he substituted, as the unsubstantial object of the lady's jealousy, *aura,* thin air (cf. 830), for the nebulous cloud (*nephele*) of the Greek original; the second was taken when the idea of connecting with *aura* the last breath of Procris faintly occurred to him, in *Ars Amat.* III, 741: *Nomine suspectas iam spiritus exit in auras;* the last, when he wrote the line identifying the beloved breeze with the breath of Procris' life.

43 (p. 85). Cf. 1, 694–698 with 474–479; 701–704 with 525–547; 710 with 558–559.

44 (p. 86). Alfred Rohde (*De Ovidi arte poetica capita duo,* Berlin, 1929, p. 9) contends that this description "nihil est nisi lumen quoddam orationis epicae."

45 (p. 86). The quarrel between Phaëthon and Epaphus may have been fashioned by Ovid after the fable told in Bacchylides' *Theseus* (no. 17 Snell). In the dithyrambus, one son of a god challenges another to prove his parentage by performing a miraculous feat.

46 (p. 86). The story of Philemon and Baucis, 8, 620–724, is a notable exception. It is told more leisurely than usual, and the circumstantial descriptions (641–650; 655–677) appear redundant when measured against the normal standard of the *Metamorphoses.* In general, Ovid's narrative admits particulars only so far as they have a commensurate relevance for the factual or emotional development of the plot; he does not indulge in a profusion of detail merely in order to round out the picture. In that story, however, he follows rather a certain trend in the Hellenistic tradition (for a collection of pertinent material see Georg Huber, *Lebensschilderung und Kleinmalerei im hellenist. Epos,* Solothurn, 1926); and from the point of view of Hellenistic taste the story deserves the renown in which it is held.

47 (p. 87). This idea is as old as Mimnermus, cf. frag. 10 Diehl.

48 (p. 88). For the sun or moon cf., e.g., Nonnus, *Dionys.* 5, 484–488 (where the phrase ἀντώπιος αἴγλη in line 485 closely resembles Ovid's *opposita imagine* in line 349); *Dionys.* 38, 113–129; Ovid, *Metam.* 14, 767–771; *Ars Amat.* II, 721–722. For the notion that the spark which kindles passion strikes the admirer in the eye and from there penetrates deeper, see the graphic description in Plato's *Phaedrus,* 251 A–C.

49 (p. 89). This is the only passage in Ovid's works, I believe, which

has a touch of sultry sensuality (see p. 71). The reason is that the water of the Salmacis pond was supposed to induce that quality, cf. 4, 385–386; 15, 319. The character of the Nymph was fashioned accordingly by Ovid. It has been remarked above (p. 183, note 37) that the fable may have been of Ovid's own invention. The invention is based on a contamination of two motifs. The androgynous nature of Hermaphroditus is explained, first, by his bath in a pool notorious for making a bather effeminate, and secondly, by a woman grafted upon him. The two motifs are then reconciled by the identification of pool and woman and by making the metamorphosis of Hermaphroditus into an aetion for the peculiar powers of the water.

50 (p. 89). Any number of little finds are waiting for him who, with close attention to the text, an open-minded response to ideas, and a fair amount of leisurely testing and pondering of possibilities, would work out a specimen commentary on some few books of the *Metamorphoses*. Rudolf Ehwald's book has distinct merits, but the scope of his observations is limited.

51 (p. 89). For Ovid's unbelief in the fables of legend and mythology, see p. 180, note 24.

52 (p. 91). This is the context (*Ars Amat.* I, 631–658) : "Be not squeamish in making promises and inviting the gods to back them up. Juppiter will not mind the false oath of a lover; in fact, he has set many a precedent himself. It is useful that there be gods, and so let us believe in them accordingly; that is, let us assume that they watch over our actions, because it will help us to abstain, among other things, from fraud. Nevertheless, you may with impunity fool women. They are for the most part an unholy lot themselves, and it is fitting and proper to retaliate, false oath for false oath. All is fair in love, but in love only ·(cf. *solas* 643)." In the whole section, one of the leading ideas is that courtship has its own code of propriety (see p. 200, note 10). The contrast, then, between two sets of standards was given by the general theme; and yet there was no reason for the author to elaborate so forcefully the postulate of divine commandments to guide us in our ordinary life. Ovid is clearly going out of his way to insert his credo, and it would hardly leave a gap if it were absent.

53 (p. 91). In the fine line 638, incense and wine seem to have been selected for two reasons. For one thing, it was a modest and quiet offering, because it involved no heavy expense, no assistance, no pomp and ostentation; and secondly, it was a bloodless offering (see p. 225, note 100).

54 (p. 91). I am disregarding the Oriental cults and beliefs for the reason indicated above, p. 27. Ecstatic piety held no appeal for Ovid.

55 (p. 91). To mention one example, Cicero says in so many words that the institute of the augurate was no more than a sham, kept up because it appealed to the superstitious mob and because it could be easily managed to suit political expediency (*De Divin.* 2, 70 and 75). This was true not only for the last days of the Republic, but for all Roman history as we know it (cf. Th. Mommsen, *Röm. Staatsrecht,* Vol. 1, 2d ed., Leipzig, 1876, p. 104).

56 (p. 92). In the Hellenistic period, even Fortune (*Tyche*) herself was widely worshiped as a mighty divine power, and the cult of Fortune referred primarily to the destinies of political organisms. (This idea dates as far back as Pindar, cf. *Oly.* 12, 2.) But Fortune, or Chance, indefinite as it is by its very nature, does not make a very suitable goddess.

57 (p. 92). Half a century later, the Christians were persecuted as rebels. The fanatical adepts of that subversive Jewish sect would not conform to the sham religion. The test was whether or not an individual was willing to go through the motions and sacrifice to the god-emperor; unless he did so, he was destroyed.

58 (p. 93). The legend that prostitution was invented on Aphrodite's island originated from the fact that prostitution was of old connected with sanctuaries of the goddess.

59 (p. 94). R. Ehwald thinks that the phrasing of line 253 is unusual because he takes *corporis* for a genetivus obiectivus; in this, however, he is misled by a fundamental change of view which has taken place since Ovid's time. We assume that love originates in the lover; but for the ancients it was kindled by what we call the object of love (cf., e.g., *Metam.* 3, 372–374). They interpreted love in terms of the lure and attraction which issues from loveliness; thus, for Sophocles, Eros resides on a maiden's tender cheeks (*Antig.* 783–784). It was a startling novelty when Plato, in the *Symposium* (199 c ff.), proposed that love was identical with the desire of the lover rather than with the magnetism of the person loved. Christianity adopted Plato's view (except that the dogma of original sin made woman responsible for man's sensual desire), and it has prevailed ever since; but in Ovid's age the older notion was still predominant.

60 (p. 95). "Softening" and "molding" are, in this symbolism, almost synonymous. Once, in a fine line, Ovid styles the sculptor "him who with skilled hand makes rocks soft" (*Fasti,* 3, 832).

61 (p. 95). The same imagery as here, wax melting and the warm sunshine of love, recurs (with a different application, however) in 3, 487–489.

62 (p. 95). Since we no longer believe that the eye emits beams of

seeing light, we cannot adequately render what Ovid says about the various *lumina*.

63 (p. 96). The story is reported from Philostephanus by Clemens Alexandrinus (*Protr.* IV, 57 = 50–51 P.) and Arnobius (*Adv. Nationes* 6, 22), with Christian indignation both for the idolatry and for the irreverence to which it testifies. From the pagan point of view, however, an image of Aphrodite was no good unless it inspired the passion of which she was the source. For some parts of his fable Ovid could use as a model the story of Admetus, who, when his wife had given her own life to save his, had a statue made of her and treated it as if it were alive (cf. Euripides, *Alcestis* 348 ff.). A similar story was told about Laodamia after the death of her husband (cf. U. von Wilamowitz, *Griechische Tragödien*, Berlin, 1906, Vol. 3, p. 91, note 1).

64 (p. 96). Aristaenetus (*Epist.* II, 10) describes the sentiments of a painter who fell in love with the picture he had made of a woman. Aristaenetus lived in the 5th century of the Christian era, but the story is probably much older. One detail in Ovid's tale (*Sit coniunx mea similis eburnae,* 275–276) may have been taken from that tradition, cf., in Aristaenetus, Ἀλλ' εἴθε μοι τοιαύτην ἔμψυχον, ὦ χρυσόπτεροι παῖδες Ἀφροδίτης, δοίητε φίλην.

65 (p. 96). Cf. *Am.* III, 12; above, p. 34.

66 (p. 96). See above, p. 83, on *Metam.* 3, 432–436, with note 35, p. 214.

67 (p. 96). See above, pp. 77–78.

68 (p. 96). For the notion that a work of art is a child of its author, cf. *Tr.* III, 1, 66, etc.

69 (p. 97). Orpheus' song in the underworld (10, 17–39) is supposed to be superlatively moving, and we are told that the very Furies wept when they heard it (45–46). The more surprising are its brevity and sketchy character. I confess that from my boyhood days I have never responded to it (except for Orpheus' touching admission that he had earnestly tried to reconcile himself to his wife's death, but love won out, 25–26), and I wonder about the reaction of others. It seems that Ovid was striving, not for "rhetoric," but for the utmost candor and simplicity (cf. 19–20) of expression, and that he relied less upon the effect on the reader of the speech than upon the force of the plot itself, with Love conquering (26) even inexorable Death. Excellent is the daring adjuration in lines 29–30, suggesting as it does that a very human voice, tender and melodious, makes itself heard over the horror and silence of Death's vast realm. But a little later (41–46) Ovid allows the delicate idea to be drowned in the din of elaboration.

70 (p. 97). Ostensibly Orpheus is the speaker, but actually Ovid is apologizing for the licentious character of his story (lines 324–331 are especially risqué). *Haec terra* in line 306 is clearly no longer Thrace but Italy (see R. Ehwald), and the lines were inspired by Vergil's laudes Italiae (compare *Georgics* 2, 139 with *Metam.* 10, 309).

71 (p. 97). See above, note 30, p. 213.

72 (p. 98). In addition, Greek thought tended to consider all nature alike to be animated by one and the same life, a portion of which might then migrate from body to body.

73 (p. 99). Perhaps there is also a sensual element in the metamorphosis theme. The possibility occurred to me when I read in André Gide's story of his own childhood (*Si le grain ne meurt,* chap. ii) a passage which I shall quote in full for whatever it may be worth in this connection: "Les thèmes d'excitation sexuelle étaient tout autres [scil., than painted nudes] ... Mais pour dire à quel point l'instinct d'un enfant peut errer, je veux indiquer plus précisément deux thèmes de jouissance: l'un m'avait été fourni bien innocemment par George Sand, dans ce conte charmant de *Gribouille,* qui se jette à l'eau, un jour qu'il pleut beaucoup, non point pour se garer de la pluie, ainsi que ses vilains frères ont tenté de le faire croître, mais pour se garer de ses frères qui se moquaient. Dans la rivière, il s'efforce et nage quelque temps, puis s'abandonne; et dès qu'il s'abandonne, flotte; il se sent alors devenir tout petit, léger, bizarre, végétal; il lui pousse des feuilles par tout le corps; et bientôt l'eau de la rivière peut coucher sur la rive le délicat rameau de chêne que notre ami Gribouille est devenu.—Absurde!—Mais c'est bien là précisément pourquoi je le raconte; c'est la vérité que je dis, non point ce qui me fasse honneur. Et sans doute la grand-mère de Nohant ne pensait guère écrire là quelque chose de débauchant; mais je témoigne que nulle page d'*Aphrodite* ne put troubler nul écolier autant que cette métamorphose de Gribouille en végétal le petit ignorant que j'étais."

74 (p. 99). The last part of the prayer was taken by Ovid from Nicander, who had Myrrha pray μήτε παρὰ ζώοισιν μήτ᾽ ἐν νεκροῖσι φανῆναι (cf. Anton. Lib. 34), that is, she was ashamed to mingle with others in either realm. Whether or not Nicander, like Ovid (482), mentioned an ulterior motive, Myrrha's fear of death, we cannot tell.

75 (p. 100). For a weaker repetition of the pattern see 11, 134.

76 (p. 100). 7, 511, *Gratia dis, felix et inexcusabile tempus,* is a glorious line, but the entire passage bears close reading. There is a mellow Attic charm in the courtesy with which the princes converse, and in the tempered contrast between the negotiations with the one and with the other

king; and as Ovid describes the arrival of the royal parties and their reception by the hosts, the blending of poise and grace reminds us of the procession on the Parthenon frieze rather than of the reliefs on the Ara Pacis, where academic heaviness is sprinkled with outbursts of florid naturalism.—The scope of Ovid's poetical achievements is perplexing; his naïve and unmethodical genius refuses to be exhausted by formulae of any sort.

77 (p. 100). Cf., for instance, the garrulous raven and crow in the Second Book (esp. 2, 535–547 and 614, 631). The motif of indiscretion plays a large part throughout the rest of the Second Book. There is Ocyrhoe who prophesies against Juppiter's will (2, 638–660); Battus who gives away information (687–707); and Aglauros who peeps into the basket (552–561) and makes improper use of the love secret to which she is initiated. The connection between the two indiscretions committed by Aglauros is indicated in 748–749.

78 (p. 101). It is indeed no more than a side light; Ovid does not follow it up with a report of Hercules' labors, because he had given that already in a different context (9, 182 ff.).

79 (p. 101). The lesser poetic value of the last books of the *Metamorphoses* is certainly in part due to the fact that the author was prevented from putting the finishing hand on them. But they also have a number of flaws which no file could have removed; rather, the entire structures would have to be melted down and cast anew in very different molds.—It is true that we have no external evidence to the effect that the last books were also the last in order of composition. But it seems safe to assume that Ovid, after first making out a sketchy outline of the whole epic, composed book after book in the order in which they now stand. The easy and coherent flow of the complex narrative, with so many intricate connections from passage to passage, could hardly have been contrived unless the poet in the main worked out his long tale as he went along and perfected it section by section. Of course he would also make minor adjustments at any later time in any of the completed parts, and he may have intended to revise all of the epic when his work on it was brought to a premature end by his banishment. At that time, as he says in *Tr.* I, 7, 22, his poem "was still rude and in the process of taking shape" (for the meaning of *crescens* see p. 195, note 3). Considering the work as we have it, this assertion seems exaggerated, except, perhaps, with respect to the last section. A little later in the same poem, Ovid says, more correctly, that "the finishing touch" and "the last file" were still missing (lines 28 and 30). The same terms (*manus ultima, summa manus*) recur in *Tr.* II, 555 and

III, 14, 22, and in *Tr*. III, 14, 23 the poet speaks of the *Metamorphoses* as an "unrevised" (*incorrectum*) work.

80 (p. 101). The line of demarcation should, of course, not be taken too literally. Already in the Ninth Book, for instance, the story of Byblis (9, 450–665) has some unusual features, such as the slow progress of the action (more than two hundred lines are used for a very simple tale) and the verbatim insertion of an epistle (530–563).

81 (p. 102). While starting out on his own miniature *Iliad*, Ovid takes his cue from the First Book of the original *Iliad* (262 ff.), where Nestor tells of the Lapiths and their fight with the Centaurs.

82 (p. 102). Not immediately after them, because Nestor prefaces his description of the battle with a metamorphosis story (12, 171–209). The subject is a change in sex, a woman being turned into a man on her own request by the god who had ravished her. Normally, Ovid would have exploited the emotional aspects of the plot, as he had done before in the similar Iphis tale (9, 666–797). In his present mood, however, the poet takes no advantage of the especially inviting possibilities for elaboration in his characteristic manner. Instead, he renders the sequence of events in a succinct and unsentimental fashion (195–203), except, perhaps, for a slight touch of dry masculine humor (201–203).

83 (p. 102). For some obscure reason, the description of the fight falls into two distinct parts. In the first section, not one reference is made to the peculiar shape of the Centaurs, with the consequence that the reader is unable to tell a Centaur from a Lapith unless he follows the narrative with unremitting and very close attention; but from 345 to the end (537) the feature that monsters fight on the one side is amply exploited. The story is tedious as well as repulsive, and its dull cruelty contrasts with the sensitive manner in which a similar fight was narrated in 5, 1–235. In fact, the narrative in the Fifth Book, although gory enough, is excellent poetry, because there all the major incidents have character and human significance. The petrification at the end is cleverly prepared for (see note 22, p. 211). Stone (the column at his back) protects Perseus in 160–161; next (170–173), it fights back for him; and at the climax, stone (by the magic of the Gorgon's head) attacks and overcomes his opponents.

84 (p. 104). The possibility that Ovid took one or the other feature from Aemilius Macer (see note 86) detracts from the value of the story as a test case for Ovid's ingenuity. On the other hand, the many elaborate artistic effects in Ovid's tale make it especially suitable for illustrating the taste in which he indulged at the time.

85 (p. 104). Ovid had perhaps the Greek name of the bird, δρυοκολάπτης (cf., e.g., Plutarch, *Aetia Rom.* 21, p. 268 ε), in mind when he wrote lines 391–392. His readers were so familiar with the Greek language that he could often, by implication, refer to Greek words.

86 (p. 104). Aemilius Macer, in his *Ornithogonia,* mentioned the transformation into a bird of Picumnus (= Picus). See frag. 1, p. 107 Morel = Non. Marc. XII (Vol. 3, p. 834, 30 Lindsay = Vol. 2, p. 170, 31 Müller).

87 (p. 104). It remains obscure why Circe, who was here supposed to be his wife (*Aen.* 7, 189, cf. also 12, 164 and Plutarch, see note 85), should have been frustrated in her love for him.

88 (p. 105). And in addition, as far as the execution of the statue is concerned, from the monument erected to Valerius Corvus by Augustus on his forum, Gellius 9, 11, 10 (see Ehwald on 14, 313).

89 (p. 105). While Ovid obliterates the divinity of Picus in the *Metamorphoses,* in the *Fasti* (3, 291 ff.) he ignores his kingship and his identity with the bird and treats him as a divine prophet only.

90 (p. 105). For Circe as a singer cf. also Vergil, *Aen.* 7, 11–12.

91 (p. 105). Circe is represented by Ovid as a sorceress rather than a goddess, and for this reason the miracles she performs require a greater effort on her part. But even so, the expense in magic is out of proportion to the results achieved. First, in order to lure the hunter Picus into a dense wood where he will have to dismount (and where the woodpecker belongs), she fashions out of air a sham boar (358 ff.); then, she creates a fog to separate Picus from his retinue (365 ff.); next, she transforms him into a bird (386 ff.); again, she allows the fog to lift (399 ff.); and lastly, in order to change the shape of Picus' attendants, she marshals an array of hellish powers, shaking into a ghastly turmoil all surrounding nature (403 ff.). This eerie agitation comes as an anticlimax for the reader who has previously seen hundreds of similar transformations (including that of Picus himself) contrived without any such spectacular concomitants. If, by way of contrast, we compare with this story the passage 7, 175–293, we find that there the magic takes up more space and yet the narrative is less loud and more simple and direct, in spite of the fact that Medea is accomplishing a singularly astounding feat.

92 (p. 106). This seems to be the case, and it would be interesting to speculate on the causes. The Triptolemus legend, for instance, is unimaginative—at least as far as Triptolemus' main achievement is concerned. It is unfortunate that we know so little of Sophocles' tragedy *Triptolemus.*

93 (p. 106). Primarily, the Greek nymphs represented the original soil of the land and its native plants and streams, although at times they were

also thought of as tending a garden and watering it from ditches (see *Göttinger Nachr.*, 1924, pp. 67–68).

94 (p. 108). The date for the institution on the Tiber island of the cult of Aesculapius was January 1 (see *Fasti* 1, 291–292); which means that Ovid came across the story of the god's migration to Rome as soon as he began to collect material for his *Fasti*. Then, however, he decided that the tale was more appropriate for the last book of the *Metamorphoses*.

95 (p. 108). Cf. *Fasti* 4, 270: *Dignus Roma locus quo deus omnis eat* (because of the political conquest of the world by Rome, 255–256). I believe that the same idea is expressed in the oracle from the Aesculapius story, *Metam.* 15, 637: *Quod petis hinc, propiore loco, Romane, petisses, et pete nunc propiore loco*, that is, "You might have found such relief [*quod = auxilium caeleste* 630] in Rome itself, O Roman. It is high time for you to have in Rome itself the healer god who can *praesens* [646] assist you."

96 (p. 108). For the chronology, three points may be considered, as follows:

1) Seneca is assumed to have been born either in 8 B.C. or in 4 or 1 B.C. When he heard Sotion, he was a *puer* according to *Epist.* 49, 2, a *iuvenis* according to *Epist.* 108, 17; that is, he was about seventeen years old. This dates his discipleship about A.D. 10, or 14, or 17.

2) Seneca practiced the teachings of Sotion at least for a year (*Epist.* 108, 22). He again gave up the vegetarian diet when, shortly after the accession of Tiberius, foreign cults were driven out of Italy (*ibid.*). In A.D. 16 (or 17 ?) the *mathematici* were banned (cf. Tacitus, *Ann.* 2, 32, 5 with Furneaux's note; Dio 57, 15, 8, etc.); A.D. 19, Egyptians and Jews were expelled (Tac. *Ann.* 2, 85, 5 etc.). It follows that Seneca studied with Sotion perhaps as early as about A.D. 10 (see no. 1) and certainly no later than A.D. 18. The latter date would imply that he discontinued his vegetarian diet A.D. 19, and the term *primus Tiberii Caesaris principatus* would cover five years; we can hardly stretch it any further. The current opinion that Seneca heard Sotion "about 20 A.D." (M. Schanz and C. Hosius, *Gesch. der röm. Liter.*, 4th ed., München, 1925, p. 681) or "in about the second *or third* decennium of our era" (J. Stenzel, in *R.-E.* 3a, 1238) has consequently to be rectified. The years 13–18 are the most probable date.

3) The last book of the *Metamorphoses* was written A.D. 7 or 8, that is, from 5 to 11 years before Seneca heard Sotion. It is not improbable that Sotion taught in Rome for 5–11 years.

97 (p. 108). The argumentation of Sotion, as recorded by Seneca (*Epist.*

108, 17–22), is all but identical with that of the Ovidian Pythagoras, and it is remarkable that both isolate from the rest the argument derived from reincarnation, rather than using it as the final climax for the arguments from cruelty.

98 (p. 109). In that case, the fine couplet in the *Metamorphoses,*

> Pythagoras poured forth his teaching to a silent crowd
> which stood in wonder at what he was saying,
>
> (15, 66 f.)

may reflect Ovid's own experience when he heard Sotion.

99 (p. 109). For instance, the work of Laberius, or the First Book of Varro's *Antiquitates,* cf. Varro frags. 36–40 on pp. 128–129 of A. Schmekel, *Die Philosophie der mittleren Stoa,* Berlin, 1892, and Schmekel's discussion on pp. 434–436. For a further possible source see the references in note 101, below.

100 (p. 109). These lines are paralleled in *Fasti* 4, 413–416. It seems that Ovid took the subject of animal slaughter much to heart at the time. He discussed it twice again in the *Fasti* (1, 337–388 and 4, 395–416) in terms very similar to *Metam.* 15, 96–142. The detail mentioned in *Metam.* 15, 135 and *Fasti* 1, 327 was perhaps taken from Callimachus, frag. 9, 10–11 Pfeiffer.

101 (p. 109). The theory as expounded by Ovid coincides with certain portions of the book ascribed to Ocellus Lucanus, cf. Richard Harder, 'Ocellus Lucanus,' Berlin, 1926; W. Theiler, *Gnomon* 2 (1926), pp. 587 ff.; R. Beutler, *R.-E.* 17, 2375 ff.

102 (p. 110). Once (15, 356–360) Pythagoras mentions feats of witchcraft (for which cf. *Am.* I, 8, 13–14 and *Fasti* 6, 141–142), but he adds *haut equidem credo.*

103 (p. 110). Note, for instance, that in this book alone are the Muses invoked by the poet (15, 622–625). The book seems also more elaborate in style than the others. I have not investigated the matter, but I should like to draw attention to one feature. It was a common practice with Ovid to tune corresponding lines to the same cadence, as for example in this couplet:

> Candidus / Oceano / nitidum caput / abdiderat / Sol,
> et caput / extulerat / densissimima / sidereum / Nox.
>
> (15, 30 f.)

The device was already used with good effect by Hellenistic poets (see *Göttinger Nachr.,* 1926, pp. 226–227), and there is nothing unusual in the fine couplet just quoted; but the sophistication goes much further in another couplet, where, in addition, all words except the last rhyme with one another:

> perquE levES aurAS HYPERIONIS urbE potitus,
> antE forES sacrAS HYPERIONIS aedE reponit;
>
> (15, 406 f.)

or in these five lines:

> Clara / fuit / SPARTE, magnæ / viguerE / MYCENAE,
> nec non et Cecropis, nec non Amphionis arces:
> vile / solum / SPARTEst, altae / cecidere / MYCENAE.
> Oedipodioniae quid sunt NISI NOMINA THEBAE?
> Quid PANDIONIAE restant NISI NOMEN ATHENAE?
>
> (15, 426 ff.)

104 (p. 110). Is the detailed story, earlier in the book (15, 565–621), of Cipus who covered his head with a laurel wreath (591) just as Caesar used to do (Suet. 45, 2), and who patriotically declined the kingship of Rome when it was offered him—is that story meant to be a parallel to Caesar's refusal of the regal diadem when it was offered him by Marc Antony (Suet. 79, 2)?

105 (p. 111). The great epic, or its last part, had not yet undergone its final revision when the poet left for Tomis (note 79, p. 221), and its epilogue, at least, was not composed until after the imperial decree. Perhaps we can lay our finger on another passage written under the cloud of impending exile, if not after the poet's departure.

There is in the last book of the *Metamorphoses* one fable with certain strange, incisive overtones, the story of the man Hippolytus (15, 493–546), who was sentenced to exile because of a hideous love affair in which he was involved through no fault of his own—nor had he committed any crime. Ovid introduces the tale with the words: "I wish it were not my own story I am telling" (495–496); for he puts the tale into the mouth of Hippolytus and makes him narrate his own death (he had been revived in the meantime), which gives a ghastly effect. The erotic tangle, which was one of the most celebrated by poetry, is reported in the fewest possible words; only the woman's guilt (like the younger Julia, she was the daughter of a notorious adulteress, 500) and the speaker's innocence are emphasized (500–504). Then we hear the banished Hippolytus say that his mind was entirely taken up by the prospect of exile and failed to register anything else (514–515, cf. *Tr.* I, 3, 7–12). Furthermore, tradition had it that Hippolytus received his mortal wounds when he was dragged over the rough ground by the bolting horses of his chariot (cf. Euripides, *Hippol.* 1236 ff.); Ovid, however, changed one detail. According to him, the body hit a tree stump and the horses tore Hippolytus apart, flesh from flesh and limb from limb (521–526). In an elegy written on his voyage to Tomis, Ovid thus describes his parting forever from Rome and from those that were dear to him:

I was being divided as if I were leaving my limbs behind,
    a part of my body seemed to break off.
Such was the pain of Mettus, when the horses that punished his treachery
    tore him in different directions.
                (*Tr.* I, 3, 73 ff.)

If we wish to push our fancy still further, we may imagine the poet indulging in some daydreaming of his own while he told of how Hippolytus, through an extraordinary act of mercy on the part of the gods, was resuscitated from death (Ovid often speaks of his banishment as a living death) and permitted to live on in modest seclusion. One or another of the Greek islands was under consideration for his future residence (540–541), but the choice fell on some place in Italy, where the exiled man assumed an alias, shedding his former self and taking on the shape of an old man. In this, however, Ovid was only following the traditional version.

It is, of course, no more than an interesting possibility that Ovid had already received his sentence and was anticipating his departure from Rome when he composed this tale. But we can point to some more unusual details. The alleged analogy (*similes casus,* 494) which serves to link up the story with the main line of the narrative is rather farfetched, and the poet admits as much (530–531). The actual connection is merely its tragic character, and in fact the tale is told in such a fashion as to solicit the deepest sympathy with the victim. Contrary to the general tendency of the Fifteenth Book, the eventual elevation of Hippolytus to the rank of an Italian god is played down, and the loss of identity which shields him from further persecution is played up (535–546).

And finally, our conjecture can be supported by a passage in the *Fasti* which contains a close parallel to the trick with the first person in *Metam.* 15, 495–496. Although it is not the first but the second person in the *Fasti,* the result is the same. Carmenta is comforting her exiled son Evander in a direct speech (*Fasti* 1, 479–496), and her solacing words avoid any and all topical references, so that they are equally valid for Ovid. Furthermore, Ovid had pretended to ask Carmenta for the facts of the story

(467), and thus Ovid as well as Evander is supposed to be listening to her oration, just as, in the *Metamorphoses,* Ovid as well as Hippolytus was saying the words: "This is my own story." In the *Fasti,* moreover, the analogy between Evander's and Ovid's own banishment is made explicit in line 540, so that this time we know beyond the shadow of a doubt what the author intended to imply.

NOTES TO CHAPTER 12, OVID'S BANISHMENT, PP. 111–117

1 (p. 111). In the first stage of Roman imperial rule, the Head of State interfered with state affairs at his own discretion and in such forms as he saw fit. The imperial prerogatives were not yet clearly defined, and it is doubtful whether Ovid's relegation should be styled an administrative or a judicial act. Nevertheless I shall apply to it, for the sake of convenience, juridical terms such as condemnation and indictment. They are meant to be taken loosely rather than with their technical connotation.

2 (p. 111). Most of the evidence is collected in S. G. Owen's edition of the *Tristia,* Book II (Oxford, 1924), pp. 10 ff.

3 (p. 112). Scholars are used to say that nine years had elapsed since the publication of the *Art,* although they accept the year 1 B.C. (cf. *Ars Amat.* I, 179 ff.) as a terminus post quem for the *Art.* They seem to have forgotten that there was no zero year. Thus A.D. 8 is eight years later than B.C. 1. Furthermore, the first two books of the *Art* may have been published A.D. 1, and the three books together as late as A.D. 2. The most incriminating passage, in the sense of *Tr.* II, 212, of the *Art* is in the Third Book (III, 611–666).

4 (p. 112). Moreover, *Tr.* III, 4 seems to indicate that Ovid met his destruction because he had dared to associate with persons of highest rank. It is true that an alternative interpretation is possible, viz., that Ovid is referring to his high ambition as a writer rather than to his social connections. This explanation, however, does not seem to agree equally well with the tenor of the elegy.

5 (p. 113). All this is predicated on the assumption that Ovid's banishment was caused by the younger Julia's adultery, an assumption which I believe to be well founded. The thesis, on the other hand, that the poet was involved in a conspiracy against the Emperor seems to me farfetched. It is based on mere speculation; all the evidence we possess points decidedly in a different direction; and Ovid was, I feel, the last man to have his hand in a political intrigue.

6 (p. 113). Augustus fell in love with Livia while she was the wife of Tiberius Claudius Nero and pregnant. Instantly he divorced his own wife

and caused Livia's husband to divorce her and to give her away in marriage to himself. When, a few months later, she was delivered of her child, Augustus sent it to its father Claudius Nero. The pontifical college sanctioned the revolting procedure.

7 (p. 114). Cf. *Tr.* I, 5, 33–34; I, 8; I, 9a; III, 5, 5–6; V, 4, 35–36; *Po.* II, 3, 29–30; IV, 3. In *Po.* III, 2, 5–24, Ovid forgives those who deserted him.

8 (p. 114). I am referring to "Ibis." For my explanation of that man's misdeed see pp. 151–152 with notes. Ovid mentions Ibis as late as in *Po.* II, 7, 62 (see p. 245, note 4).

9 (p. 115). This is probably meant by *utilitas* and *auxilium, Tr.* I, 3, 88 and 102. The later epistles show that Ovid hoped his wife would successfully intercede with Livia (see p. 135).

10 (p. 115). As an emotional act with no practical consequences, the burning of the *Metamorphoses* is in line with the conception of useless epistles composed by women of legend.

11 (p. 116). Other manuscripts, however, seem to have been irreparably destroyed on the same pyre, and Ovid later regretted their loss (cf. *Tr.* I, 7, 15 and IV, 10, 63–64).

12 (p. 116). To pick at random from the overwhelming evidence, cf. Ovid, *Tr.* I, 1, 39–44; V, 12, 3–4; *Her.* [XV] (Sappho), 14 (*vacuae carmina mentis opus*) with Palmer's note; [XV], 195–198; Horace, *Carm.* I, 1, 30 with Heinze's note, and *Epist.* II, 2, 77 ff.; Tacitus, *Dial.* 9 (*in nemora et lucos, id est in solitudinem, secedendum est*), and chapters 12 and 13 of the *Dialogus.* This is, in a nutshell, the *raison d'être* for pastoral poetry (cf. p. 9 with note 26, p. 175).

13 (p. 117). For the precise meaning of *Tr.* I, 11, 11–12, compare the elaboration in IV, 1, 37–52 with the notions *hoc studium, stupor,* and *insania* recurring as *hoc studium* (37), *stupet* (42), and *furor* (37 and 38).

14 (p. 117). The line *Tr.* I, 11, 12 is to be read in the shape in which the inscription *C.I.L.* VI, 9632 (= *Carm. Lat. Epigraph.* conl. F. Bücheler no. 89) reproduces it, *Omnis ab hac cura cura levata mea est;* cf. *Rem.* 170 and 484 (see A. E. Housman, *Manilius,* Vol. 1, p. LX). Exactly parallel is *Po.* III, 9, 21: *Scribentem iuvat ipse labor minuitque laborem* (see p. 139). Ovid is not punning, but playing off against one another the pleasant and the unpleasant aspect of the same thing, *care* or *exertion.*

NOTES TO CHAPTER 13, OVID IN EXILE, PP. 117–142

1 (p. 118). In this note I shall account for my description in the text of Ovid's journey to Tomis.

Three voyages are explicitly mentioned in *Tr.* I, 10 and 11, namely: (1) from Italy to Lechaeum, in December (11, 3-4); (2) from Cenchreae to Samothrace, on the *Minerva* (10, 1-20; 11, 5-8); and (3) from Samothrace to the Thracian coast (10, 21). An overland journey through Thrace was to follow (10, 23). One more voyage (4), from some Black Sea port to Tomis, is indicated in *Tr.* V, 2b, 18. I believe that it was also made on the *Minerva* because 10, 41-44 make better sense if the poet is supposed to be on board when the boat arrives at Tomis, and because *sitque* in line 1 indicates that Ovid hopes for his own protection by the patron goddess of the boat even for the future, although he has already left the ship (cf. also the present tense of *fida manet* in line 10). Elegy 11 (with the *nunc quoque* in line 19) was written on the fourth voyage. Its position at the end of the book, and the concluding line ("I shall write no more"), suggest that it is the latest of the travel elegies; the "short hop" from Samothrace to Thrace would not warrant so much excitement; the *portus* of line 25 is more likely to be identical with Ovid's final destination; and the words *laeva pars* in 31 reflect the official term (cf., e.g., Owen's note on *Tr.* II, 197) for the west coast of the Black Sea.

Now for the chronology. In 11, 13-16, star dates are given. I have found them nowhere discussed or explained and am no expert in the ancient star reckoning; thus my own explanation has a tentative character only and is open to correction.

When constellations are mentioned to designate a date, it seems that ordinarily, unless otherwise specified, reference is made to the heliacal rise of the constellation. Thus, for instance, the "dog days" are those at which the star of the Dog rises shortly before the sun and ushers in the day. The date for the heliacal rise of the *nimbosi Haedi* (13, = *pluvialis Capella*) is the 1st of May, according to *Fasti* 5, 113. The corresponding date for the Pleiades (= *Steropes sidus* line 14) is May 13 (cf. *Fasti* 5, 599-600). Line 15 I take to mean (not, as it is commonly explained, that the days were cloudy, but): "Arctophylax, when rising, extinguished the day and brought dusk with it," which is an apt circumlocution for the acronychal rising. The actual date is March 4 or February 24 (slight variations are to be expected for a number of reasons), according to Euctemon or Eudoxus respectively (cf. F. Gundel in Roscher, *Lexicon der Mythologie* Vol. 6, p. 889). In the *Fasti* (3, 403-406), however, Ovid made the mistake of marking March 5 as the date for the heliacal setting, instead of the acronychal rising, of Arctophylax (see H. Peter's note on *Fasti* 3, 406; in *Fasti* 5, 733, on the other hand, May 26 is correctly mentioned as the date of its heliacal setting). *Serae* in line 16 likewise seems to indicate the "late" or acronychal rising of the Hyades, which takes place on May 5 according to *Fasti* 5, 163–164. Thus we have two heliacal dates, May 1 and May 13; and then two acronychal dates, March 5 and May 5. The slip in the *Fasti* casts the shadow of a doubt on the lone March date, but I propose to accept it because, while the *Fasti* was merely based on some book calendar, the voyages gave Ovid ample occasion to watch the stars directly and to discuss with the crew the weather which their rising and setting portended. Since no one of the voyages can have lasted from December to March, or from early March to the middle of May, we can assign the December to the voyage on the Adriatic and the Ionian Sea (II, 3–4); March to that on the Aegean; and May to that on the Pontus.

One difficulty remains. If *Tr.* I, 11 was written in May, how then could Ovid, in connection with verbs in the present tense, speak of *brumalis lux* (39) as well as of *hiems* (43), and *hiberni fluctus* (33)? The answer is, first, that winter was longer in Thrace than in Italy (Ovid considered Thrace as an arctic country, cf. *Tr.* III, 4b, 1–2); and secondly, that, since this elegy is the epilogue to the whole book, the present tense in its last part covers the time of the entire journey which lasted from December to May. The pronoun *haec* in lines 35 and 37 clearly refers not to this poem alone, but to the entire book (cf. 1–2, and *haec* in 3); and the *carmen* in the last line can equally well be taken either way because both the elegy and the book end with that line. The last part, then, of the poem reflects in the mirror of the present situation the author's writing of verse at any time of his winter journey.

The structure of the elegy is this. "The present book was composed under the trying circumstances of my journey into exile (1–2). In part, it was written while I crossed the Adriatic (3–4, first voyage); in part, while I sailed on the Aegean (5–8, second voyage); and indeed it was strange that I could compose verse at all on shipboard in inclement weather (9–18; the past tenses cover the journey up to the present moment). Even now, while the journey is drawing to its close (fourth voyage) and I am writing the last elegy of the series, a storm rages (19–24). Moreover, I know that at the place of my destination still worse hazards await me (25–34). Thus I have been writing under a severe strain, and my readers ought to be lenient in criticizing the book which I am now concluding (35–44)."

2 (p. 118). For reasons of style and literary convention, Ovid concentrates on the personified ship, but doubtless he felt the same way about the crew.

3 (p. 120). For the truthfulness of Ovid's statements on the locale and climate of Tomis, cf., e.g., Kurt Regling, *Die antiken Münzen Nordgriechenlands,* Berlin, 1910, Vol. I, p. 588, note 2. I do not think that Ovid exaggerates much in picturing his sufferings. For one thing, he describes them in a fairly concrete and very plausible manner; and secondly, even if we had no word from him, we would still know, the susceptibilities of Balkan enthusiasts notwithstanding, that Tomis was not a healthful or congenial place of residence for an aging Roman poet as delicate, cultured, sensitive, and social as Ovid happened to be.

4 (p. 120). The Ovid of the exile is bound to annoy any historian. The historically minded biographer will regret that Ovid gave a sentimental rather than objective picture of his own life among the "Goths." The historian of the Balkans will resent it that Ovid disliked and maligned that part of the world. And the historian of Rome will censure it that Ovid did not make enough of a unique opportunity for shedding light on a dark corner of the Empire.

5 (p. 120). Of course we have to make due allowance for the obvious exigencies of Ovid's situation. For this reason, we are not obliged to believe his professions of heartfelt affection for all members of the imperial family (especially *Po.* IV, 9, 105–124; cf. also p. 135), although he may have nourished the fanciful hope that it would help to bring about his release if he actually felt that way and may therefore have tried to talk himself into it.

6 (p. 120). For the wish to die on terra firma rather than be drowned, the commentators cite *Fasti* 3, 597–598; *Metam.* 11, 539–540; Vergil, *Aeneid* 1, 94–96. The earliest instance is *Odyssey* 5, 306–312.

7 (p. 120). It is natural for a man in Ovid's situation and with his mentality to use the prison bars of his misery as a protection from further attacks; cf. also *Tr.* III, 11, 25; *Po.* II, 7, 42; IV, 16, 51–52; *Tr.* V, 6, 31–34, etc.

8 (p. 121). Apart from the touch of humor, the sentiment in these lines is of the same type as in the strikingly modern (see p. 210, note 16) passage of Simonides' *Danaë,* frag. 13, 18–19 Diehl: Κέλομ' εὗδε, βρέφος, εὑδέτω δὲ πόντος, εὑδέτω ἄμετρον κακόν. When Ovid wished that *hiems* should cease, he probably thought not of the storm alone, but of all his adversity, his own ἄμετρον κακόν (cf. *hiems* in *Tr.* III, 8, 30). In *Tr.* I, 2, 103–110 the supposed subsiding of the storm is turned into a wishful oracle pre-

dicting the subsiding of the imperial disgrace (compare line 110 with line 4, each in its context).

9 (p. 121). For *Tr.* III, 8, 29-30 cf. *Fasti* 6, 149-150 in its context.

10 (p. 121). *Caelum* in *Tr.* III, 8, 23 is both "climate" and "the fire of the heavenly bodies"; cf. also III, 3, 7-8. The drinking water at Tomis was brackish, cf. *Po.* II, 7, 73-74; III, 1, 17-18.

11 (p. 122). The fine lines we just quoted from *Tr.* III, 8 seem identical in their thought with a passage from Ovid's earliest work, *Am.* III, 6, 13-20, but at closer inspection we see that the sort of realism which wins out over legend is different. In the *Amores,* Ovid had turned with his *potius* (19) from miraculous legend to a personalized river, asking it to relent; now, in the *Tristia,* he turns from miraculous legend to the Emperor, asking him to relent.

12 (p. 123). For the notion that all the adventures as Odysseus told them to the Phaeacians were not true, cf. Pindar, *Nem.* 7, 20 ff. (see *Gnomon* 6, 1930, 12), and Lycophron, *Alexandra* 763-765 (see U. von Wilamowitz, *Hermes* 62, 1927, p. 278). Ovid frequently likens himself to Odysseus (*Tr.* V, 5, 3 and 51; *Po.* I, 3, 33, etc.), to Philoctetes (*Tr.* V, 1, 61; V, 2, 13; V, 4, 12; *Po.* I, 3, 5; III, 1, 54); to Orpheus (*Tr.* IV, 1, 17), and to other characters of legend, according to the aspect of his life to which he is referring.

13 (p. 123). For the geography cf. *Dobrogea 1878-1928, Cintizeci de 50 ani de viețǎ Româneascǎ,* Bucharest, 1928, pp. 455-456. According to *Encyl. Britann.* s.v. *Constantza,* the harbor is well protected from the north but dangerously open to southerly winds. K. Regling (see above, note 3), p. 588, note 1, suggests, without indicating his reasons, that the ancient harbor was situated in a crescent-shaped indenture of the cape itself rather than where the present harbor is situated. This does not seem very plausible.

14 (p. 123). For the historical background cf. A. von Domaszewski, *Neue Heidelberger Jahrb.* I (1894), 190 ff; (Weiß, *Die Dobrudscha im Altertum,* Sarajewo, 1911, was not available to me); Carl Patsch, *Beiträge zur Völkerkunde von Südosteuropa,* Sect. V, Pt. I, in Wiener Sitz.-Ber., phil.-hist. Klasse 214, 1 (1932); *R.-E.* sub vocc. *Getae, Sarmatae, Sarmatia,* and *Thrake.* Many points are controversial or conjectural.

15 (p. 124). We possess little evidence for the economic life of Tomis, cf. Regling (note 3), p. 595; my statement rests in part on conjecture only.

16 (p. 124). The incumbent had already protected and befriended Ovid while he was traveling through southern Thrace; see above, pp. 118-119.

17 (p. 124). δορυφόρος τῆς ἡγεμονίας, according to the text *Sylloge Inscr.*

Graec. ed. W. Dittenberger, 3d ed., Vol. 2, no. 798, 4 from A.D. 37, when Rhoemetalces, son of Cotys (cf. *Po.* II, 9) and Antonia Tryphaena, had become the last suzerain king of Thrace.

18 (p. 124). In the year 15 a reorganization took place which seems to have improved the political conditions (cf. Regling—note 3, above—p. 593, note 1).

19 (p. 125). See Patsch (note 14), pp. 115–116; Max Fluss, *R.-E.* 15, 2373.

20 (p. 127). Moreover, we cannot expect Ovid to write his elegies in the manner of Horace's *Iter Brundisinum* or, for that matter, of Katherine Mansfield's letters. Neither his own nature nor that of the genre would have permitted such an attitude. His concern for dignity of style can be inferred from the fact that in his descriptions of the place and population he never mentions such things as filth, stench, vermin, bad manners, and the like.

21 (p. 127). When one of Ovid's correspondents, with friendly curiosity, inquired about the people of Tomis and their habits (*Tr.* V, 7, 9–10), just as Cicero wanted to hear from his brother about the *gentes* in Gaul and their *mores,* the *situs* and *naturae rerum et locorum* (*Ad Qu. fratrem* II, 15, 4), the poet painted both the inhabitants and the country in the most dismal colors.

22 (p. 130). In *Tr.* IV, 1, 21, Ovid speaks of "a plot" and "a soldier's sword" that threatened him (one word in the line is unfortunately corrupt), and later in the same elegy he writes (65–66): "I shall not tell the story of a plot against my life; true as the tale is, it will sound too wild for finding credence." In *Tr.* V, 2, 30, we read again: "... not to mention the armed hand raised to destroy me ..." (*ut taceam strictas in mea fata manus*), as distinct from the fact that he lived in a barbarian land and in a place surrounded by savage enemies (31–32). Perhaps Ovid believed that some people hoped to oblige the Emperor by eliminating him, or that Augustus had given secret orders to have him murdered, but of course he could not openly voice a suspicion of this sort.

I should think that the poet, obsessed with fear of violence as he was, would at all times have one of his slaves near him as a bodyguard.

23 (p. 131). In this couplet, Ovid doubtless had in mind Sophocles, *Philoctetes* 936–949 (compare ὦ καταρρῶγες πέτραι, 937, with Ovid's *voce fatigaret Lemnia saxa sua*), or a similar passage from another tragedy. For *querula Progne* (line 60), Sophocles frag. 583 (Pearson) may be compared; and Niobe (line 57) was also the heroine of a number of tragedies. Ovid had previously published another collection of poetic epistles, the

Heroides, which were likewise akin to tragic monologues or arias (see p. 190, note 1).

24 (p. 131). The idea, with its emphasis on the subjective side of a narrative poem, sounds surprisingly modern. With it Ovid goes beyond Horace, who compared his own poetry not to a likeness of the author's features, but to a pyramid in which a king is buried (*Carm.* III, 30; cf. Tr. III, 3, 77–80). For Ovid's wish to write personal rather than perfect verse see above, pp. 7–8. *Po.* IV, 13, 9–10 shows that Ovid was sensitive in "observing the marks" of an author's individual manner.

25 (p. 132). Evidently Ovid's married condition did not interfere with his amatory poetry, nor does anyone seem to have taken exception to that incongruity. Although the Romans did, at least in theory, mind the faithlessness of a wife, they were far from squeamish about the amours of a husband. But the two spheres had to be kept neatly apart, and it is a surprising exception that Ovid included in his *Amores* an elegy (III, 13) in which he mentioned his wife (line 1).

26 (p. 132). Ovid wrote his autobiography in order to paint for his readers his own portrait as a background to his erotic verse (I do not understand why he fails to refer to the *Metamorphoses*). The ancient idea of a biography was (cf. Friedrich Leo, *Die griechisch-römische Biographie nach ihrer literarischen Form,* Leipzig, 1901, pp. 96–97) that the personality ("das Sein, das Wesen, die Handlungen, in denen sich Anlage, Gesinnung, Ausbildung spiegeln") was to be represented in terms of "life and actions" (βίος καὶ πράξεις, cf. *vitae acta* line 92). The main point of Ovid's autobiography is that poetry, commonly considered as "useless" (*studium inutile,* line 21; cf. above, pp. 9–10), gave him both eternal fame and a purposeful life even in banishment; thus, after all, it was anything but useless. (In deference to the theme, *Musa triumphans,* the fact that his poetry had contributed to his ruin is here suppressed.)

I feel that the elegy is somewhat spoiled by the author's attempt to blend into one person Ovid the bourgeois and Ovid the bohemian and poet. Like many other writers, he was not entirely the same man in his prosaic and his poetic life. The interesting topic is discussed by Ovid himself in his apology, *Tr.* II, 348–360. But the passage there has to be taken with a grain of salt because it is tainted by the author's purpose, for obvious reasons, to dissociate his own person from the amatory verse he had composed. How far can we accept as true what he asserts? We may well take his word for it when he contends that he has broken up no marriage (348–352) and that, in this sense, his life was clean (354); and we know anyway that the adventures which figure in his erotic poetry were in part imaginary (355–356). But we are only half convinced when he says (353) that his poetry was not in line with his *mores,* that is, with his actual character and behavior. The author is trying to convey the impression that the real Ovid had little in common with the personality displayed in his erotic verse, and that the latter personality was largely an artistic fiction (357–360). In this form the thesis is hardly correct. Both characters were equally real. The conscientious bourgeois, and the poet responsible to his art alone, existed within the same person side by side. Inevitably, the two characters would frequently clash with each other, and some compromise would have to be decided upon from case to case. We have no means of knowing on what basis Ovid compromised.

27 (p. 132). Occasionally, he also grew defiant and ironically contended that his poetry ought to be as barbarian as the life to which he was condemned, so as faithfully to mirror his sufferings (this seems to be the meaning of *Tr.* V, 1, 69–74).

28 (p. 133). This is the text of *Po.* III, 5, 33–34:

> Namque ego qui perii iam pridem, Maxime, vobis
> ingenio nitor non periisse meo.

The vexed question of punctuation and interpretation can perhaps be answered in the following fashion. In his own epitaph Ovid had said (*Tr.* III, 3, 74): *Ingenio perii Naso poeta meo,* and he had used the same phrase in *Tr.* II, 2 (cf. also *Po.* II, 7, 48). No doubt the author expected his readers to remember those epigrammatic lines and accordingly to take *ingenio meo* with *perii* as well as with *non perii.* It follows that *vobis* is likewise meant to go with both verbs, and the meaning is this: "Through my poetry I have brought about my relegation and long since become a dead man in your eyes; but through my poetry I also strive now to keep alive in your eyes." Our explanation of *perii vobis* is confirmed by the concluding distich of *Po.* I, 5, in the hexameter of which the same construction recurs in an identical context:

> Vosque quibus perii tum cum mea fama sepulta est,
> nunc quoque de nostra morte tacere reor.

The trend of the pentameter, however, is different this time, because Ovid is now in a despondent mood (see pp. 156–157). The context shows that *tacere* refers to a conspiracy of silence: probably no one is willing to praise Ovid's poetry from his ignominious exile. The distich says: "I became a dead man for you at the time that I was banished, and I suppose you will also ignore the verse which the dead man is still writing."

29 (p. 135). Ovid was perhaps not very adroit in his struggle for libera-
tion, but everything else seemed also to operate against his burning desire. The influential man to whom he sent the arrows died just when he
was about to see the Emperor and ask him to pardon the poet. This made
Ovid feel as if a contagious curse were upon him (*Po.* IV, 6, 7–14).

30 (p. 135). Cf. also *Tr.* III, 8, 13–22.

31 (p. 135). He composed an elegy on the triumph of Tiberius (*Po.* II,
5, 27–34; III, 4) and wanted to have it published, although he was diffident about its quality, because he was not in the right mood for the description of a joyous event (*Po.* III, 4, 45–50). Furthermore, he wrote a
poem on the deification of Augustus with the avowed purpose of earn-
ing his release from Tomis (*Po.* IV, 6, 17–20; 8, 63–86; 9, 131–134). For
the poem in the Getic language see below, p. 250, note 5.

32 (p. 136). In his happier times Ovid had written this: "It is not proper
to hear a poet as if he were a witness in court; I wish my words had no
weight with you" (*Am.* III, 12, 19–20). Now, however, he declares (*Po.*
III, 9, 47–50): "Other poets may mold and change their stories, . . . but
my verse has the weight of a deposition made by an incorruptible witness."

33 (p. 139). For this passage see above, p. 173, note 18; and for line 21,
p. 229, note 14. Cf. also *Po.* I, 5, 9–20.

34 (p. 139). Dancing and reciting were more closely related in Ovid's
time than they are in ours. Dances were mimic, and we remember that
Ovid's poetry was being rendered on the stage by dancers (see above,
p. 47, with note 4, p. 195).

35 (p. 140). For the context (the poet is pleading that his miserable
condition ought to protect him from further attacks) see above, p. 232,
note 7.

36 (p. 140). Alcaeus, it is true, had also complained of the "ills of exile"
(cf. Horace, *Carm.* II, 13, 28), but his poems were of a different genre
and, as a recently discovered papyrus shows (*Oxyrhynchus Papyri* XVIII,
London, 1941, no. 2165), both his situation and his reaction were totally
different.

37 (p. 141). In this chapter we have exploited Ovid's epistles from exile
merely from the biographical point of view, neglecting the ideas they
convey and the art with which they are constructed. Any closer analysis
of single elegies (provided we do not conduct it on the lines of school
rhetoric) reveals surprising poetic qualities. This is true not only for the
best-known poems from the first books (like *Tr.* I, 3), but for the later
and latest elegies as well.

38 (p. 142). The whole tenor of the elegy *Tr.* V, 12 shows that Ovid's

correspondent was not exhorting him to write more or better personal epistles, but rather to compose poetry of a different and more elevated character.

NOTES TO CHAPTER 14, THE "FASTI," PP. 142–151

1 (p. 142). In *Tr.* III, 14, 37–44, Ovid complains that he has no access to books or persons which he could consult for "a word, a name, or a place," and he indicates that this makes the writing of verse difficult. Although Ovid may have known his Rome intimately, he was bound to forget details.

2 (p. 143). The *nuper* in *Tr.* II, 551 indicates that the *Fasti* was Ovid's most recent project at the time when he was banished. For parallels between the *Fasti* and the last books of the *Metamorphoses* see p. 103; note 94, p. 224; and note 100, p. 225. H. Peeters (*Les "Fastes" d'Ovide,* Brussels, 1939, pp. 28–31) believes that Ovid began to prepare the *Fasti* at a far earlier date, namely, about the year 8 B.C.; but his reasoning seems none too clear. When in this connection Peeters twice (pp. 28 and 31) calls attention to the fact that in *Fasti* I, 645 an event of 8 B.C. is called *recens,* he overlooks three points. (1) Ovid styles the campaign of Tiberius *recens* by comparison with an event of about 400 B.C., so that the term need only mean "in modern times, within our own lifetime." (2) The couplet addresses not Augustus, but Tiberius, and was therefore probably written later than A.D. 14. (3) The subject of the passage in which *recens* occurs is the anniversary of an event which took place on January 16, A.D. 10, and Peeters himself correctly lists (p. 84) the section I, 637–650 among those which Ovid added in his exile.

3 (p. 143). If we care to divide Ovid's career into periods, we shall best begin a new period with the twelfth volume of the *Metamorphoses* and the time when he began to work on the *Fasti.* For the inadequacy of the conventional trichotomy of his career see above, p. 199, note 1.

4 (p. 144). Not only did the subject of the *Fasti* require a different treatment, but the author too had changed since he wrote the first eleven books of his *Metamorphoses.* Sentimental love no longer plays a role in the *Fasti;* wherever an erotic affair is narrated, the passion is not of the delicate and tender sort, but rather in the way of stark sensuality.

5 (p. 144). See above, p. 91.

6 (p. 144). Ovid himself gives a more idealistic reason in a fine passage in which he explains that contemplation of the celestial bodies draws the human mind heavenward and makes it impervious to lust, greed, and worldly ambition (I, 295–310. The suggestion that this eulogy of the

nong the passages inserted later in honor of Ger-
; Ovid makes it plain that he has a man in mind
al pursuit, including politics and soldiering; see
ift Joh. Vahlen, Berlin, 1900, pp. 381 f.). His actual
stars fail to express so elevated a spirit. His star
ertaining and amusing than edifying and lofty.
uch of humor in 2, 247–266 (note also that in line
declares: *Non faciet longas fabula nostra moras,*
t that *mora,* cf. lines 256 and 259, is the point of
unknown to us, Ovid wrote a poem with the
he described all the constellations. The list
lent hexameters of frag. 4 Lenz.
ompliance with the imperial policy appears,
for example, in 2, 139, as contrasted with *Ars Amat.* I, 131–134. An indication that Augustus was likely to approve of the theme of the *Fasti* can
be seen in the fact that the Emperor hired as tutor for his grandsons the
same Verrius Flaccus who arranged the Fasti of Praeneste (cf. Suetonius,
De Gramm. 17; *Corpus Inscr. Latin.* I, 2d ed., no. 230; F. Peeters [see
note 2], p. 23, note 3.)

8 (p. 145). Most scholars have adopted the suggestion that the preface
to the Second Book (II, 3–16) was originally written to open the First
Book (with *ite* instead of *itis* in line 3; see E. Thomas, in *Festschrift
Joh. Vahlen,* Berlin, 1900, pp. 373–374) and received its present position by the hand of the editor of the posthumous work. This theory,
however, overlooks the fact that the passage in question preludes II,
119–144. When Ovid says, in lines 15–16: *At tua prosequimur studioso
pectore, Caesar, nomina, per titulos ingredimurque tuos,* he is both hark-
ing back to I, 587–616, where the *nomen* (line 608, etc.) and *titulus* (line
602) *Augustus* was celebrated and, even more so, looking forward to the
nomen (cf. *nomen,* and twice again *nomina,* in II, 127–130) and title of
pater patriae which will be extolled under the date of February 5. The
two passages II, 3–16 and II, 119–144 are introduced with the same em-
phatic *nunc;* the same notions and words recur in both, but their weight
is increased in the second. Thus the *vela maiora* (the more elevated subject) of line 3 becomes *maiora viribus* in line 123; the higher task which
is set for the *elegi* in the preface (3–16) turns into a task almost too heavy
for mere *elegi* in 125–126; and line 7, *sacra cano signataque tempora fastis,*
is echoed in 121–122: *dum canimus sacras alterno pectine Nonas; maximus hic fastis accumulatur honor,* with the superlative *maximus.* It follows that Ovid put off to the Second Book the discussion of his switch

from dallying love elegiacs to the dignified elegiacs of the *Fasti* because in that book the *Fasti* was to reach the highest dignity (*maximus honor*).

9 (p. 145). One line of the *Fasti,* for instance (6, 176, *nec quae Pygmaeo sanguine gaudet avem*), is directly translated from Callimachus (see *Hermes* 63, 1928, p. 305, line 14: αἵματι πυγμαίων χαιρομένη γέρανος). A more important detail is this. In contrast to earlier poetry, Callimachus represents the Muse who inspires him as if she were standing before him in the flesh and actually conversing with him, cf. *Oxyrh. Pap.* XVII, 1927, no. 2080, 58–59: Ὡς ἐφάμην· Κλειὼ δὲ τὸ δεύτερον ἤρχετο μύθου, χεῖρ’ ἐπ’ ἀδελφείης ὦμον ἐρεισαμένη. Ovid pretends to converse with the many gods he says he has consulted in the identical fashion. In *Fasti* 5, 7–110, for instance, all the Muses are supposed to be present and to discuss the poet's problem, not only with him, but also to their mutual benefit (cf. lines 10; 55–56; 107).—Callimachus had also written a prose book on the Greek calendar, and even before him the Hellenistic writer Simias of Rhodes had composed a poem, in elegiacs, on the months of the year and the reasons for their names. (Cf. *De Simia Rhodio,* Göttingen, 1915, pp. 40–41.)

10 (p. 146). For the concluding couplet (4, 385–386) see note 24, p. 242. Another anecdote of the same general type is 4, 681–712. This story is similar to Callimachus, *Aetia* frag. 8, 1–25 Pfeiffer. The Hellenistic style required that the setting include some topical detail which, though adding nothing to the substance of the exposition, makes the little scene appear more real and personal. As with all anecdotes, it is beside the point to ask whether the incidents are true or fictitious.

11 (p. 146). Cf. the programmatic phrase *tempora cum causis,* 1, 1 = 4, 11. The author lays his finger on the aetiological character of the *Fasti* when in 3, 723–725 he all but says: "I shall not describe here the transformation of the Tyrrhenian sailors, because it is not the *Metamorphoses* in which I am at present engaged but rather an aetiological work."—It would perhaps be worth while to investigate the principles on which Ovid's explanations are based. The *nam* in 1, 90 betrays the notable fact that in the poet's mind a deity which had an equivalent in the Greek pantheon needed no further elucidation. As this was not true for Janus, the author (or his source) found it difficult to interpret the nature of the god and took recourse to identifying Janus with a notion taken from Greek philosophical speculation (103, see note 6, p. 209; cf. also the atrocious etymology *Ionio Iano* in *Metam.* 14, 334). The Romans owed their spiritual life so largely to the Greeks that when they wanted better to understand their own deities they were obliged to explain them in terms of Greek ideas.

12 (p. 146). Very many times was Ovid obliged to express date intervals of the type "Three days after this celebration..." or "When the next day rises...," but he managed with great ingenuity to avoid verbal repetition; he has ever new phrases for the same thing, one finer than the other. Another sport in which he successfully indulges is to make up for the dullness of trivial topics by a piquant wording; this is a characteristic Hellenistic device.

13 (p. 146). The First Book in general does not make smooth reading. In striking contrast to most of the rest is the easy and natural flow of the passage 663–704. The probable reason is that the subject appealed to Ovid (see p. 208, note 7).

14 (p. 146). Whenever in the *Aetia* the author raises his head to speak of himself and to give his own views, the reader immediately feels that he is in the presence of a powerful personality. In the *Fasti,* by contrast, the personal elements are in general shadowy and unimpressive, and the few times this is not so strike the reader as exceptions. Among these exceptions (they are, characteristically, on the sentimental side) are the fine couplet 6, 771–772; the tender reference to the author's own family in 6, 219–220; and the prelude to the Fourth Book (see p. 146). For a witty personal remark in 2, 248 see above, note 6.—The references to the author's own exile which were inserted later are in a different category; we are now dealing with the original version of the *Fasti.* For 1, 479–496, probably also written after Ovid's banishment, see pp. 227 f., note 105.

15 (p. 146). In 6, 3–8, Ovid says: "Some people will think I am lying when I tell of my conversations with gods; actually, however, I am inspired by gods and, if anyone, the bard of the *Fasti* has a right to behold gods face to face" (cf. also the short evasive remark in 3, 167–168). In 6, 253–256, the poet goes a step further and makes an explicit point of no longer pretending that a god appeared to him in person. At the end of the book (6, 797–812), however, he reverts to the manner of Callimachus (see note 9).

16 (p. 146). In 3, 1–10, for instance, Mars is teased by the author because as a soldier he lacks a liberal education and takes no interest in poetry (cf. 3, 99–120 on the ineptitude for science of a soldier nation). In lines 171–172, eventually, the god half follows the poet's invitation to lay down his arms for a while (1–2; 7–8): he takes off his helmet but still keeps his lance.—In the First Book, Janus is represented like a good old uncle, as it were, rather than a god. The humorous explanation in 103–114 (see note 6, p. 209) is put into his own mouth, and in 129 he says directly that his own cult names are funny.

17 (p. 147). Some of the superstitions which Ovid mentions have survived to our own days, for instance, the notion that the month of May is not appropriate for a wedding, while June is auspicious (cf. 5, 489–490 and 6, 219–234; Ripert—see p. 169, note 9—p. 141).—Interesting is the custom mentioned in 5, 671–692: a trader sprinkles with sacred water both himself and the wares he expects to sell in order to wash off any fraud by which he may previously have acquired them. This is a religious parallel to the juridical norm that no one can validly sell an object which was unlawfully acquired.

18 (p. 147). Rational habits of etymology were not evolved in the Western world before the 19th century, in contrast to India, where this art was highly developed at a far earlier date. In fact, it was under the influence of Indian grammatical tradition that Western scholars trained themselves in scientific methods of etymology.

19 (p. 147). *Ars Amat.* III, 121; see above, p. 64.

20 (p. 148). Greek religion was, of course, not entirely free from ritualistic and superstitious elements; thus Ovid was able to quote, in the passage to which we were referring, examples of lustration from Greek legend (2, 37–44). But these elements were not preponderant there, as they were in the Roman religion.

21 (p. 148). Lightly and *en passant* Ovid now also uses the fiction of a night shortened in order to expedite the arrival of a joyous day (4, 673–676; 5, 545–548), by contrast to the poem on *The Dawn (Am.* I, 13).

22 (p. 148). It happens to be a Greek, not a Roman, miracle tale which Ovid is here rendering. Greek myth also contained a number of crude, archaic stories (cf. note 20), but in the *Metamorphoses* Ovid either avoided tales of this kind or mellowed their rawness.

23 (p. 148). To mention a rather small detail, Ovid is sometimes cavalier about the marking of dates. Thus he uses a mere *quoque* to indicate that another festive event is celebrated on the same day (6, 183 and 193; 637); or he vaguely says *hinc* when he means *die abhinc tertia* (4, 393). The text we have gives no date at all for the Feralia (2, 533 ff.). At other places, the datings are elaborated (see note 12).

24 (p. 148). Sometimes Ovid strained his ingenuity in order to connect the various items with one another. Examples are 6, 463–466; 6, 785–790 (for the drunkenness of the man who looks up to the skies on his way home cf. line 778); and, most felicitous, 4, 385–386. There were three entries for April 6: anniversary of the Battle of Thapsus; setting of Libra; and rainy weather. Ovid combines them by the invention that a rainstorm, caused by the setting of Libra, cut short the loquacity of the old

gentleman when he was explaining about the battle. In the preceding passage, 4, 373–376, the phrasing (*qui dicet ... verus erit*) is rather artificially assimilated to what follows (*mihi quidam senior ait ... 377–379*).

25 (p. 150). The following lines, 627–630, are gratuitous, not because terms of legend are used to describe bad relatives, but because they draw out the list too long and carry too loud colors into the picture.

NOTES TO CHAPTER 15, THE "IBIS," PP. 151–155

1 (p. 151). The text of the *Ibis* indicates that the poem was written after Ovid's arrival at Tomis (cf. lines 27, 638, etc.) and before he learned of the death of Augustus (cf. *idem* in line 27), that is, between spring, A.D. 9, and autumn, A.D. 14. On the other hand, the book also says that the poet is fifty years old (line 1), which he ceased to be in March, A.D. 9; and it gives the impression that at the time of Ovid's writing (cf. the present tenses in lines 8–22) Ibis is both inveighing against the poet and pursuing his financial scheme which, as can be seen from *Tr.* I, 6 (cf. note 4), was frustrated before Ovid reached Tomis. The conflict of dates shows that it is merely a poetical fiction when Ovid pretends that Ibis is at present trying to rob him of his money (and, concurrently, that the author is still fifty years old). The fiction, which is quite proper and legitimate, was certainly not designed to mystify the reader, but rather to give the pasquil the air of immediate actuality. The poem has greater force when it is assumed that the fight is still on and the issue still in doubt on both fronts, the financial as well as that of Ovid's reputation.—For the date of Ovid's *Ibis* see, further, notes 8 and 9.

2 (p. 151). The ibis bird was supposed to feed on refuse and to administer clysters to himself by way of his beak; to the latter habit Ovid alludes, in discreet phrasing, in line 450. For the evidence see R. Ellis, *P. Ovidi Nasonis Ibis,* Oxford, 1881, p. xxxv.

3 (p. 151). See above, pp. 114 f. That Ibis had previously been on a friendly footing with Ovid can be inferred from the terms *gratia rupta* (40); *caput male fidum* (85); and *perfide* (130). On the other hand, if Ibis had been one of Ovid's *close* friends (like the addressee of *Po.* IV, 3, see below, note 6), Ovid would have stated that aggravating circumstance in no uncertain terms.

4 (p. 151). Ovid spreads a veil of mystery over the main offense by which the so-called Ibis had outraged him, but his hints are, I believe, definite enough to give us an approximate idea of the misdeed.

Some scholars are of the opinion (see R. Heinze, *Berliner Philol. Wochenschr.,* 1921, p. 895) that Ibis tried to aggravate the Emperor's ire against the poet, in the hope that the relegation would be changed to exile; exile entailed the confiscation of the culprit's property, and Ibis expected that he, as the man who had brought about Ovid's conviction, would receive the customary share of the proceeds. This conjecture, ingenious as it is, cannot be accepted. In 19–20 Ovid complains that Ibis "attempted to loot the poet's burning house rather than extinguishing the sudden blaze"; "not extinguishing" is a far cry from fanning the flames and wreaking new, and worse, havoc. The couplet implies that Ibis did nothing about Ovid's punishment, one way or the other, but tried to exploit it for his own advantage. In 13–14, the author accuses Ibis of "speaking ill [for *iactat* cf. *Am.* III, 1, 21] of Ovid in the forum [cf. 232] and harassing the wound which ought to be left alone [so it could heal]"; that is, Ibis kept alive the public indignation (not the Emperor's ire) over the poet's mistake instead of allowing his deed to be forgotten (cf. *delituisse,* 12; *Tr.* III, 11, 62–66, etc.). Not even the word *vexat* gives the impression that Ibis tried to deepen the "wound" and to give it a new and decisive turn for the worse; and Ovid, in his bitter resentment, is not likely to have understated his grievance either here or where he speaks of the conflagration.

Lines 17–21 make it plain that Ibis jeopardized Ovid's subsistence in exile by trying to wrest from him a sizable part of his fortune. The distress on which he attempted to capitalize is likened by Ovid not only to a fire but also to a water hazard (17–18): "While I cling to the shattered remnants of my ship, Ibis fights to possess the *tabulae* of my shipwreck." *Naufragium* was an accepted symbol for financial ruin (Cicero, *Phil.* XII, § 19); but why should Ibis be interested in "planks"? The answer is, I believe, that *tabulae* is also to be understood as "ledger" or "IOU" (cf. R. Heinze on Horace, *Sat.* II, 3, 70). Ibis pressed a claim against Ovid at a moment when the poet could only settle it with a substantial loss to himself and a commensurate gain for Ibis. Ovid may have borrowed money from Ibis; we know how often Romans of the time lived on borrowed money. We also know to what degree any man of property in Rome was expected to stand security for obligations into which his acquaintances entered in the course of their business transactions. Thus Ovid may, for instance, have mortgaged real estate or offered other property as security for an obligation of his own, or for the obligation of one of his friends; the obligation fell due and the security was forfeited to Ibis unless Ovid settled the claim by a cash payment; in the stringent state of his affairs, Ovid did not have the cash at hand; and Ibis counted on acquiring the property in lieu of a debt which amounted only to a fraction of the value of the security. Ibis may even have bought someone's claim on Ovid for the purpose of ruthless exploitation.—I have elaborated the story in detail, not because I contend that it happened exactly so, but in order to indicate, by way of concrete illustration, the kind of scheme I have in mind.

From *Tr.* I, 6, 7–16 we can glean information about the way in which the maneuver was frustrated. In this passage, Ovid charges "someone" (line 13) with the attempt to rob him of his property at the time of the poet's catastrophe. Everything mentioned here agrees exactly with the proœmium of the *Ibis,* and one line (8) is almost identical with the *tabulae* line from the *Ibis* (18). It is therefore safe to assume that the anonym of the elegy is Ibis. From the elegy we can thus learn that Ovid's wife, with the help of his valiant friends, warded off the attempt; let us say, the friends advanced the necessary cash, or they contested the claim of Ibis successfully (*fortis,* in line 15, can either mean that they had the courage to help a man whom the Emperor hated, or that they gallantly fought Ibis in the legal contest). This explains, in turn, the distich *Ibis,* 15–16; it does not mean that Ibis "durch seine Zudringlichkeiten die Gattin des Dichters belästigte" (as E. Martini says, *Einleitung zu Ovid,* p. 56), but that the poet's devoted wife, instead of mourning in peace for her husband's banishment, was compelled to attend to his affairs and protect him from financial ruin.

Since the First Book of the *Tristia* was composed in the winter A.D. 8/9, the difficulty was overcome soon after it had arisen.

The line *Po.* II, 7, 62 (cf. *spolia,* as in *Tr.* I, 6, 7 *spolium*) refers also to the outrage of Ibis, and so probably does *comitum nefas* in *Tr.* IV, 10, 101. For other references see below, note 6.

5 (p. 152). *Si perges,* in line 53, receives its precise meaning from lines 13–14; cf. also *Tr.* IV, 9, 7–8, where Ovid admonishes Ibis (see next note) to desist from his hatred. Because of the poetical fiction that the *Ibis* was written before the financial scheme was frustrated (see note 1), it is possible that Ovid also pretended to deter Ibis from pursuing his maneuver (17–21). The Hellenistic poet Euphorio had written a learned invective, with the title *Chiliades,* against certain persons who had defrauded him of a sum of money he had deposited with them (cf. John U. Powell, *Analecta Alexandrina,* Oxford, 1925, pp. 28–29). He predicted that the embezzlers, or their offspring, would at some time receive the punishment they deserved, and cited legendary examples of such comminations which had come true even after a thousand years. His ostensible objective was evidently to frighten the evildoers into restoring the property. The same Euphorio also composed a poem of execrations against a person

who had stolen a cup from him. A fragment we possess contains four curses, and three of them have the shape of legendary examples—just as in the main section of Ovid's *Ibis.* Unlike the *Ibis,* however, the fragment is in hexameters; moreover, Euphorio was evidently in the dark with respect to the identity and sex of the thief, since the four curses envisage their victim alternately as a man and as a woman. (This explanation, I think, resolves a difficulty which has puzzled students of frag. 9 Powell.)

6 (p. 152). This is the gist of the elegy *Tr.* IV, 9: "Your name and your misdeed I do not yet disclose, and they shall remain hidden provided you repent your damnable crime. But if your hatred against me prevents you from doing so, I shall use my art as a weapon, and in a new poem reveal to all the world and to all posterity who you are and what you did. The present elegy is only a faint prolusion of the attack to be delivered, unless you heed my warning." All this is identical in every respect with the first 61 lines of the *Ibis* (and the first line of the elegy is similar to *Ibis,* line 9; lines 8 and 10 of the elegy resemble *Ibis,* line 86, see note 25); therefore I have no doubt that the elegy is directed to Ibis.

Tr. III, 11, on the other hand, and *Tr.* V, 8 are different. Just as the preceding elegy is directed to anyone (cf. *si quis, Tr.* III, 10, 1) who may still remember Ovid with sympathy, even so *Tr.* III, 11 is addressed to anyone (cf. *si quis es,* line 1) who may still speak ill of the poet, with the implication that such baseness is abnormal and exceptional (cf. *uno iudice,* 38). The poem thus apostrophizes, not a given individual, but whomever it may concern (cf. *quicumque es,* 63). *Tr.* V, 8 rebukes in a similar fashion a man who gloats over the poet's downfall, but this time the author seems to address a definite person whom he has in mind rather than wondering whether such an individual exists. Nevertheless, again Ovid does not specify the addressee beyond charging him with malicious joy over his misfortune, so that whoever was guilty of the charge would have to refer the elegy to himself. Evidently, Ovid was aware that in Rome some animosity against him was still lingering on, and he wrote the two bitter elegies in order to deprecate the ill feeling against a man who was already punished with incommensurate severity.

And, lastly, *Po.* IV, 3. This elegy is certainly not directed to Ibis. Ovid says that he will not mention the man's name, but will expose his crime. What he had done was, that, after he had been one of Ovid's intimate friends from the days of their youth (see note 3), he disowned their relationship as soon as the poet was disgraced, and never wrote a polite, if short, note of sympathy; worse still, it has been reported to Ovid that he had made unfriendly remarks when the blow had fallen.

7 (p. 152). In *Tr.* IV, 9, 3, *vincetur* (*clementia*) is corrupt; the scribe miscopied the word because the phrase *victa est clementia* was still lingering in his mind from 8, 39. A possible emendation is *ducetur,* cf. *Po.* I, 3, 15.

8 (p. 152). The reverse order is unlikely because the elegy has no point after the *Ibis,* while there was a point in doing the same thing over again with far greater artistry and elaboration. The *Ibis,* then, was composed between spring, A.D. 10, and autumn, A.D. 14 (see note 1, above).

9 (p. 152). For *Ibis* 1–8 cf. *Tr.* II, 563–568. In *Po.* IV, 14, 44, Ovid repeats again the contention of a clean record. This can be explained in three ways. Either the *Ibis* was not yet written at that time (which is unlikely); or it was as yet unpublished; or Ovid ignores the existence of the *Ibis.*

10 (p. 153). Ovid is thinking of the pasquils by means of which Archilochus is supposed to have driven Lycambes (54) to suicide. The modern reader will also think of Archilochus frag. 79 Diehl, which, like Ovid's *Ibis,* contains a curse against a former ἑταῖρος (a member of his band?) who had wronged and deserted the poet.

11 (p. 153). According to the ancient theory of magic, curses would not take effect unless the identity of the accursed was patent. The name of the victim is written out clearly even in those texts in which the rest is made intentionally illegible (cf. G. Zipfel, *Quatenus Ovidius in Ibide Callimachum aliosque fontes imprimis defixiones secutus sit,* Diss. Leipzig, 1910, p. 12).

12 (p. 153). Ibis will be punished throughout his life and after his death in all eternity (161–162; 195–196), and Ovid will not cease to harass his enemy even after his own death; his ghost will stretch out "cold hands" against Ibis (154), and his "bony shape" (144) will pursue the villain. Is this the first time in extant literature that a ghost is represented in the shape of a skeleton?

13 (p. 153). The words are, however, not entirely clear. Possibly Ovid meant to say that the day of Ibis' birth was as unauspicious as the day of the *Clades Alliana.*

14 (p. 154). Cf. the curse tablet no. 38, 26 Audollent (from Zipfel [see note 11] p. 22): ʼΕπέκλωσε γὰρ αὐτῷ ταῦτα ἡ... Γῆ χθονία.

15 (p. 154). With line 232 compare line 14.

16 (p. 154). We are not entirely groping in the dark, because remnants of an ancient commentary have come down to us. Without explanatory notes, the third section must at many places have remained unintelligible for the ordinary reader. It has therefore been suggested (see U. von

Wilamowitz, *Hellenistische Dichtung,* Berlin, 1925, Vol. 2, p. 100) that the extant scholia are derived from a commentary which the poet himself had caused to be compiled and for which he had personally furnished the material. Lines 57–64, however, of the *Ibis* rather give the impression that Ovid did not care to make the solution of his puzzles easier.

17 (p. 154). Twice, the author himself stresses the lurid exaggeration by piling upon it a still more fantastic exaggeration. In 197–204 and 641–642 he announces that all he will say or has said should only be an infinitesimal part of his enemy's actual punishments.

18 (p. 154). This is the more remarkable since it was an established practice in antiquity that a person wished the evils with which he was himself confronted upon his enemies (e.g., the last couplets of *Tr.* III, 11 and V, 8; *Po.* I, 10, 17–20; *Fasti* 3, 494; Horace, *Carm.* I, 21, 13–16; or upon "other people" in general, e.g., Aesch. *Agam.* 1571–1573 Wilamowitz; Theognis 351–354). See Otto Weinreich, *Tübinger Beiträge* 5, 1929, pp. 169–199.

19 (p. 154). Some few execrations carry a faint taste of that same poison which vitiated Ovid's own life at Tomis. I am thinking of the passage 107–126, where 107–110 have a direct counterpart in *Tr.* III, 3, 7–8 and III, 8, 23; in 113 we read *exul;* lines 123–124 have a parallel in *Tr.* III, 8, 39–40, etc. The passage occurs not in the grotesque section, which floats, as it were, in a vacuum, but in the romantic part, which contains a number of topical references.

20 (p. 155). The two couplets *Ibis* 205–208 are among the most passionate lines that Ovid ever wrote; not since his early youth (see above, p. 188, note 63) had he expressed himself with such frenzy.

21 (p. 155). Truly Ovidian, however, are the fine lines 421–424; they stand strikingly out from the dry context in which they occur. For once, Ovid was unable to suppress his natural manner; one of the things in which his poetry is great is the expression of frustration.—It goes without saying, on the other hand, that the manner of presentation would still preserve in a measure the Ovidian character. For one thing, Ovid was always in the habit of borrowing from his own previous works. Compare, for instance, *Ibis* 431 with *Metam.* 1, 165.

22 (p. 155). Excavations have brought to light a great number of execrations from antiquity, written on metal tablets or papyrus. G. Zipfel (see above, note 11) has culled from these texts many parallels to Ovid's *Ibis,* and has been led by the similarities to conclude that Ovid, when he was preparing his *Ibis,* familiarized himself with the orthodox methods of cursing as practiced by those who believed in the efficacy of execrations.

Zipfel's material, however, fails to bear out the inference. Before we can draw it we have to eliminate from the list of coincidences the following three categories: such patterns as were inevitable in any ancient curse; such patterns as were commonplace in colloquial cursing; and third, such patterns as are likely to have been used in Ovid's literary models. So far as I can see, all parallels noted by Zipfel fall in one or another of the three classes (for the connection in Hellenistic literature of prophecies with curses see above, note 5). There are two characteristic features by which the bona fide execrations are distinguished from their literary counterparts: the invocation of apocryphal deities or demons, and the hocus-pocus of ceremonious obscurantism (use of nonsensical formulae; performance of symbolic acts, such as mutilation of the writing material, burying of the text, destruction of an effigy of the accursed person, etc.). These features are not represented in Ovid's *Ibis* (for the poet's dislike of magic see p. 203, note 27). There is no reason, then, to assume that Ovid studied from folkloristic sources the fine art of elaborate cursing, or that he had any other ambition than to live up to the standard of his models from high literature.

23 (p. 155). Ovid's direct model, the *Ibis* of Callimachus, is completely lost, but in point of obscurity we can compare with Ovid's poem the long fragment we possess from Lycophron's *Alexandra*. In addition, we know a little about the two poems in which Euphorio heaped learned execrations on his enemies (see note 5), and the similarity between Ovid's *Ibis* and these poems is indeed very great. Perhaps Ovid imitated Euphorio as well as Callimachus.

24 (p. 155). The threat, however, of such a pasquil would not have been serious if Sulla's *lex Cornelia de iniuriis* was at that time already interpreted in the sense indicated by Ulpian *ad edictum, Dig.* 47, 10, 5, 9 and 47, 10, 15, 27. This interpretation gave an *actio iniuriarum* both *Si quis librum ad infamiam alicuius pertinentem conscripserit* and *Si carmen conscribat ad infamiam alicuius.* So far as the *Ibis* was concerned, however, it could be written with impunity even if such an *actio* was admitted, see *Dig.* 47, 10, 15, 9: *Si incertae personae convicium fiat, nulla executio est;* the exemption would obviously apply to *diffamatio* as well as to *convicium.*

25 (p. 155). Cf. the similar function of *dolor* and *ira,* also with respect to Ibis, in *Tr.* IV, 9, 8 and 10.—The *dolor* as an entity half detached from the person reminds us of Seneca's tragedies, cf. Otto Regenbogen, *Schmerz und Tod in den Tragödien Senecas,* Vorträge der Bibliothek Warburg 8, Leipzig, 1930, p. 192.

NOTES TO CHAPTER 16, OVID'S LAST YEARS, PP. 155–159

1 (p. 156). Digestion seems to have been sluggish, cf. line 14. In a previous acute illness he had pains in his *latus* (stomach ?), cf. *Tr.* V, 13, 5.

2 (p. 157). In *Po.* III, 7, 21, the second *iuvat* is certainly corrupt. A word like *fugit, abit, perit,* or *cadat* is required.

3 (p. 157). In *Po.* III, 7, 33, *repetita forma locorum* does not mean 'the repeated description of this place.' For *repeto* 'I recall,' cf. *Po.* II, 10, 6; for the *loca* Ovid recalls cf. *Po.* I, 8, 33 ff.; and for the experience to which Ovid refers, a dream journey to some "happier country" he had known before (and especially to Rome), followed by a harsh awakening to reality, cf. *Po.* III, 5, 47–56 and *Po.* I, 2, 49–54.

4 (p. 158). In contrast to *Tr.* III, 12, 50–54 (above, p. 126).

5 (p. 158). The subject of the Getic poem was the deification of Augustus, probably adapted from Ovid's Latin poem in honor of that event (see p. 237, note 31), and it ended in a eulogy of the imperial family (*Po.* IV, 13, 23–32). This was indeed a unique piece of propaganda for the Empire among the natives, and the poet hoped to be rewarded with his release from Tomis (37–38).

6 (p. 159). In *Po.* III, 2, 41–98, Ovid goes on to have a man who was born in the Tauris region tell the story of Orestes and Pylades at Tauris. The fiction that a Greek legend is rendered, in the guise of a local tradition, by an aged native of the place is in the style of Callimachus' *Aetia* and of Ovid's own *Fasti*. (Alexander Pushkin, in turn, in the poem from his own exile, *Tsygany* [*The Gypsies*], used the same device to recall Ovid's stay in Scythia.)

7 (p. 159). The question of the territories assigned to each of the two rulers is disputed, but Ovid is quite specific in indicating that the region around Tomis was given to Cotys (cf. *finitimi Po.* II, 9, 4; *tua terra* line 10; *iacens intra tua castra* line 37). Cf. also M. Rostovzeff, *Gnomon* 10 (1934), pp. 7–8.

8 (p. 159). Cf. Tacitus, *Annals* II, 64; Antipater of Thessalonica, *Anthol. Palat.* 16 (*App. Plan.*), 75.

9 (p. 159). Ovid also ingratiated himself with Vestalis, a centurio primipilaris of Gallic extraction who had been sent to the region in an administrative capacity (*Po.* IV, 7).

10 (p. 159). Cf. Ripert (see p. 169, note 9), p. 245.

NOTES TO CHAPTER 17, THE "HALIEUTICS," PP. 160–162

1 (p. 160). He studied the geography and hydrography of the Black Sea and set forth in one of his elegies the reasons why it froze over in the winter cold (*Po.* IV, 10, cf. above, p. 134). A parallel to his sympathetic interest in the fish is his desire to learn to talk to the oxen of the Dobrudja so they would understand him (*Po.* I, 8, 55–56, see above, p. 131).

2 (p. 160). That the fishermen whom Ovid consulted were Greek can be inferred from the fact that he mentions no native fish names.

3 (p. 160). There is no explicit evidence that Ovid studied the fish by means of direct observation and inquiries from fishermen, but, living as he was in a fishing center and having so much time on his hands, it is safe to assume that he did so (he loved to chat with sailors, according to *Tr.* III, 12, 21 ff.). Moreover, we read in Pliny's *Naturalis Historia* (32, 34, § 152) this: *His adiciemus ab Ovidio posita animalia quae apud neminem alium reperiuntur sed fortassis in Ponto nascentia, ubi id volumen supremis suis temporibus inchoavit:* (a list of eleven kinds of fish follows). Two facts, however, cast doubt on Pliny's suggestion that Ovid knew those kinds of fish not from literary sources, but from direct observation. Five of the eleven species listed by Pliny (provided they have been identified correctly by modern scholars) do not now occur in the Black Sea; and several of those which, according to Pliny, were mentioned by no other author are recorded in other ancient books; five of them, in fact, are mentioned by Pliny himself in other parts of his work. Cf. Georg Schmid, *Philologus* Suppl. 11, Leipzig, 1907–1910, pp. 334–337.

4 (p. 160). Ovid might have named his last project *Ars* (cf. line 82) *Piscatoria* (*piscatorius* was an accepted term), but that name would have recalled the ill-starred *Ars Amatoria,* and *Halieutica* was also shorter. Other Greek titles were *Heroides* and *Metamorphoses;* neither of them could be replaced by a one-word Latin name. On the other hand, Ovid preferred two-word Latin titles, such as *Medicamina Faciei* and *Remedia Amoris,* to Greek words coined *ad hoc,* like *Prosopopharmaca* and *Erotiatrica.* Hellenistic literature was fond of neologisms, but the Augustan writers, including Ovid, were chary of them.

5 (p. 160). Theodor Birt's (*De Halieuticis Ovidio poetae falso adscriptis,* Berlin, 1878) criticisms of the fragment seem in large part justified, but I cannot assent to his conclusion that the fragment was written by some other author. For one thing, our text agrees fully with the detailed paraphrases by Pliny from Ovid's last and unfinished work. Furthermore, the hypothesis fails to explain the fact that the fragment is

excellent in its greater part, while in spots the wording is so bad that not even a mediocre writer would have let it stand.

6 (p. 160). Cf. S. G. Owen, *Class. Quart.* 8 (1914), p. 267; R. Keydell, *Hermes* 72 (1937), p. 423. For details see the following notes 7–10.

7 (p. 160). Th. Birt (see note 5), pp. 21–22, objects to the phrasing of line 62 but does not go far enough. *Emisso telo* is hardly correct; the context shows that the boar is throwing itself upon a spear which the hunter is holding in his hands (cf. Xenophon, *Cyneget.* 10, 11–12). Ovid seems to have written, or intended to write, something like *pressoque immissus moritur per viscera telo.* For *presso* cf. Vergil, *Aeneid* 10, 347, and ἀντερείσαντα ἐρρωμένως Xenophon § 16; for *immissus* cf. προωθῶν αὐτόν *ibid.* In his hastily written draft, Ovid may have used symbols for endings, preverbs, and *que* or *et,* and the editor deciphered them incorrectly.

8 (p. 160). The first few lines of the fragment consist, I believe, of what originally were mere cues for later elaboration, metrical only in part; these odds and ends were combined and done into a semblance of running hexameters when the fragment was put into shape for publication. We cannot reconstruct what Ovid would eventually have made of it, but we can still make out the general idea: <*Hanc*> *accepit mundus legem* <that each animal be able to survive>; <*natura*> *dedit arma per* (?) *omnes* <*feras*>; *natura ipsa sui admonet* (see note 10); *iam* (the *iam* has been transposed to the following line) *vitulus sic* <*vana*> *minatur qui nondum gerit in tenera* <*fera*> *cornua fronte....* It seems that Ovid's manuscript contained notes and verses in various stages of perfection, and the editor selected for publication those parts which were comparably readable and coherent. In subsequent tradition the text was in part further adjusted and in part further corrupted.

9 (p. 160). Some gaps, however, are due to subsequent mutilation of the text. Pliny's text was more complete than ours is.

10 (p. 160). I suggest that line 52 is made up of two such doublets. *Ipsa sequi natura monet* hardly makes sense, but emended to *ipsa sui natura monet* it may be another version for the fragmentary phrase, in line 2, *admonuitque sui* (nature causes each animal to understand its own nature). The second half, *vel comminus IRAER* (or *IRATE*) duplicates *nec comminus acri* of line 44. In Ovid's own manuscript, the two phrases were probably written together somewhere at the top or bottom of a page; since they seemed to make a line, that line was tentatively inserted later both after line 51 and after line 65. (R. Keydell, *Hermes* 72, 1937, p. 424 note, thinks that the *natura* of line 52 refers not to the game but to the hunter; but why and how should Ovid discuss the instincts of hunters?)

11 (p. 160). Some of the gaps have to be bridged by mere conjecture, while other lacunae can be filled out confidently from similar passages in other authors. Ovid based his exposition on a certain set tradition which is also represented in several extant works, and most of his ideas and examples recur somewhere else. The parallels make it possible to clear up a number of obscure passages (cf., e.g., R. Keydell, *Hermes* 72, 1937, pp. 421 ff.). I have not, however, studied the complex problem thoroughly, and for that reason my remarks on the *Halieutics* have in part only a tentative character.

12 (p. 161). According to *Dobrogea* (see p. 233, note 13), p. 455, the promontory on which Tomis was situated is bordered by a cliff from 9 to 35 meters high. The nearest sandy beach is 6 kilometers distant (cf. *Enciclop. Italiana,* Vol. 11, p. 635), and Ovid is not likely to have ventured out so far from the city.

13 (p. 162). The *mitis* of line 16 is a slight exception, motivated by the character of the story; the fable belonged, as the parallels show, to the stock-in-trade of naturalists.

14 (p. 162). The *Nux,* although ascribed to Ovid in the manuscript tradition, is certainly not by him. Its merits as well as its defects have little in common with either the good or the less good passages that Ovid wrote, or with what we know of his school declamations. While Ovid, for instance, frequently overworks his points and repeats them with only slight variation, the author of the *Nux* often fails to make his points, but dwells instead on edgeless generalities. (Similarly, the supposed parallel in line 26 is no parallel at all; Clytaemestra was assassinated by her child, while the tree is harmed because people want its fruits.) If the poem (unlike the chapter on laurel and olive in Callimachus' *Aetia,* frag. 9, 209–302 Pfeiffer) is meant to be symbolic (which I doubt), then the modest nut tree in a roadside grove represents, not a world-famous genius relegated to a wilderness at the fringe of the Empire, but some humble artisan, shopkeeper, or the like who conscientiously serves the chance customers that come his way but is thoughtlessly insulted and exploited by them.

Notes to Chapter 18, The End, pp. 162–163

1 (p. 162). The latest certain date for Ovid's life is December, A.D. 15, or January, A.D. 16, because Ovid hoped that his epistle *Po.* IV, 9 would reach its addressee by May, A.D. 16 (see lines 3–4). Jerome reports that the poet died A.D. 17, but his dates cannot be relied upon (see R. Helm, *Philologus* Suppl. 21, Heft 2, 1929, pp. 56–57). On the other hand, we

have no means of proving Jerome wrong, and on independent grounds
it is unlikely that Ovid lived very much longer than to the autumn of that
year. He probably died, or ceased to be able to write poetry, no later than
in the first half of the year 18. Here are my reasons for these assertions.

a) In *Fasti* I, 223–226, Ovid has Janus declare: *Nos quoque templa
iuvant, quamvis antiqua probemus, aurea; maiestas convenit ipsa deo.
Laudamus veteres, sed nostris utimur annis.* The lines obviously refer
to the modernization of a Janus temple in Rome. It is commonly argued
that the poet cannot have written them before he learned of the dedication, in October, A.D. 17, of the rebuilt temple, and it is therefore assumed
that he was still alive in the year 18; the news, it is being said, would take
half a year to reach Tomis (see under *d*). The inference, however, is
far from stringent. The lines in the *Fasti* are justified if Ovid only knew
that a modernization of the sanctuary was planned or under way; for
him, there was no point in waiting for news of the dedication. Now we
happen to possess evidence that Augustus began to beautify the temple;
Pliny, in *Nat. Hist.* 36, § 28, mentions a *Janus pater in suo templo dicatus
ab Augusto ex Aegypto advectus . . . , iam quidem et auro occultatus.*
It follows that the lines in question may well have been written during
the lifetime of the first emperor.

b) Many scholars contend that the poet cannot have begun his remodeling of the *Fasti* before, in the spring of the year 18, he learned of
Germanicus' arrival in the East. This reasoning, however, is still less convincing. Ovid already had good reasons to appeal to Germanicus before
the Prince was sent to the East (see above, p. 142); but even if that appointment was the poet's only ground for the rededication to Germanicus
of the *Fasti,* he did not have to wait with his work on it for the news
of the High Commissioner's actual arrival.

c) A terminus ante quem, rather than a terminus post quem, for Ovid's
death or incapacitation can be derived from the chronology of Germanicus' office. The news that Germanicus was appointed must have made
Ovid very anxious to complete as fast as he could the remodeling of the
Fasti, and yet he has hardly progressed beyond the First Book. It follows
that Ovid was not able to work for very many months after he heard of
the appointment of Germanicus.

d) When did that news reach Tomis? When students try to ascertain
the time at which Ovid wrote certain passages, they are accustomed to
proceed on the assumption that it took any intelligence half a year to
travel from Rome to Tomis. The assumption is based on two passages,
Po. III, 4, 59–60 and IV, 11, 15–16, where the poet says that a year will

go by before a reply will have arrived at its destination. For one thing, however, the poet gives no more than a round figure, and a maximum figure at that (*annus abisse potest* III, 4, 60); moreover, the time for composing an elaborate poem is included in both cases. Secondly, he is speaking of his private correspondence, which was likely to suffer a number of long delays on its way (see above, p. 134); he is also speaking of *fama* and *rumor* (III, 4, 41 and 59), that is, a report by a traveler who had witnessed the triumph or had received from someone else a detailed and precise description—and it might take any amount of time before such a traveler made his appearance at Tomis. It was a far different matter with simple news items of great interest for everyone, such as intelligence of the Emperor's death or of the appointment of Germanicus. News of this kind was immediately carried by speedy couriers to all officials and many others in the provinces and, unlike a corporeal letter, it would be spread far and wide by word of mouth through every traveler who moved anywhere from one place to another. The appointment of Germanicus was made in June or July, A.D. 17, and I think Ovid must have known of it a month or two later.

2 (p. 163). See pp. 11–17. The lines quoted here are *Am*. I, 13, 12 and 5–8.

INDEXES

I. INDEX TO OVID

FOR THE CONVENIENCE of the reader, sections A, B, and C of this index register certain matters somewhat more systematically than could be done in the book proper, although both the listings and the references are meant to be suggestive rather than exhaustive. The register is sometimes rounded out by statements for which no specific page reference can be given.

A. OVID'S LIFE AND LITERARY CAREER

His autobiography (132 with 235 n. 26). Chronology of his life and writings (175 nn. 1 and 2; 193 f. n. 1; 195 n. 1; 204 n. 3 to ch. 8; 204 n. 2 to ch. 9; 221 n. 79; 226–228 n. 105; 230 f.; 238 n. 2; 239 f. n. 8; 243 n. 1; 245 n. 4; 247 nn. 8 and 9; 253–255 n. 1). The conventional division into three periods is inadequate (199 n. 1; 283 n. 3).

He was born March 20, B.C. 43, the son of well-established middle-class parents, and inherited equestrian rank (4); his father was over forty when he was born; his only brother died in his youth (174 n. 21).

He was interested only in poetry, but his father forced him into training for a career; his rhetorical schooling (5–7).

Journey to Athens (8); other travels (174 n. 20).

He began to recite his own verse in public at about the age of eighteen (10–11; 175 n. 1).

He started on his political career, but gave it up at the age of about twenty-five, preferring "leisure" and poetry to senatorial dignity (8–10).

His three marriages (132).

He wrote the *Amores* in his teens (?) and twenties; before they were completed, he composed the *Heroides* and tried his hand at tragedy. He planned to write tragedies for the rest of his career, but was loath to part with the theme of love. He published the *Heroides,* and soon afterward the *Amores* in five books, which he later reduced to three. He composed one tragedy, *Medea* (46–47 with notes).

He won fame immediately (47) and was looked upon as the foremost elegist of the nation (72); his elegies were acted out on the stage (47).

For five to nine years he remained inactive (47); at the age of forty-one he reverted to the theme of love, but in a different spirit (53–54), and produced within about two years five (or four) volumes of didactic poetry: *Ars Amatoria* I and II (54–63), to which he then added Book III (65); *Medicamina Faciei* (63; date uncertain: 204 n. 3 to ch. 8); and lastly, bidding his farewell to love, *Remedia Amoris* (67–71). He embarked immediately on a more ambitious plan (71–72).

The *Metamorphoses* may have been an old project (cf. 210 f. n. 17)—we cannot tell when Ovid began to prepare it,—but he seems to have worked on it primarily between his forty-fourth and fifty-first year (72; 221 n. 79). When he had completed about eleven books and had attained the critical age of the late forties (143), he gave up his old manner and experimented, in the last four books, with a number of new themes and styles (101–110). At the same time (238 n. 2), he worked out six or more books of the *Fasti*, which was to be his public service because it dealt with national traditions (142; 145).

At the age of fifty (A.D. 8), when the *Metamorphoses* was lacking only the final revision (221 n. 79) but the *Fasti* was still uncompleted (142), he was relegated to Tomis (111–114).

His banishment created a sensation (134) and further enhanced his fame (163); but many people turned their backs on him; he had financial difficulties, and one of his acquaintances ("Ibis") tried to trick him out of a considerable sum (114–115; 243–245 n. 4).

His reaction to the stern sentence (114–116); departure from home (116); journey into exile (116–117); some slaves accompanied him, but his wife remained in Rome (115). He continued to write verse (*Tristia* I) on his way (116–117).

He arrived at Tomis in spring (?), A.D. 9 (230–231); found the place and people utterly uncongenial; collapsed, and fell seriously ill (121).

The town of Tomis: political conditions (123–125); Rhoemetalces and Cotys, kings of Thrace (159); Tomis twice threatened by an invasion of savages (130–131); climate (121; 125–126); landscape (129; 253 n. 12); population (123–125; *Po.* III, 8:134–135).

The state of Ovid's health (121; 155–156); discomforts and vexations (121–122; 125–130); the language barrier (124; 126; 127; 128; 158); difficulty of correspondence with Rome (134).

His futile attempts to bring about his release (134–138; 157).

His frame of mind during the first years: haunting memories, self-reproach, frantic appeals, and spells of apathy (141). Lest he should give up his own self, he struggled to remain a sullen stranger to Tomis (126–127).

He wrote *Tristia* and *Epistulae ex Ponto* (125; 131; 135; 137; 140–141); reasons why he composed the personal elegies (131–139). He wrote *Ibis* (155); three encomia in honor of the dynasty (135), one of them in the Getic language (158; 250 n. 5); worked on *Fasti* (142–143); and began *Halieutica* (160–162).

As time went on, the years wore him down (137–140). He touched the bottom of despondency (156–157), even while acclimatizing himself in body and spirit; he tentatively compromised, and looked with some friendliness on the people of the land; he appreciated that he was liked and honored by them (155–160).

He died A.D. 17 or 18 (?), at the age of fifty-nine or sixty (162–163; 253–255).

Influence of his poetry on his contemporaries (170 n. 5); its popularity in Antiquity (169 n. 4); its powerful appeal to the Middle Ages (2 with notes;

188 n. 62; 213 n. 33; 214 n. 37), for which it served as a "modernizing" factor (169 f. n. 10); one of his poems gave rise to a medieval genre (11–12; 175 n. 5); his works were much read and used in the Renascence and later, but have been under a cloud since the nineteenth century (2).

B. Ovid's Personality

Ovid the artist and bohemian, and Ovid the private man and bourgeois, were not quite the same person (235 f. n. 26).

HIS DISPOSITION
(See also p. 100 on characters in *Metam.*)

Ovid was hardly a masterful and domineering personality (241 n. 14), nor was he swayed by grand passions; but he was sensitive, responsive, quick, subtle, warmhearted and kindly.

The instances of emotional abandon are few but distinctive: the youthful lover's frenzied anguish (30–31; 188 nn. 63 and 64) and inordinate contrition (18–21); the mature man's righteous wrath against Ibis (248 n. 20); the sentenced offender's recurrent fits of dejection (156–157; 162–163), during which he would wantonly destroy his own handiwork (115; 132).

Instances of fretting displeasure and indignant protest abound in his personal elegiacs.

Much brooding bitterness in the misery of his exile; grief became a habit (137–139 etc.); spells of numb apathy (115; 141).

Stark physical fear of violence ever since his banishment (129–130, etc.); his want of fortitude was bound up with his best qualities (140).

He lacked the nerve for finality (46–47; 48; 65; 101); was irresolute (3; 112–113; 135); and had a propensity for undecisive compromises (78–79; 90–91; 99–100).

Ovid was mild but stubborn. Obstacles were circumvented, or blandly ignored, or transformed into avenues of approach. This is patent in all his erotic works. He discouraged a gambler's approach to love and assigned a strictly limited part to violence (58); he demanded, instead, intelligent subordination, understanding forbearance, and steadfast application (58–61 etc.).

In exile, he showed a time-proof tenacity which surprised himself (139); his affliction was turned into a mantle of tragic dignity (139–140) or into a shield to protect him from further blows (120; 162; 232 n. 7; 237 n. 35). He remained long stubborn in his refusal to adjust himself to the conditions imposed on him (126–127), and was very assiduous in his attempts to bring about his release, clinging to hope whether or not it was justified (137–138 etc.). At times, at least, he could aver that his spirit and will had conquered adversity (122; 132; 156).

His industry as a writer (141–142; 158; 174 n. 25) is attested by the great amount of good poetry he produced from early youth to his last days, except, it seems, for a period of from five to nine years in his thirties (47).

He was naïve (100) in the freshness and brisk directness of his poetry, the ingenuity of his imagination, and the unhampered flight of his fancies (24; 30 etc.); in his ready response to each of many characters and events from life or from fable (90; 184 n. 40; *Am.* II, 4; etc.); in his indifference to the imperial policy (23; 64–65; 92); in his unconcern for conventions and the candor with which he voiced his novel experiences (23). His frankness in matters of sex (3) is likewise rather naïve than bold (71).

His most significant trait is his warm, gentle, understanding kindliness, a kindliness of a novel sort (21–23; 59–61; 90 etc.).

He was a devoted son and brother (132), and was proud to have a heart susceptible to Cupid's darts (132). He had a fond sympathy for his fellow men (*passim*), including the characters of his stories (99–100), and even for animals (80; 109; 162; 225 n. 100).

His anger was prone to relent as soon as it had been vented (29); he eventually forgave the friends who had deserted him when he needed them most (229 n. 7); the cure he proposes for misplaced love is as lenient and gentle as possible for both partners (except for one passage: 68–69). His one attempt to write aggressive verse was not successful (153).

He was proud only of his descent from a good family (170 n. 1) and, much more so, of his art and the renown he earned through it (33; 71–72; 110–111 etc.).

For his good-natured humor see below, p. 265 (near bottom).

HIS TASTES

Ovid was indifferent to such practical pursuits as business, politics, and litigation, and he hated sordid greed and brutal war (10; 13; 28; 33; 70; 92; 186 n. 53; 208 n. 6).

Although he had no inclination for the pastoral idealization of country life, he was responsive to the tender charms of nature, and loved to work in his garden (70–71 with 208 n. 7). In his last years, he took an interest in sea life and fishing (160). He seems to have enjoyed traveling (70).

He liked things neat, pleasant, and meaningful rather than pompous, spectacular, or formal (65; 76; 86; 127; 220 f. n. 76); he did not share the current veneration for the past, but was happy to live in an enlightened and cultured age; the Augustan reform movement left him, therefore, cold (64–65; 147; 203 n. 31).

HIS HABITS

We have spoken of his industry before; not even in adversity and boredom did he care to dull his grief by getting drunk, or to kill time with senseless games and excessive sleep (138).

He was evidently very sociable and loved to talk (100; 133; 251 n. 3); he went out of his way to tell his readers about the author (46; 71–72; 131–134). His poetry shows many examples of mental communion at a distance (38; 50; 153 etc.); in exile, he used to take mental travels to Rome and enjoy a conversation with one of his friends, dramatically imagining both his own and the other's words (133; 250 n. 3).

He must have been given to daydreaming (122; 131). He often took the possible for the real (30; 187 n. 59); he manufactured wishful oracles for himself (232 f. n. 8). He indulged in illusions and self-deception in order to spare his own feelings and to enrich and embellish his emotional life (17; 30–31; 138), and he knew how to trick himself into being sensible (69; 132–133).

HIS VIEWS

His views will not be itemized here. For his views on love see 9–72, *passim;* 238 n. 4; etc. He demurred at homosexual love, because it victimizes the one partner for the benefit of the other (185 n. 46). He hated the idea of philters and drugs that interfere with the free will (62; 104; 203 n. 27; cf. 248 f. n. 22). For the notion of love's self-sufficiency see 50 with 196 f. n. 7; 198 n. 17. For the changes in his attitude toward love see 53–54; 65–67; 67–68 (all with notes); 238 n. 4; 159.

He was not philosophically minded (3; 73; 92), although, as an educated man, he had a smattering of the various schools (e.g., Epicurean: 90; Stoic: 187 f. n. 62; Neo-Pythagorean: 108–110; 224–225 nn. 96–97 and 99–101). He did not believe in mythology, miracles, or the magic potency of rituals (89; 147–148; 180 n. 24); he was an agnostic but practiced a mild traditional piety, which had a Greek rather than Roman tinge (90–92; 148; 150). But he believed fervently in man and in art (92–93).

HIS MODERNITY (169 f. n. 10)

His poetry shows the marks of both the decline of Antiquity and the emergence of a new world (3; 163). Among the more specific modern features are these:

His habit of moving on more than one plane of reality (see below, p. 265, bottom).

His openness to the phenomenon of fluid identity (21; 79–81; 99): double identity (215 n. 42); two natures in Hercules (81–82, with notes); the self divided (79; 227); interplay of sameness and otherness (82–85; 88); the identities of lovers merged (21; 183 n. 37); separation from the self (99); Ovid felt he had lost his identity when he was banished (133; 236 n. 28).

His particular sort of loving-kindness (21–23; 59–61; etc.).

His capability of contrition and mortification (18–21); the vehement self-condemnation of Charisius in Menander's *Arbitration* (lines 558–604 in A. Koerte's 3d ed., 494–540 in earlier editions) is comparable, but Ovid's plunge into frantic remorse appears more spontaneous because he made it on account of a trivial mistake. There seems to be a touch of flagellantism in Ovid's raging against his own verse children, "flesh from my flesh" (115; 132; cf. *irata sibi, Tr.* IV, 1, 101).

C. Ovid's Art

THE WRITING

Verse came more natural to young Ovid than formal prose, and even his prose
had a poetic complexion (5–6); he was a born poet (8), given to writing
like an addict to a drug or a lover to his passion (*Tr.* IV, 1, 27–36); he used
to compose on a couch in a garden pavilion, but after his débâcle found
himself writing verse even under the most harassing circumstances (116–
117); from then on, he experienced the necessity of unburdening his grief
in verse (137), seeking relief, not renown, and singing like a convict in a
chain gang (136); he kept on writing because there was nothing else for
him to do (138–139). For the honest work he put into his writing see pp.
174 n. 25; 261 (bottom); 266 (end of fourth par.); 267 (last par.).

Some reasons why he composed: the *Amores* (9–10; 26–28; 32–34); the *Art
of Love* (54–55; 65); the *Metamorphoses* (99; 210 n. 17); the *Fasti* (143–
145); the *Ibis* (155); the *Halieutica* (160); the epistles from exile (131–
139); *Po.* IV, 14 (158); *Po.* I, 8 and II, 9 (159); *Po.* IV, 7 (250 n. 9); poems
in honor of the dynasty (135; the poem in Getic: 250 n. 5); poems of a non-
personal character (141–142).

His pride in his "immortal" verse (*Amores:* 33; *Metam.:* 110; *Tr.* and *Po.:*
131; 152; 163). He felt he was rising to an unexpected new height when,
at the age of thirty (?), he began the *Medea* (46–47); and when, at the age
of forty-three, he began the *Metam.* (72); and when, at the age of about
fifty, he began the *Fasti* (145 with 239 f. n. 8); and eventually felt he was
chosen by fate to sing of living death (131; *Tr.* V, 1, 7–24). But by then he
became diffident of the quality of his verse, had fits of acute despondency,
and destroyed his own manuscripts (115; 132–133), whether good or bad
(229 n. 11); at last, he lost interest in perfection (138–139; 156–157).

He was unwilling to part with a subject once he had it under his hand (cf.
Am. III, 1, 16), and composed more and more poems on the same theme
(*Am.:* 46–47; more erotic epistles: 48; return to love poetry after a solemn
farewell: 47; 53; a third volume added to the *Art of Love:* 65; *Metam.* drawn
out too long: 101; *Tr.* concluded and resumed: 137). He took up a new
project before the previous one was completed (wrote *Her.* and prepared
Medea while completing *Am.:* 46–47; prepared *Fasti* while completing
Metam.: 103; 224 n. 94; 238 n. 2). A number of fallow years were followed,
in his early forties, by a spurt of production (53); *Tr.* and *Po.* were produced
at the average rate of one acceptable elegy a month (140).

He made a second edition of the *Amores,* reducing it by two-fifths (194 n.);
he sanctioned publication of *Metam.* in an unrevised form (116); the extant fragment of *Hal.* is no more than a sketchy draft, published after the
author's death (160 with notes). The titles he gave to his works (196 n. 2;
251 n. 4).

THE SCOPE OF HIS ART

His poetry is not as shallow as is generally assumed (4; 73 etc.); it sometimes approaches profundity (83–85; 93–96; 213 n. 30 etc.); it conveys significant views and ideas (4; 16–17 and *passim*), consistently developed throughout his career (35).

His originality (15–16; 45–46 with 193 n. 15; 51–52; 72; 95–96; 104; 140–141; 183 n. 37; 200 n. 9; 211 n. 22; 214 n. 38; recasting commonplace topics: 119); he often gave a traditional theme a novel cast.

His naïve and unmethodical genius defies exhaustive description (221 n. 76); he sometimes exceeded his normal range (description of splendor: 86; of dignity: 100). Uneven quality of his work (68; 73; 97; 105–106; 132; 241 nn. 13 and 14; 242 n. 24; 248 n. 21).

Few but forceful instances of ecstatic manner (18–21; 30–31; 188 nn. 63 and 64; 248 n. 20); spirited exuberance in *Amores* (26); clair-obscure sketches give place to precise pictures (49); ripe style (70; 76 etc.); some mature wisdom in *Rem.* (70) and in *Tr.* and *Po.* (132); differentiation between elegiac and epic style (74); his pride in turning from erotic to patriotic elegy in *Fasti* (145); a touch of the grotesque in *Metam.* (80); realistic, romantic, and grotesque sections of *Ibis* (152–155); romanticism yielding to realism in the period of exile (122–123; 125–126; 136; 156–159; 237 n. 32).

His creative powers began to decline with *Metam.* XII (101); declined further after his banishment (132; 138–139); were rising again, it seems, when he started on the *Hal.* (161–162).

At times, he used themes and styles out of character for him: a hideous passage in *Rem.* (68); ambition for grandeur in the last books of *Metam.* (101–102; 110); a brutal tale (102 with 222 n. 83); magic in operatic profusion (105 with 223 n. 91); philosophy (108–110); *Fasti* (145–149); *Ibis* (155).

Some influences and models: Once he imitated Tibullus to the point of spoiling a passage (181 n. 30). Hellenistic elements in *Am.* (12); *Epist.* (49; 196 f. n. 7; 51–52); *Metam.* (216 n. 46; 220 n. 74 etc.); *Fasti* (145–146; 151; 240 nn. 9 and 10; 241 nn. 12 and 14); *Ibis* (151; 153; 155; 245 f. n. 5; 249 n. 23); in a passage of *Po.* (250 n. 6). Tragic lyricism in the elegies (*Her.*: 190 n. 1; 210 f. n. 17; *Tr.* and *Po.*: 131 with 234 f. n. 23).

SOME TRAITS OF HIS ART

One of the virtues of his art is its charm; another, the priceless sense of humor it displays. The humor (14–15; 20; 24; 28; 34; 44; 76–77; 85; 90; 120–121; 146; 148; 149; 239 n. 6) is gentle and good-natured rather than rowdy or sarcastic (215 n. 42; one caustic passage: 204 n. 3 to ch. 9); dialectical wit (88; 215 n. 42). Irony, tragic or otherwise (37; 90; 198 n. 11; 215 f. n. 42).

He was fond of building up his poetry in two strata, representing two distinct mental attitudes (150–151); his verse often moves on more than one plane of reality (17; 35; 38; 45–46; 89; 110; 152–155) or dwells in in-between regions (46; 90; 99–100; 163). He took delight in the fabulous and utopian (34; 90; 92–93; 99).

A favorite theme is the protest of the heart against the exigencies of practical life (10; 16–17; 33), against the mechanical laws of nature (17; 87; 89), and against unsatisfactory realities (30–31; 45; 96). Entreaties are often directed to one who cannot be supposed to listen (192 f. n. 14; 45; 120; see also 158). Sentimental illusions (37–38 etc.), self-deception (see above, p. 263, near top), and inconsistencies (190 f. n. 3) play a large part.

The use he made of myth and legend (17; 19; 24; 41; 45; 89–90; 144; 154; 181 nn. 26 and 28). Human interpretation of nature (12; 17; 87–89); of a mechanistic theory (176 n. 13); mythological logic (93). Remolding of legends: mellowing a crude story (76–78); reinterpreting in a modern spirit (79 with 211 n. 18; 81–82); radical recasting (95–96). His treatment of Italian myth and legend (56; 103–108; 110; 144–150); humanizing and secularizing (105; 106–107; 146; 223 n. 89; 241 n. 16). Legend losing out against the realities of his exile (122–123; 125–126).

PRESENTATION AND STYLE

His presentation is distinguished by its lucidity (56; an exception: 146 with 241 n. 13), fluency, and grace (74; 85–86; 89–90; 97; 237 n. 37). He has coined many quotable sayings, and could be as concise as he wanted to be (204 n. 3 to ch. 9); but he suffered from *embarras de richesse,* and it was hard for him to discipline his ideas and to observe a definite order (3; 8; 200 n. 10), or to relinquish a point once it had been successfully made (8 with 174 n. 19; 214 n. 37; 219 n. 69; 243 n. 25). He made up for his lack of methodical arrangement by his ingenuity in improvisation (74–75) and the elegance of his transitions (203 n. 28; 242 f. n. 24). The apparent ease of his presentation was due, no doubt, not only to his natural gift and his lively response to his themes, but also to hard, honest work: *ars* (which includes labor) *adeo latet arte sua.*

Ovid's tales are dyed deep with sentiment (86); sometimes he intercedes in his own narrative and talks sympathetically to his characters (79; 83; 99–100; 214 n. 35). He excels in depicting frustration (37–38; 80; 248 n. 21).

His settings are graphic (74) but never overdrawn; he strictly subordinates descriptive detail to plot and sentiment (86; 119; 213 n. 34; exception: 216 n. 46).

Was Ovid a "rhetorical" poet? Some general remarks on the problem (167–169 n. 3); he borrowed conceits from Latro (170 n. 3; 186 n. 55); his critical attitude toward school rhetoric (6–7 with 170–171 nn. 6–9; 58–59); the *Her.* are no *"suasoriae* in verse" (190 n. 1); his discretion in not using "rhetoric" (77 with 210 n. 12; 86; 196 f. n. 7; 215 n. 41; 219 n. 69).

Whenever Ovid uses a striking figure of speech, he does so to bring out a striking pattern of fact or mood (172 n. 14; 183 n. 38; 196 n. 7; 197 n. 10; 215 n. 42; 229 n. 14; 236 n. 28; but see also 241 n. 12).

Some specific stylistic devices: apostrophe (79; 83; 214 n. 35); double entendre
(198 n. 11; 215 f. n. 42); zeugma (197 n. 10); preludes and echoes (77–
78; 176 n. 11; 209–210 nn. 9 and 10; 211 n. 22; 222 n. 83); corresponding
lines attuned to each other (209 f. n. 10; 225 f. n. 103).

THE AUTHOR AND HIS AUDIENCE

The personal character of his poetry is obvious in *Am.* and the epistles from
exile (cf. *Am.* III, 1, 15–16 and *Tr.* V, 1, 7–24); impersonal elements in
Am. (11); interdependence of his life and art (32–34); personal elements
in *Ars Amat.* (54; 61); he thought of *Metam.* as, in a sense, his own portrait (131 with 235 n. 24); personal treatment of the material in *Fasti*
(145–146); the author's face behind the mask of a character in *Metam.* and
Fasti (226–228 n. 105); strange combination of the personal and impersonal in *Ibis* (155).
His craving for a response from his readers (48; 71; 133–134); "dancing in
the dark" (139); he was a considerate author (102); his poetry is to be translated by the reader into terms of his own experience (34–35; 80).

THE POET AND HIS CRITICS

Ovid recited his verse, before publication, to selected audiences (10–11); he
sent advance copies to his literary friends (48); and he discussed his poetry
with other men of letters (7–8). He may have been amenable to some of
their suggestions, but he balked at others, because he preferred native individuality to academic correctness (172 nn. 14 and 15; 173 f. n. 18). Contemporary and later critics are agreed that he knew, but cherished, his own
faults and, instead of commanding his talent, chose to yield to it (47; 172 f.
n. 17; another criticism: 174 n. 19). He resisted the criticism that his erotic
poetry was too licentious (71). He wanted his verse to be expressive of
its theme (*Rem.* 387–388), to appeal to the reader, and to be personal, in
contrast to Horace, who in theory and practice looked to Good Taste as
the one guiding principle.

THE POET AND HIS ART

Self-criticism: He tried his hand at tragedy before he decided to compose the
Medea (46); he also seems to have experimented with poetry in the grand
style (*Gigantomachia*) and to have found that it was uncongenial to him
(32–33 with 189 n. 68). In *Tr.* IV, 10, 61–62 he indicates that he had often
committed to the "correcting flames" such verse as he felt to be "faulty";
one of the reasons why he attempted to destroy the *Metam.* was that the epic
was not yet revised (and he despaired of perfecting it: 115–116). There are
passages where, bothered by his artistic conscience, he tries to justify what
he is doing (102; 105; 146 with 241 n. 15; why he is writing *Rem.*: 67;
why an invective: 152); in *Tr.* and *Po.* he often apologizes for the imper-
fections of his elegies (132 with 236 n. 27; 134; 138–139; 156–157); at times

he wrote only to burn to ashes what he had composed because it was not good enough (*Tr.* V, 12, 61–64, see pp. 132–133). The tedium of correcting (139 with 173 f. n. 18).

Handicapped by current prejudice (8–10; 26–28; 116–117 with 229 n. 12; 189 n. 67), Ovid had no very definite idea of the place to be assigned to his art (10; 32–33; 46), but he saw clearly some basic facts: that creative art is personal (see above) as well as objective; that it is not tied to reality, but builds up a spiritual world of its own (34–35; 93–96); and that the work of art, once it has come into being, has an existence independent of its maker (94).

D. INDEX TO OVID'S WORKS AND PASSAGES CITED OR DISCUSSED

The numbers of poems and lines are those of the Teubner edition; variations are sometimes given in parentheses.

II, 7, 19–22: 171 n. 6
II, 8 (discussed): 184 n. 40
  9–14: 171 n. 6
II, 10, 31–38: 186 n. 53
II, 11, 10 (discussed): 172 n. 14
II, 12: 28
  9–16 (discussed): 28; 196 n. 7;
    201 n. 21
II, 13, 6: 30
II, 16 (discussed): 175 f. n. 9; 185
  n. 45; 208 n. 7
II, 17, 11–20: 179 f. n. 18
II, 18: 32; (discussed): 46
  13–14 (discussed): 195 n. 3
  19: 175 n. 4
  27–34: 48
Amores III, 1 (discussed): 46–47
  10: 172 n. 15
  16: 264 (fourth par.)
  21: 244
  25: 173 n. 17
  III, 2, *The Chariot Race* (dis-
    cussed): 23–24; (structure):
    175 n. 6; (quoted in *Ars*): 56
  60: 31
III, 3, 12: 31
III, 4, 3–5: 187 f. n. 62
III, 6, 13–20: 180 n. 24; 233 n. 11
  89 (*quid si*): 178
III, 8 (discussed): 28
  55–56: 186 n. 55
III, 9: 10; 32
III, 10 (structure): 175 n. 6
III, 11, 19–20: 189 n. 70
III, 12 (discussed): 34
  15–16: 33
  19–20: 237 n. 32
  21–42: 180 n. 24
III, 13: 208 n. 7; 235 n. 25
III, 14 (discussed): 30–31; 188 n.
  63
  37–40 (genuine): 188 n. 64
  45–50: 30
III, 15:46–47

Ars Amatoria: 53–67
  (put on the index by Augustus):
    111; 114
  (organization): 200 n. 10
  (leitmotif): 78
Book I: 54–59
  I, 1–30: 54–55
  31–34: 201 n. 14
  92: 200 n. 11
  101–134: 56; 239 n. 7
  164: 102
  269–342: 58
  290–292: 172 n. 15
  381: 58
  [From here on, line numbers
    vary; subtract two for Bor-
    necque's edition]
  435: 201 n. 14
  437–486: 49
  457: 195 n. 1
  459–462: 203 n. 28
  459–486: 58
  466 (explained): 201 n. 18
  525–end (subject and arrange-
    ment): 200 n. 10
  551 (zeugma): 197 n. 10
  587–588: 201 n. 15
  609–610: 59
  611–616 (discussed): 57
  624–627: 204 n. 6
  631–658: 217 nn. 52 and 53
  637–642, *"religion is useful . . ."*
    (discussed): 90–92
  643–658: 57
  665–714: 58
  669 ff.: 58 with 201 n. 16
  739–754: 189 n. 70
  766–768: 200 n. 8
  767–770 (explained): 58 with
    201 n. 17
Ars Amatoria II: 59–63
  II, 14: 59
    24, *semibovemque virum . . .*
      (discussed): 183 n. 38

II. GENERAL INDEX